Christianity's Quiet Success

LISA KAAREN BAILEY

Christianity's Quiet Success

The Eusebius Gallicanus Sermon Collection
and the Power of the Church in Late Antique Gaul

University of Notre Dame Press
Notre Dame, Indiana

Library of Congress Cataloging-in-Publication Data

Bailey, Lisa Kaaren, 1974–
Christianity's quiet success : the Eusebius Gallicanus sermon
collection and the power of the church in late antique Gaul /
Lisa Kaaren Bailey.
     p.   cm.
Includes bibliographical references (p.   ) and index.
ISBN-13: 978-0-268-02224-2 (pbk. : alk. paper)
ISBN-10: 0-268-02224-0 (pbk. : alk. paper)
1. Eusebius Gallicanus collectio homiliarum. 2. Preaching—
Gaul—History—Early church, ca. 30–600. 3. Sermons, Early
Christian—Gaul—History and criticism. 4. Pastoral care—
Gaul—History. 5. Gaul—Church history.   I. Title.
BV4208.G26B35   2010
251.00944'09021—dc22
                                                      2010033410

C O N T E N T S

CCSL	*Corpus Christianorum series latina*
CSEL	*Corpus scriptorum ecclesiasticorum latinorum*
FC	*Fathers of the Church*
GC	*Liber in gloria confessorum*
GM	*Liber in gloria martyrum*
LH	*Libri historiarum X*
MA	*Miscellanea agostiniana*
MGH AA	*Monumenta Germaniae historica: auctores antiquissimi*
MGH SRM	*Monumenta Germaniae historica: scriptores rerum Merovingicarum*
PL	*Patrologiae cursus completus series latina*
SC	*Sources chrétiennes*
VJ	*Liber de passione et virtutibus sancti Iuliani martyris*
VM	*Libri de virtutibus sancti Martini episcopi*
VP	*Liber vitae patrum*

For the reader's convenience I have referred to published translations wherever these are available. Any alterations have been noted in the references. Scriptural translations are those of the Revised Standard Version unless the primary source departs substantially from that text. All other translations are my own. Names of authors are given in Latin versions except where there is a widely accepted Anglicised alternative.

ACKNOWLEDGMENTS

I owe thanks to more people than I can possibly name and to those I do name, I owe more than I can possibly say. My advisor, Peter Brown, displayed all the qualities of the best pastor, bestowing kindness and encouragement when he perceived it was necessary, but always pushing me to think harder and do more. He is a leader by example in his dedication and excitement. William Jordan challenged, provoked and inspired me. He is a model of scholarship. I count myself extremely fortunate to have spent time working with such great historians.

Many people have aided, over the many years, in making this a much better project. For their patience, their ideas, their corrections, their generosity in sharing work and their willingness to read drafts, I particularly wish to thank: Kutlu Akalin, Rob Bailey, Angela Bell, Scott Bruce, Malcolm Choat, James Cunningham, George Demacopoulos, François Dolbeau, Deanna Forsman, Campbell Grey, Holly Grieco, Yitzhak Hen, Chris Hilliard, Robert Kaster, William Klingshirn, Anne Lester, Emily Mackil, Jaclyn Maxwell, Volker Menze, Kim Phillips and Kevin Uhalde. Zoë Smith provided invaluable assistance over the course of a summer scholarship to get the manuscript material in order, while Barbara Hanrahan and the anonymous reviewers for UNDP have been wonderful in helping me transform a dissertation into a book. Any errors which remain after the efforts of all these are, of course, my own.

A number of institutions have provided me with financial assistance over the years. This project would never have begun were it not for a Fulbright scholarship sending me to America, and while there I was supported by the History Department at Princeton University, the Center for the Study of Religion, the Group for the Study of Late Antiquity and the Mrs Giles Whiting Foundation. Since my return to New Zealand, the University of Auckland, the Faculty of Arts and my two departments have been extremely generous with funds to enable me to travel to the other side of the world for research and conferences. I am very grateful to them all.

I owe thanks to many libraries and research institutions for allowing me to use their facilities, especially the Bibliothèque nationale de France, Institut de recherche et d'histoire des textes, Institut d'études augustiniennes, Biblioteca Apostolica Vaticana, Biblioteca nazionale centrale di Roma, Biblioteca Vallicelliana, Newberry Library and the Bodleian Library. I have received invaluable assistance from staff at Firestone Library and the University of Auckland Library and in the latter I particularly want to thank Philip Abela and the patient people working in the Interloans department.

My colleagues and students in the departments of History and of Classics and Ancient History at the University of Auckland have been very supportive and provided a stimulating environment for research. Many friends in New Zealand, America and around the world have kept me sane. Philip Rousseau made me love late antiquity in the first place and helped me see that it was possible to spend a life studying it. He has been a constant guide and supporter ever since. Valerie Flint was another early inspiration and is sorely missed. My family have been ever tolerant of my passion for strange times and places and my parents have always encouraged me to seek knowledge. Thank you.

This book is for Drew, whose arrival slowed it down in the best possible way, and for James, my love.

Introduction

The sermons of the Eusebius Gallicanus collection were popular and important from late antiquity right through to the high Middle Ages. There are 447 manuscripts which contain copies of the sermons and their influence can be traced throughout Western Europe, yet today they are largely unknown. They are unknown because they are quiet, unassuming, and anonymous, and we have always preferred the noisy, charismatic, and knowable. Yet the Eusebius Gallicanus collection gives a picture of late antiquity both fascinating and revealing. These sermons, from fifth- and sixth-century Gaul, provide a glimpse of one of the most important developments in European history: the process by which the Christian Church came to a position of true power in the West—no longer a small sect, but a force and a presence in the lives of all Western Europeans, even those who were not part of it. This process was long and slow. It did not begin in the fifth and sixth centuries and it certainly did not end with them. These centuries were, however, a crucial time of transition, and one which would shape much of what was to follow. The

1

Eusebius Gallicanus collection lets us inside the workings of this process. It deserves our attention.

The Eusebius Gallicanus is a source surrounded by confusion and dissensus. Scholars who have worked on it cannot agree on who wrote the sermons it contains, who put it together, what it was for, or even what it should be called. As a result it has been relatively neglected and its evidence seldom cited in studies of early medieval preaching or late antique Gaul. This is unfortunate for two reasons. First, it excludes a source which was clearly important and influential from the moment of its inception right through the high Middle Ages. The Eusebius Gallicanus collection was used by clergy as a preaching guide, and by monks and pious lay people as devotional reading. The large number of surviving manuscripts containing sermons from the collection is testament to its popularity, influence, and ongoing relevance.[1] Second, the Eusebius Gallicanus serves as a useful counterpoint to the evidence which dominates scholarly analysis. It is one of the anonymous, multiauthored "handbook" collections which became increasingly important from the fifth century on, and which mark a significant shift not only in styles of Christian preaching, but also in the development of the late antique Church. The Eusebian sermons therefore both enlarge a meagre source base and challenge and complicate the current picture. They give us a fresh view of how pastors sought to balance the needs of community against individual responsibility and they illustrate how some Christian leaders exerted indirect but effective power over their communities. They demonstrate the Gallic adoption and adaption of the pastoral strategies of Augustine of Hippo and they form a fascinating contrast with the contemporary but much more familiar preaching of Caesarius of Arles.

The Eusebius Gallicanus collection has not been ignored completely. Paul-Laurent Carle and L. A. van Buchem have produced studies of sermons seventeen and twenty-nine, examining their contributions to the development of the theology of the Eucharist and the confirmation rite.[2] Achille M. Triacca has surveyed the use of the term *cultus* in the collection and the imagery comparing the Church to the Virgin Mary.[3] Clemens M. Kasper and Rosemarie Nürnberg have studied the Eusebian sermons to monks as part of their work on the monastery of Lérins, and the sermons on saints have attracted the attention of scholars working on saints' cults in late antique Gaul.[4] Jean-Pierre Weiss has studied the collection for evidence of whether priests preached in the fifth century.[5] Antonella Bruzzone used it as a case study in her work on the use of simile and metaphor in preaching.[6] As yet no one has written on the nature of the collection as a whole, its function, or how it was used. No one has studied the pastoral care it provides, or compared it to other examples of preaching from the period.

In large part this has been because of the ongoing debates over the sermons' authorship, which have proved a paralysing distraction.[7] It is not necessary, however, to resolve this question before using the Eusebius Gallicanus as evidence. Most scholars now agree that the sermons date from the mid-late fifth century in their original form, that Faustus of Riez wrote at least one of them, and that most of the sermons to monks can be linked to the monastery at Lérins. My reconstruction, which I defend at greater length in chapter 2, is that the collection as we currently have it was put together in the sixth century and circulated as a series of useful models. In the process of editing and compilation, many of the original details and specificities in the sermons were undoubtedly stripped out, which is why they have been so difficult to situate. It was precisely this universality and genericness, however, which accounted for their appeal. Studying these sermons can therefore tell us much about what pastoral strategies were seen to "work" in late antique Gaul, and also show us how some quite simple texts could have had an extraordinarily broad impact.

The Eusebius Gallicanus as it stands in the *CCSL* edition consists of seventy-six sermons.[8] Glorie, the editor, presents them in the order found in two of the more extensive manuscripts, the first half of which follows the liturgical year.[9] Sermons for Christmas, Epiphany, Lent, Easter, Ascension, and Pentecost are interspersed with those for the feast days of saints Stephen and Blandina; two sermons on the creed, placed before the Easter series; a sermon on the litany; and one on the penance of the Ninevites. This arrangement takes us up to sermon twenty-nine. Sermons thirty to seventy-six include nine more on saints and martyrs, a series of ten homilies directed to monks, sermons on theological issues, exhortations on proper Christian behaviour, and sermons to be spoken on specific ecclesiastical occasions, such as the founding or anniversary of a church, the ordination or burial of a priest, and the address of a priest to an audience which includes bishops. The sermons are not exegetical in focus.[10] That is to say, although they are dense with scriptural reference, they do not take exegesis and explanation of scripture as their primary role, nor are they organised around a sequence of readings, thus differentiating the collection from some contemporary homiliaries and preachers.[11]

Like some other contemporary collections, however, the Eusebius Gallicanus includes a selection of sermons directed to monks.[12] These have a different rhetorical style and employ some distinctive pastoral strategies, although they are connected to the rest of the collection in important respects.[13] Indeed, the integration of these sermons to monks with the rest of the collection is one of its most interesting features, as it demonstrates the congruity of monastic and lay communities in this period and the overlap of pastoral anxieties and strategies in both contexts.

Most of the other sermons were directed to the laity. They are simple and straightforward in style. Though they do not embrace the Christian *sermo humilis* with as much enthusiasm as Caesarius of Arles was later to do, there is nothing in them which would not have been comprehensible to a broad urban audience in fifth-century Gaul.[14] The sermons are well constructed, so that they flow clearly. They often end with a summary of the main points. Sentences are usually short and repetition is used to create rhythm and focus attention. The authors use rhetorical devices, especially metaphor and simile, to draw interest and facilitate understanding.[15] The few learned references to Cicero, Pliny, and Virgil are commonplaces, and if audiences missed their origins this would not have impeded their understanding of the arguments offered.[16] Their discussions of theology are clear and assume no prior knowledge. They deal with common anxiety-creating enigmas such as the virgin birth, the exact workings of the Trinity, and why the good continue to suffer.[17] The questions which the preachers put into the mouths of their audiences are those which they might imagine a lay congregation to have. The collection includes sermons for saints' feast days and the instruction of catechumens, as well as urban litanies. The preachers address the problems of worldly wealth, barbarian invasion, and proper Christian observance. They deliberately and explicitly extend the concept of Christian brotherhood beyond the monastic context.[18] The style and content of the sermons are consistent with an urban pastor addressing a lay audience.[19] They are liturgical in nature and populist in tone.[20] Sample introductions were intended to guide clergy in preaching techniques, but none of the full sermons was aimed at a clerical audience. Although the collection was ultimately used in a number of different ways, it was originally intended to aid those required to preach to the Christian laity.[21]

The Eusebius Gallicanus sermons had the impact they did because of particular contexts which have also dominated the historiography of the period. First, they appeared at a challenging moment of transition for the Church. Since the conversion of Constantine, the Church had allied itself to the institutions of the Roman state, using its resources and structures to effect the transition from a minor cult to an official religion aspiring to universality. The support of central government put money, manpower, and influence at the disposal of those deemed to be orthodox, and facilitated the suppression of those who were not.[22] Though no single, unified, universal Church resulted, it was a possible dream. To Eusebius of Caesarea and many others besides, it was self-evident that the empire had been constituted by God to this eventual end.[23] In the early fifth century Orosius reiterated Eusebius' confidence, but his stridency already felt hollow.[24] Rome was faltering and its presence in the provinces was fading. The warlords, chieftains, and landowners who filled the vacuum could not be relied upon for consistent support, intent as they were upon self-preservation in a newly fluid world. Against Orosius, Augustine of Hippo urged his readers to place no trust in the institutions of this world, revealed now as palpably vulnerable.[25] As the Church in the West was forced to disengage from the empire, local environments loomed larger.

These local environments were increasingly isolated. Horizons narrowed. Everything became further away—Rome, Constantinople, the next town along. The ideal of a universal Church was still present, but consistency across vast geographical areas was impossible to achieve without a central authority capable of enforcing it. The bishops of Rome laid increasingly vociferous claim to such a role in the West, but their rhetoric was as yet neither widely accepted nor realisable.[26] Local pressures required local solutions, representing an opportunity for some clergy to assume positions of power and patronage within their communities by taking over roles previously handled by secular authorities.[27] Opportunity also arose in a less celebrated respect. As Julia Smith puts it, "In institutional terms . . . Christian modes of organization remained decentralized and could be easily replicated everywhere . . . A religion with an avowedly universal message managed to localize itself in a multitude of cultural contexts."[28] The resulting variety of local responses paved the way for the Church's success in many different environments. Although consistency was the Church's goal, its failure to achieve this proved a strength.

For most local clergy, however, the sense of opportunity may have been overpowered by feelings of vulnerability. The Church had yet to develop extensive infrastructures to support its representatives. Church councils in late Roman Gaul were irregular.[29] Contact between bishops and the scattered lower clerics under their authority depended upon episcopal energy and initiative.[30] While some Gallic bishops were drawn from social elites, many others and most of the lower clergy had more humble backgrounds, might be minimally educated, and received inconsistent training.[31] Only in the fifth century did they begin to receive regular stipends, and the finances of the Church in many districts were still dependent upon the generosity and support of their congregations.[32] These clergy were thrown back upon their own resources by the increasing localisation of the Church, and yet it was also they who were the face of the Church for most of the faithful, and who undertook the daily work of pastoral care upon which the integration of Christianity into Gallic communities depended. It was a weighty burden.

These troubles and strategems of the late Roman clergy, particularly the episcopate, have been the subject of many excellent studies, and Gaul has loomed large in their analyses. Gaul is seen to exemplify two of the critical developments in this period, both of which served to establish or solidify the charismatic authority of bishops who might have shaky institutional supports. The first is the exploitation or deployment of the cult of the saints by bishops who recognised its power to create associations of holiness, provide a focus for community identity, and bring wealth and prestige to particular towns or churches. Springing off Peter Brown's *Cult of the Saints,* scholars including Raymond Van Dam, Brigitte Beaujard, and Jill Harries have demonstrated how central the local cult was to the development of the Gallic Church.[33] The Eusebius Gallicanus sermons provide another set of examples, but also demonstrate how the cult of the saints formed one part of a broad pastoral community-building project. They show us how veneration of a town's heroes could be made a vehicle for larger arguments about ideal interpersonal relations and local religious loyalties.

The second important context for the Eusebius Gallicanus sermons, one which looms large in scholarship on this period, is the relationship between ascetic and episcopal models in the development of religious authority. Here, the East has a been a major focus of recent monographs, as in the works of Claudia Rapp and Andrea Sterk.[34] However, scholars focusing on Gaul, including Friedrich Prinz, Martin Heinzelmann, Raymond Van Dam, Philip Rousseau, and Ralph Mathisen, have long recognised both the power and the complications of combining episcopal with ascetic authority.[35] Gallic examples form key studies in two recent works on religious authority, by Conrad Leyser and George Demacopoulos, respectively, both inspired by the discussion of the Gallic situation in Robert Markus.[36] Studies of individual Gallic bishops and monks have also been very influenced by this perspective.[37] But while this area of scholarship has almost completely ignored the Eusebius Gallicanus sermons, their evidence is of central importance. They combine sermons preached by abbots to their monks and sermons preached by bishops who used to be monks to their lay congregations. They show "monk-bishops" in action, and demonstrate that such movement between communities did not have to be as tense or problematic as it appears from some modern scholarship. In the Eusebian sermons, both types of Christian community—those within the monastery walls and those without—were approached with very similar pastoral techniques. The theme of authority, meanwhile, did not loom as large in these sources as it does in the scholarship. Instead the concerns expressed in these sermons are about community cohesion, salvation, and relationships. The Eusebius Gallicanus sermons therefore both contribute fascinating new evidence to the discussion and change our current picture.

These two historiographical frameworks for late antique Gaul have been useful and productive. A third prevalent framework, however, has distorted more than it has contributed: the idea of the "semi-pelagian controversy." Discussion of Gallic writers, bishops, ascetics, and pastors has been dominated by the spectre of this controversy, even though almost all scholars now agree that it was largely an early modern invention.[38] According to the traditional view, Pelagius' heretical emphasis on the role of human free will in achieving salvation was answered by Augustine of Hippo, who maintained that salvation was the always unmerited gift of divine grace, the recipients of which were predetermined by God. The monastic "semipelagians" of southern Gaul, finding Augustine's position unpalatable, sought a compromise which retained some role for human action, but the bishop of Hippo's views were eventually reinstated as Gallic orthodoxy at the council of Orange in 529, under the auspices of Caesarius of Arles.[39]

This simple account has been greatly emended by subsequent work.[40] Scholars now emphasise that there was no unified or sustained controversy over grace and free will in Gaul, but rather irregular outbursts of debate. They recognise also that these debates did not carry the weight in the fifth century with which post-

Reformation writers invested them, influenced as the latter were by the disputes of their own day. The tone of the discussion was, they conclude, "determinedly irenic."[41] The two positions, moreover, are now deemed to have been closer together than previously thought. Indeed, the views of the "semi-pelagians" are now interpreted as slight moderations of Augustine's own, and have been hailed as an attempt to find a balanced, workable solution to a difficult question.[42]

Even with these revisions, however, the standard scholarly view of the structure of the controversy has remained. Scholars are ever tempted to see a neat debate with clear-cut sides.[43] On the one side was Augustine, motivated by the desire to safeguard the sovereignty of grace.[44] On the other side was John Cassian, concerned that passivity bred indolence and motivated by the desire to safeguard the relationship between human action and human destiny.[45] The contrast between Augustine and John Cassian is then seen to be neatly echoed by the contrast between Faustus of Riez and Caesarius of Arles, moved closer together but still representing different "sides" in a debate. Faustus appears as the key spokesman of the "Gallic position" on grace and free will, as articulated in his treatise *De gratia*.[46] As a bishop who had once been a monk, he is depicted as translating Cassian's position into a congregational setting, seeking a middle ground in which the essentials of Augustine's views were retained, but with their most troubling implications alleviated.[47] The path to compromise was then supposedly completed by Caesarius, who enshrined a modified and moderated Augustinianism and brought the controversy to a tidy close.[48]

This schema continues to influence the interpretation of the works of Cassian and Faustus of Riez as well as of the Eusebius Gallicanus sermons, all of which have been seen as coming out of the heartland of "semi-pelagian" resistance to Augustine's doctrines.[49] As A. M. C. Casiday has recently pointed out, however, it would be a mistake to see either "Augustinianism" or "anti-Augustinianism" in late antiquity—both were developments of later ages.[50] They, along with the concept of semi-pelagianism, result from a reading back of subsequent heated controversies and polarised positions into an age in which neither were evident. The Eusebius Gallicanus sermons, indeed, demonstrate the distorting effect of such anachronism. The sermons were not self-consciously part of any theological debate, nor did they articulate a consistent position within a spectrum of views. They did, however, expose certain assumptions, pastoral concerns, and strategies reflecting an environment in which grace and free will were matters under discussion. Sermons within the collection expressed an optimism about human capacity, contained an emphasis on individual responsibility, and articulated the view that human effort is both required and rewarded by God. Much of this they shared with other Gallic writers of the time who found Augustine's approach pastorally problematic. Much of it they also shared, however, with Caesarius of Arles, Augustine's supposed Gallic disciple, and with Augustine himself, who took a quite different approach to the issues of grace and free will in his sermons than he did in his treatises.[51] There are interesting divergences in emphasis between the Eusebius Gallicanus sermons, Caesarius of Arles, and Augustine, but to view any of these sermons as statements in a theological controversy would be to miss the point. These were *pastoral* works. They responded to theological anxiety on the part of Christian congregations and they were informed by views being aired at the time, but they were not "position pieces," nor do the sermons attempt to offer a coherent response to the issues. The Eusebius Gallicanus preachers were not on one side of a "camp." They were on the coal face of theological explanation. Sermons were late antique theology in practice.

Just as an understanding of the issues under discussion in this alleged controversy can help us to place the Eusebius Gallicanus sermons in a richer context, so also they help us to understand the situation of the Gallic Church in the fifth and sixth centuries. Gallic clergy were aware of what was going on elsewhere in the Christian world, but, within limits, they made their own decisions about what to think and what to do. Gallic pastors explained theology as they best saw fit and Gaul retained its own liturgies throughout the period under discussion.[52] Gallic councils could be called to assess matters under dispute, but the impact of their decisions on practical pastoral care is very difficult to trace.[53] The picture remains one of localisation and diversity and this was not to change for a long time.

All of these considerations make it difficult to talk of a "Christian Church" as though it were a singular and unproblematic entity. There was more than one Church in late antiquity and more than one way of being in it. This work is concerned with what became known as the Roman Catholic Church. The Arian, Donatist, and Eastern churches all considered that they had more claim to be the "one true Church," but none succeeded in persuading the majority of the inhabitants of Western Europe to agree. The term "Church" functions here as a shorthand for the institution which prevailed.

Even the "Catholic" Church, however, was "neither centralized nor systematized."[54] Instead it consisted of the multitudes of people who considered themselves members of it. The most visible of these were the clergy. These were the paid and unpaid religious professionals serving in offices with clearly delimited responsibilities and nominal authority over particular regions, realms of behaviour, and metaphysical questions; they were supposedly marked out from other Christians by the sacrament of ordination. Yet the clergy did not constitute "the Church"—they were members of the communities they guided, not separate from them.[55] Moreover, like any other corporation, the Church was more than the sum of its parts. It survived the deaths of its constituent members and developed a memory, or set of traditions, which perpetuated its identity.[56] The machinery of this corporation provided the sacraments, raised money, built buildings, dispensed charity, regulated orthodoxy, and protected its own. In this sense, the Church was an institution. People kept the institution running and made the decisions which form a large part of what we study, but the Church was more than them. Finally, the Church could be seen, and was perhaps most often seen by late antique Christians, as an ideal. It was the pure bride of Christ, the fecund virgin mother, the personified representation of the Christian community, and the expression of its cohesiveness. In the "true" Church there could be no schism or disunity, and outside of it there could be no salvation. This idea of what the Church could and should be lies behind all the attempts to forge Christian communities in late antique Gaul. These ways of viewing the Church in Gaul, as throughout Europe, were not mutually exclusive. They coexisted, even if they did not always perfectly meld.

The centrality of pastoral care in the development of this Church has now come in for renewed attention. Scholarship on the history of pastoral care had long been conducted with an eye on the imperatives of ministerial training, resulting in an ahistorical approach.[57] The work of Henry G. J. Beck nonetheless represented a pioneering attempt to establish and explain what pastoral care meant in its late antique context, with an emphasis on practical rather than theoretical sources.[58] More recently, the work of Jaclyn Maxwell and Demacopoulos, among others, has brought pastoral care to centre stage. Maxwell treats the pastoral context as the fundamental interpretative framework for understanding the sermons of John Chrysostom, and for Demacopoulos pastoral care under the guise of "spiritual direction" becomes the key dynamic in the development of Christian communities.[59] It is this sense of pastoral care as a relationship, but one governed by particular imperatives on the clerical side, which underpins my interpretation of the Eusebius Gallicanus sermons.

From the side of the pastors, whose efforts the sermons reflect, these imperatives were fourfold. The first was to make sure that the faithful got to heaven. This involved dispensing the sacraments to them, and ensuring that they believed the right things and behaved the right ways. The second was to communicate the Christian message. This involved reading and expounding scripture, explaining an immensely complicated theology, and laying out the terms on which the adherents of the faith should understand their world. The third was to provide for the flock materially. This involved encouraging and dispensing charity, administering justice, and interceding with other powers, both terrestrial and celestial. The fourth was to build the structures of the Church—the "institutionalised" expressions of religion. This involved establishing respect for and obedience to clerical authority, fostering a sense of common identity and defining that common identity in Christian terms. Pastoral care, in other words, comprised the ordinary, day-to-day interactions between clergy and laity, but also between abbots and monks. It was the necessary engine of all Christian communities and one which drove the growth of the Church as a whole.

Very little evidence of this pastoral care survives. Most often it left no textual record, or was too ordinary to warrant commentary or description. One of its primary vehicles, however, was preaching, and a number of late antique sermons survive as witness to its forms. It is these sermons which form the subject of this book.

The first two chapters set the scene. Chapter 1 places sermons into the various contexts which make sense of them as historical sources: the nature of the texts, their function, their audiences and the environments in which they were written, preached, heard, and read. From this discussion, sermons emerge as key vehicles of pastoral care in late antique Gaul. Their role as vehicles, and not just witnesses, elevates their usefulness to the historian, but also necessitates careful interpretation when using them as evidence. Chapter 2 turns the focus onto the Eusebius Gallicanus sermon collection. Very little work has been done on these sermons because of crippling disagreements over the collection's authorship and provenance. It is both important and possible to move past these disagreements and use the Eusebius Gallicanus as a source on pastoral care in Gaul. Chapter 2 suggests a way out of the quagmire, and examines the nature of the collection, what it was for, and how it was used.

The next three chapters examine some particularly important elements of the pastoral care offered in the Eusebius Gallicanus. Chapter 3 focuses on community. Community building was a central imperative for a Church which needed to integrate itself into the structures and society of late antique Gaul. Pastors went about this task in their own ways, however, and did not share a single vision of what an ideal Christian community would look like. The Eusebius Gallicanus preachers emphasised the value of consensus, harmony, and mutuality in community relations and facilitated this by encouraging tolerance, playing down or eliding difference, and constructing their own leadership as situated within rather than above the congregation. These characteristics give an overall impression quite distinct from that of some other contemporary preachers. The Eusebius Gallicanus sermons on local saints, moreover, illustrate how adaptable pastoral care could be.

Christian community required common basic beliefs. Chapter 4 explores how the Eusebian preachers fulfilled their pastoral duty to explain the faith to their congregants so that they might believe what was necessary to get to heaven and to feel connected to their religion on earth. In the absence of any coercive power, preachers relied on rhetorical mechanisms to persuade their audiences. They strove at the same time both to make the faith accessible to all Christians and to keep it under clerical control—to maintain the authority of the Church. Through a series of case studies, chapter 4 illustrates the divergences within the Christian tradition in how the faith was explained, but also shows that these divergences did not always fall along expected lines. The explanations were ultimately determined by the demands of pastoral care.

Chapter 5 examines how the Eusebian preachers sought to maintain Christian community in the face of inevitable sin. By showing their congregants how to atone for their transgressions and cleanse their souls from the stain of guilt, pastors hoped to clear the path of their flock to heaven, and keep them within the Church. Augustine of Hippo's thinking on penance and expiation was very influential, but the authors of the sermons in the Eusebius Gallicanus collection adapted it to the needs of their own congregations and to suit their pastoral priorities. The sermons reveal their own distinctive understanding of what membership in the Christian community entailed.

Chapter 6 moves on to those sermons within the Eusebius Gallicanus collection which were directed to monks. It argues that the style of pastoral care which the Eusebian preachers offered to the laity was consistent with that which they offered to ascetics. The preachers' understandings of mutuality, leadership, and self-reliance, as well as their ideals of interaction between the individual and the group, did not change, whether they addressed monks or lay Christians. The collection makes clear, however, that asceticism was not understood in a monolithic manner. Different strands within it and individual interpretations of it fed into lay pastoral care in a variety of ways. While other Gallic bishops came to their congregations with expectations of ascetic behaviour, the Eusebian preachers emphasized the ideals of monastic community. These became the foundation for the pastoral care which they offered to lay Christians.

Sermons show religious elites engaged in the pastoral work which laid the foundation for the success of the Christian Church. Western Europe became "Christendom" not only because of dramatic conversions, heroic missions, and violent coercion, but also due to the slow, quiet work of innumerable individuals, facing their congregations every day, every week, or every month, and forging, with them, a Church. Theirs is a story worth telling.

Preaching in Late Antique Gaul

Scholars encounter sermons as words on a page. They float in manuscripts and editions, far from the churches and libraries of late antique Gaul. They can seem abstract—ideas without an audience and without a context. It is easy to forget that these sermons were an integral part of the liturgy, and therefore of the ritualised acts through which the Church attempted to impress its power and majesty, to convey the fundamentals of the faith, and to build a Christian community. Sermons were also one of the main vehicles of pastoral care, the mechanism by which clergy sought to mold the lives and thoughts of their flocks. This chapter therefore sets the scene, illustrating the nature of late antique Gallic sermons, their functions, their audiences, and the environments in which they were written, heard, and read. These were living texts. They were used. If we cannot see how and why they were used, we will not understand the role they played in the cultural integration and empowerment of the Christian Church.[1]

For the baptism of Clovis, king of the Franks, wrote Gregory of Tours, "the public squares were draped with coloured cloths, the churches were adorned with white hangings, the baptistery was prepared, sticks of incense gave off clouds of perfume, sweet-smelling candles gleamed bright and the holy place of baptism was filled with divine fragrance. God filled the hearts of all present with such grace that they imagined themselves to have been transported to some perfumed paradise."[2] Sidonius Apollinaris found the festival of St. Justus, by contrast, less divine. "There was an enormous congregation of both sexes, too great for the very spacious church to contain, even with the expanse of covered porticoes which surrounded it . . . Owing to the cramped space, the pressure of the crowd and the numerous lights which had been brought in, we were absolutely gasping for breath."[3]

Sermons were preached amidst the cacophony of sights, sounds, and smells which filled the late antique church:[4] vaulted ceilings, domes, and colonnades;[5] walls decorated with gilding, coloured marble, mosaics, inscriptions, gold and silver ornaments, frescoes, and impressive wall paintings;[6] light from windows, oil lamps, and candles, the scent of which mixed with smoke and incense;[7] liturgical vessels of precious metal, altar cloths of silk and gold, clergy in white robes, a congregation dressed in its finest.[8] The air was filled with chanted psalms, murmured prayers, and holy words,[9] and the church either crammed with men and women of all classes, or frighteningly empty and still.[10] The faithful were encouraged to think of churches as the closest thing to paradise on earth.[11] They were encouraged to think of them as places where miracles happened.[12] They were encouraged to think of them as sacrosanct sites—free of violence and worldly cares.

We learn of the congregation's behaviour in church, however, chiefly when it violated these ideals. A preacher had to compete with gossip, chatter, flirtation, and the conduct of business.[13] His congregation might recline when it should be standing, remain upright when it should be genuflecting, leave early, arrive late, complain of his sermon or even where he stood.[14] The faithful milled about during the service, pressed upon the altar railings, and shouted responses to the preacher, both approving and disruptive.[15] The festival of a saint might be accompanied by singing, dancing, feasting, drunkenness, and games.[16] The churches of Gregory of Tours were full of violence and intrigue.[17] The preacher spoke into a fraught space filled with visual and aural noise, which could distract from the sermon, but could also reinforce its message and the air of authority which the preacher was trying to convey.

In late antique Gaul, preaching was a standard part of the church service.[18] The Gallic mass reserved a place for a sermon, sermons are mentioned in all expositions and descriptions of the rite, and councils commanded that preaching happen every Sunday at least.[19] Caesarius of Arles urged that it be even more frequent, though it is unclear how many preachers followed his example.[20] It was certainly more common in the cities than in the countryside, where congregations depended upon visits from their bishop, or were at the mercy of local priests.[21] Most preaching would have been heard in the context of a liturgy.[22] The sermon would have been surrounded by processional entries, collective prayers, invocations and responses, chanting and singing, readings from scripture, the offering of the host, recital of the names of the dead, the kiss of peace, fraction of the host, and communion itself.[23] Special occasions were more elaborate, daily ones less so.[24] The laity were not yet passive spectators of this ritual:[25] they prayed, gave responses, sang psalms, and were required to take communion at least three times a year, to observe the major feasts, and to attend on Sundays as often as they could.[26] Some may have come to church every day,[27] others doubtless less often.[28]

The liturgy in which they took part was an idealised expression of Christian community,[29] an attempt to create a harmony and consensus which were not always manifest in practice.[30] The examples of Augustine's dispute with the congregation in Carthage over where he should stand to preach, and Caesarius locking the doors of his church to prevent people from leaving the service, illustrate that, as Catherine Bell argues, ritualisation permitted the continued possibility of resistance and appropriation.[31] Ceremony did not automatically create cohesion, and participation did not necessarily imply an internalisation of the values expressed.[32] Nonetheless, the appearance of consensus could sometimes help to create that consensus, and this was clearly the goal of those who conducted liturgy.[33] Liturgy was an argument for community, as reflected in the story of Germanus of Auxerre forcing a public confession from a liar in the course of the service, or of Gregory the Great preaching on even as his congregants dropped dead from plague.[34] These stories reflect the ideal that liturgy forged and bound community, and that sermons were preached as part of this effort.

Their liturgical context also influenced how sermons would have been heard and understood by their audiences. They were one part of a ceremony which culminated in the preeminent ritual of the faith, in which God was believed to be made flesh and was consumed by members of his community. Every part of the liturgy, sermon included, was potentially charged with the power of that moment. Moreover, the sermon was surrounded by formalised words and actions. These could make less structured speech dramatic by contrast, but they could also invest preaching with an air of *auctoritas* over and above the actual content of what was said. Sermons were not ordinary speech, but were rather ritualised in order to "distinguish and privilege" them in relation to other forms of speech.[35] Their formal structures, repetitiveness, and lack of spontaneity were strategies aimed at the coercion of consent.[36] Sermons were also, however, the one part of the service when pastors could directly address their flocks. As such, they were part of the liturgy, yet also distinct from the rest of it. They were used to discuss the scriptural readings which congregations had just heard, to explain theological issues, to encourage the laity in their hope for salvation, and to exhort them to do better, chastise them on their faults, urge repentance for sins, celebrate the saints, and mark the circuit of the liturgical year. They were the ideal teaching tool in a society with low levels of literacy and a high regard for oral communication.[37] Thus a persuasive, explanatory role coexisted, sometimes uneasily, with the status of sermons as ritualised utterances.

Because of their teaching role, most sermons were delivered in simple, straightforward Latin, comprehensible to the majority of the Christian community. Recent work has emphasised that the division

between Latin and the vernacular was a result of the Carolingian reforms which supposedly restored the ancient pronunciation of Latin
and initiated the phonetic spelling of the spoken language.[38] The
language of the late Roman and Merovingian sermons was a formal
version of the same language which ordinary people spoke.[39] Some
festal sermons were elaborate, some preachers were known for showing off their rhetorical skills, and some special audiences demanded
special efforts.[40] For ordinary, weekly preaching, however, pastors
generally followed the principle outlined by Augustine in *De doctrina christiana:* that there is no point to correct speech if it does not
meet with the listener's understanding, and that a teacher should
therefore avoid all language which does not communicate.[41] This
was of primary importance in preaching, where, as Banniard argues,
intercomprehension was fundamental to the act.[42] It was the essential responsibility of the preacher to ensure that his audience understood him, and elaborate typologies were developed to ensure that
both the language of preaching and the subject of the sermons themselves were appropriate for specific audiences.[43] Some preachers expressed this goal in programmatic statements, while others were less
explicit:[44] either way, clear language, common analogies, simple messages, repetition, and summary of the main points were the preacher's stock-in-trade.[45] Sermons could be very long—Hilary of Arles
was once reputed to have kept his congregation standing for four
hours, and Augustine preached an epic work to prevent his flock
from joining in the celebrations of the Kalends.[46] Usually, however,
sermons were kept short to ensure attention and to enable recall.[47]
The point of preaching was to be understood, and preachers strove
hard to make sure that they were.[48]

Caesarius may be taken as the high-water mark in any estimate
of how important preaching was for the late antique Church. He
insisted, repeatedly and in stern tones, on the bishop's obligation to
preach.[49] He urged his colleagues to do so as often as possible, in
church and out of it, to the willing and the unwilling.[50] He encouraged them by circulating model sermons and extending the right to
read these to priests and even deacons.[51] He instructed his congregation to attend church, listen carefully, demand preaching if they did

not get it, and discuss the lessons afterwards.[52] He attacked those who left before the sermon or objected to its content.[53]

For Caesarius, preaching was at the very heart of his pastoral mission. Few others were as dedicated, but preaching was nonetheless an important and highly valued skill in a Gallic pastor. Gennadius of Marseille made it a category of distinction in his praise of contemporaries and forebears, Sidonius Apollinaris lauded the abilities of Faustus of Riez, and Gregory of Tours recounted the achievements of Nicetius of Trier and Gregory the Great with awe.[54] Arator praised the number of preachers in sixth-century Gaul, and preaching was frequently mentioned in saints' lives as a signal of their virtue and pastoral ability.[55] Sermons by Valerian of Cimiez, Hilary of Arles, Faustus of Riez, Caesarius of Arles, Avitus of Vienne, as well as the Eusebius Gallicanus collection, have survived from the fifth and sixth centuries. Many more have doubtless been lost, or remain amidst the myriad anonymous and unedited sermons in medieval manuscripts.[56] Preachers of the time also drew on and used the circulating sermons of Ambrose of Milan, Augustine of Hippo, Maximus of Turin and others. By the Carolingian period, sermons were the natural vehicle for reform, and for communication with the Christian laity.[57] The preachers of the eighth and ninth centuries were able to draw upon a vast reservoir of Christian homiletics which had been produced and preserved by their late Roman and Merovingian predecessors.[58]

While preaching was valued and encouraged in late antique Gaul, the Church hierarchy recognised nonetheless that it was both a difficult and a dangerous practice. The levels of "pragmatic literacy" in Merovingian Gaul may have been higher than previously thought, but this did not guarantee that clergy were capable of producing the quality and quantity of composition required for preaching.[59] The educational system was no longer training young men in the skills required to churn out oratory, while the structures necessary to inculcate in the clergy a competent knowledge of the scriptures, exegesis, and apologetic technique were only beginning to emerge.[60] Unguided or illegitimate preaching was a potential cause of error and challenges to authority.[61] For this reason, the Church struggled with the preaching of subepiscopal clergy who might lack sufficient education or supervision. There was a long-standing Gallic custom of allowing priests to preach or to write sermons for others—the priests Salvian and Musaeus of Marseille were both praised by Gennadius for their homiletic output, and the "prologue" sermons in the Eusebius Gallicanus collection may have been written for priests preaching before their superiors.[62] This practice of using others' sermons was condemned by Pope Celestine and discouraged by some bishops, who linked it to heresy and disobedience,[63] but Caesarius of Arles, an ardent believer in the importance of preaching as a tool for spreading the "right" forms of the faith, encouraged priests and even deacons to read sermons written by established preachers.[64] Typical clergy might not be trusted to compose their own exegesis or to formulate their own theological explanations, but Caesarius maintained that if the lower clergy could read the sacred scriptures in church, they could also read the words of Ambrose or Augustine, and he pushed for confirmation of this right at the Council of Vaison in 529.[65]

This goal, of enabling preaching but also controlling its content, fuelled the proliferation of homiliaries. These were collections of model sermons which provided sound exegesis in good style, samples of moral exhortation, and exemplars for all the major liturgical festivals. Bishops put them together from their own and from patristic sermons, or commissioned copies of preexisting collections, which they distributed to clergy under their care.[66] Preachers unsure of their compositional abilities could simply read them out and the Church hierarchy could be sure that what they said was "safe." Set in this context, homiliaries emerge as conservative documents. They represent an attempt at stabilisation and control of preaching which reflects the power and importance of sermons in late antiquity and also represents an important stage in the development of the Church as an institution.[67]

For all these reasons, the sermons which scholars find in manuscripts occupy an especially indistinct position between oral and written forms of communication.[68] These texts are not transcripts of what preachers said, but versions produced before or after the event.

Some may never have been spoken aloud at all, though most were intended to be.[69] They both reified a fluid oral medium and democratised it, leaving congregations no longer dependent upon the increasingly rare compositional skills of their pastors, or upon the missionary fervour of unusual individuals. By writing, collecting, and copying sermons, scribes gave them an additional life. A sermon no longer had to be heard and it was no longer a singular event; it could be read, studied, and meditated upon. Homiliaries became devotional reading and intellectual resources as well as liturgical handbooks. As a result, even when preaching was less frequent, sermons lived on.

R. Emmet McLaughlin has argued that these homiliaries sounded the death knell for spontaneous, zealous preaching, and he is right.[70] Freely composed or extemporaneous sermons were increasingly discouraged in the liturgy, being regarded as dangerous or even improper. McLaughlin's lament, however, misses the significance of this change. The explosion of homiliaries from the sixth century on indicates a broad shift by the Christian Church towards consolidation of all that had been achieved so far.[71] By copying patristic sermons, bishops and scribes were setting out to create an orthodox tradition—dictating appropriate thought, responses, exegesis, and pastoral methods. When any clergy used these collections as a basis for their own preaching, they were presenting the carefully chosen combinations of words which the collections' compilers believed were the right way to represent Christianity to the world. During this same period, scribes were also compiling and consolidating other parts of the Church's intellectual heritage into *florilegia,* lectionaries, commentaries, anthologies, capitularies, and collections of Church council canons.[72] They were molding the Christian past and turning it into a handbook for the future. In these efforts lay the beginnings of an intellectual tradition and the necessary basis for the development of a Church—an institution which could sustain itself over vast periods of time and space.

The nature of the sermon texts which survive reflect this process. They are formulaic, plagiaristic, and often anonymous. Maurice Bloch has noted that religious speech, if it is to be perceived as authoritative and sacred, must conform to fixed patterns, and that sermons are carefully formalised religious oratory.[73] They were, it should be remembered, one act in the liturgy, itself hardly an impromptu or unstructured performance. They are filled with set phrases, expected arguments, and standard endings,[74] and an experienced preacher like Caesarius of Arles could churn them out as if on a production line.[75] The use of formulas entailed the risk of outright plagiarism, as the phrases, ideas, and entire homilies of those who had gone before were freely taken by preachers who had no sense for the rights of an author or the integrity of a text. If Augustine had said it properly and well, his words would suffice. Late antique sermons were constructed from a dizzying variety of references, quotations, borrowed phrases, and reworked passages, all unattributed. As a result, sermons, often the least-studied part of a famous author's oeuvre, could be the most influential. As Adalbert Hamman observes, while Augustine's controversial works lost their relevance and his theological works became the preserve of the elite, his sermons continued, often anonymously, to instruct the Christian people long after he was gone. "Mortuus adhuc loquitur."[76]

This formalisation and plagiarism was not necessarily restrictive for preachers. Although the intent of homiliaries was to fix and control preaching in accepted forms, they in fact facilitated diversity. By the fifth and sixth centuries, preachers could choose from "a veritable thesaurus" of approved actions and conventions.[77] Sermons are often variations on a theme, but each is a distinct variation, so that manuscripts are filled with what has been, for scholars, a maddening multiplicity of versions.[78] Indeed, part of the distaste with which some scholars view sermons from this period may be attributed to the complications and frustrations of studying them. The unembarrassed plagiarism of the age makes it almost impossible to tease out the exact contributions of any given preacher to any given text, and raises the problem of how words first spoken in fourth-century North Africa were understood by audiences in sixth-century Provence. It also means that those scholars who value originality and spontaneity in preaching find late antiquity and the early middle

ages "a remarkably fallow period."[79] Those who do work on late antique sermons naturally gravitate to known individuals with secure
corpuses. In the late antique West this has meant that scholarship
dwells on Ambrose of Milan, Augustine of Hippo, Caesarius of
Arles, and Gregory the Great, and to a lesser extent on Leo the Great,
Maximus of Turin, and Peter Chrysologus of Ravenna. As the only
representative from Gaul, and a marvelous source to boot, Caesarius
has often stood as the representative of all Gallic preaching in this
period.[80] While each of these preachers is important, influential, and
worthy of study, we should not forget that these are the people
whom the medieval Church subsequently deemed to be saints: charismatic leaders, wonder-workers, influential theologians, and zealous
missionaries. Few late antique Christians had a great rhetor or charismatic ascetic as their bishop; most would have heard preaching
based on anonymous or rehashed sermons, read from homiliaries or
other collections such as the Eusebius Gallicanus. Scholars who neglect these sermons provide a distorted picture of preaching in late
antique Gaul.

Some of these scholars have sought to play down the role of
preaching in the late antique Church.[81] Yet, as we have seen, it was a
highly valued skill and a potentially powerful and effective tool of
communication which the Church hierarchy expended great effort
to regularise and control. This fact becomes clear when sermons are
situated within the contexts of the church and the liturgy, and once
the nature of the texts is clearly illustrated.

Having surveyed the circumstances in which sermons were written, heard, and copied, and having illustrated something of the nature of these texts, the final context into which sermons need to be set
is their function. First and foremost, sermons were attempts to communicate with and persuade an audience.[82] For the sermons studied
here, that audience was most often the lay congregation standing in
a church, but it could also be fellow clergy or the inhabitants of a
monastery.[83] These people needed to be persuaded to behave as the
preacher was asking, to believe as he instructed, or to feel what he
intended them to. This need to persuade defined and delimited

what the preacher could say and how he could say it. It meant that sermons existed as part of a relationship, and not as stand-alone performances.

This relationship was a pastoral one. In other words, it was molded by the clergy's obligation to provide pastoral care for those under their charge.[84] This determined how preachers could and could not speak to their audiences. Having no real power, the clergy could not necessarily rely upon secular support and their religion was not yet at the stage where its dictates were automatically believed and followed, if indeed they ever were. Any members of the clergy who were not simply serving their time, who took their pastoral obligation at all seriously, were forced to *persuade* their congregations. The efficacy of their words was consequently at the forefront of preachers' concerns.[85] Sermons are thus not polemics, not theological statements, not celebrations of faith, and not abstract, contextless words on a page. They are constantly calculated appeals to their audiences; they exist to persuade, and this central function has concrete repercussions for how they should be read as texts.

As a first stage, scholars who use sermons as sources need always to be aware of the elements of audience and reception. This does not mean reconstructing lay piety and the behaviour of ordinary Christians, a different and quite separate project for which sermons are only partial evidence, but rather being aware of how preachers tried to reach their audiences and how their strategies were shaped by the reactions of those audiences. Some scholars have already recognised this. In the field of Augustinian studies, Theodore De Bruyn and Éric Rebillard have focused their attention upon the need to gauge audience reaction to episcopal preaching and to understand the efforts at mutual communication made by preacher and congregation. Rebillard has argued that Augustine's preaching on death changed in the face of audience despair, and that the arguments he eventually put forward were the result of pressure from his flock to articulate a message more amenable to their conceptions of Christianity.[86] De Bruyn has maintained that Augustine's sermons on the fall of Rome failed in their pastoral intent precisely because he was unable or unwilling to alter a message to which his audiences objected.[87] Both authors have placed the interaction between Augustine and his audience at the centre of their studies. Rebillard calls preaching an "interactive dialogue," and he and De Bruyn have been building on the work of those earlier historians who emphasised that Christianity was not a uniform monologue, dictated by elites, but perpetual debate.[88] This perspective also underpins Jaclyn Maxwell's recent book on John Chrysostom, where the dialogic nature of sermons is understood as a means to explore the "interaction and disagreements" between preacher and audience which resulted in the "democratization" of fourth-century Christian culture.[89] The efforts of these scholars have highlighted the agency of the laity in the formation of the Christian Church.

While preaching functioned as a dialogue, however, this was seldom the preachers' intent. Their goal was in fact to limit severely the interpretative autonomy of their audiences—to control the discourse itself and the ways in which their congregants thought about and understood their world.[90] The "formalisation" of the language of preaching, as Bloch points out, was part of this effort.[91] Highly formalised language is coercive, attempting to dictate appropriate responses and reactions and, in its most effective forms, making contradiction or negation impossible by virtue of its internal structures. It is efficacious because it is intangible.[92] It communicates without explanation and therefore cannot be argued with.[93] We should not assume that the preachers of the Eusebius Gallicanus or any other sermons achieved this aim, but it is essential to recognise it as their goal. As I will illustrate in subsequent chapters, they sought to determine the assumptions which Christians held, the grounds on which they reasoned and the conclusions which they reached.

Formalisation had limits: beyond a certain point it could be too constraining.[94] When preachers needed to engage with their audiences' anxieties in an active manner, they had to take a step closer to them. They did not want to engage in a dialogue, but they were often forced to do so. The persuasive strategies of the Eusebius Gallicanus preachers need to be understood in this light. They appeared to use reason, but sought to direct its use down precisely controlled channels, appealing to emotion in ways which outlined and delimited appropriate emotional responses. They sought to state and thereby shape the terms of the relationship between preacher and audience. This function of sermons directly determined the nature of the historical evidence which they provide.

Sermons pose significant challenges to any scholar who would use them as sources. These challenges are worth addressing, as they also provide opportunities. Sermons were one of the main vehicles of late antique pastoral care and are some of the only surviving evidence for it. The very characteristics which make them difficult for historians to work with—their anonymity, their plagiaristic and formulaic character, and the crossover between oral and written forms of communication—also point to their contemporary importance as part of an attempt to build power. They help us to understand exactly how that power was built—what mechanisms of attempted coercion and control were employed—but also to understand the limitations on that power. Freedom remained.[95] The audiences of sermons could and did respond to them as they chose. This meant that the clergy were in a situation of continual pressure. The texts we have were their carefully crafted responses to the challenges. They are far from abstract.

The Eusebius Gallicanus Sermon Collection

The Eusebius Gallicanus is a key example of an important genre: the anonymous collection, designed as a preaching handbook. As such it represents some widely practiced sermon models and preaching styles. We know that it was used and that it was popular.[1] It should loom large in scholarly discussions of early medieval preaching and the development of the Gallic Church, but to date it has not. This is, in large part, because of the seemingly unresolvable arguments over its authorship, an obstacle which has occupied the attention of scholars investigating the collection and scared off others from using such a contentious source. Such problems are endemic to sermon studies in general. As Dolbeau has shown, the confusion surrounding the sermons of Augustine has contributed to the relative neglect of the works of even so examined an individual.[2] Unsurprisingly, scholars have been even less inclined to dabble in the muddy waters of the Eusebius Gallicanus, and it has remained a peripheral source.

This chapter outlines the state of debate over the collection and why it has stalled on key issues. Some plausible solutions are suggested, but other questions are recognised as unanswerable. The latter arise from the nature of the source and from the extent to which late antique attitudes towards authorship and originality differ from our own. Rather than seeing these problems as roadblocks, however, I treat them as opportunities. Recognising the nature of the source and the context from which it emerges makes it possible for scholars to talk about and use the Eusebius Gallicanus not in spite of the problems it presents, but because the problems themselves are evidence for the history and character of the late antique Church.

It is characteristic of the state of Eusebian scholarship that even the collection's proper name is the subject of dispute. "Eusebius Gallicanus" was the designation granted it by a seventeenth-century editor based on the recurrence of the name Eusebius in manuscripts of the sermons and on their apparent Gallic origins.[3] No Eusebius of Gaul has emerged from the historical record to claim responsibility for the texts. Few medieval scribes seem to have known who the author was. They term him *Eusebius episcopus,* identify him with known Eusebii such as the bishops of Caesarea, Emesa, and Vercelli, and even suggest that the works were translated from Greek or Hebrew.[4] All of these scribal conjectures have been subsequently dismissed.[5] Instead, scholars argue that the name Eusebius may have been a pious pseudonym, a way of giving the collection an "oriental" flavour, or a result of confusion with a collection of sermons circulating under the name of Eusebius of Alexandria.[6] They also point out that the scribes just as frequently claimed the sermons for Augustine, Caesarius, Faustus, Faustinus, Gregory, Jerome, Maximus, and others.[7] As a result the collection has been known, among other things, as the "pseudo-Eusebius," the "Collectio Gallicana," and the "collection attributed to Eusebius of Emesa."[8] This proliferation of titles has only added to the confusion surrounding the text and the difficulty for scholars in accessing information about it. The collection is designated the "Eusebius Gallicanus" in this study because this is the name under which it has now been edited in the *CCSL*. This choice does not imply a specific claim about the sermons' authorship but is simply in the interest of standardisation. Scholarly circumlocutions, though accurate, are in this instance unhelpful.

What Jean Leroy terms the "nomenclature luxuriante" of the Eusebius Gallicanus manuscripts resulted in a complicated publishing history prior to the *Corpus Christianorum* edition.[9] In 1531 the ten sermons *ad monachos* were published in Cologne under the name of Eusebius, bishop of Emesa.[10] Jean de Gaigny published fifty-six of the homilies under this same attribution in 1547 and eighteen of them were published by Lievens under the name of Eucherius of Lyon in 1602. These two editions were then published together by André Schott in 1618 under the name Eusebius Gallicanus and reissued in 1677 as part of the *Maxima Bibliotheca Patrum*. Sermons included in the *CCSL* edition by Glorie have also appeared in editions of the works of other authors, particularly Faustus of Riez, Eucherius of Lyon, Caesarius of Arles, and Maximus of Turin.[11] Leroy and Fr. Glorie's work has been invaluable in clearing up this confusion, and providing a stable and clear corpus.[12] Their work provides the evidentiary foundation for this study.

The problem of attribution arises because, like most other sermons of this period, those in the Eusebius Gallicanus collection were not *ex nihilo* original compositions. Their authors drew extensively on the words and phrases of a number of different authors, most especially Ambrose of Milan, Augustine of Hippo, Faustus of Riez, Jerome, Hilary of Arles, Maximus of Turin, and Tertullian.[13] These derivative works were in turn excerpted and absorbed by Caesarius of Arles, Columbanus, Defensor, Isidore of Seville, and many others.[14] Authorship was not as important and sacrosanct a concept to late antique preachers as it is to us. Their unoriginality was what gave the Eusebius Gallicanus sermons the stamp of authority and was one of the main reasons for their ongoing popularity.

However, this "plagiaristic habit," common to all late antique preachers, makes the process of determining authorship extremely difficult and has been the root cause of much of the confusion surrounding the collection. The dissensus has thus far centred on who

wrote the sermons in the Eusebius Gallicanus collection, and the differing solutions to this problem have spin-off implications for the
dating and nature of the compilation process. There are two main
schools of thought on the collection's provenance. One theory holds
that the sermons are the work of Faustus of Riez (ca. 410–490/500).
In his unpublished thesis, Leroy advances the most complete and
uncompromising version of this case. His argument has two stages.
First, he maintains that the sermons in the collection possess a stylistic and thematic unity and that this unity can only be explained
if they all share a single author.[15] Second, he argues that this author
is Faustus. Almost everyone, he notes, agrees that at least one sermon in the collection, sermon thirty-five on Maximus of Riez, was
the work of his successor Faustus. If we accept the stylistic unity of
the collection, therefore, *all* the sermons should logically be attributed to Faustus. Leroy bolsters this case by dismissing a series of
other possible candidates and by pointing out that Faustus fits the
circumstances—he was acclaimed for his preaching, he had opportunities to preach to both monks and laity, and he was abbot of
Lérins, which has been seen by many as a likely original setting for
the sermons to monks. Leroy also argues that the sermons are consistent with Faustus' theological views and with the style, cadence, and
expression of his letters and treatises, an argument which Leroy supports with a long list of textual parallels to the bishop of Riez's known
works.[16] He explains the lack of a clear attribution by arguing that
the sermons lost their association with the bishop of Riez after his
views on grace and free will were deemed theologically unsound by
subsequent generations.[17] Leroy expresses his case with great confidence and vast documentation, and his argument has been accepted
by a number of scholars. His support of Faustus' candidacy is shared
by August G. Engelbrecht, Élie Griffe, Bernard Leeming, Alexander
Souter, Buchem, Carle, and Nürnberg.[18] Variations on it were advanced by both Germain Morin and Clare Stancliffe, who argue that
the collection in its present state was the product of someone who
compiled the sermons of Faustus subsequent to their composition,
perhaps working from the episcopal archives of Riez.[19] For Morin
and Stancliffe, this supposition explains the signs of editing and the

elements of later composition found in the texts, as well as the re-hashing of some passages. Stancliffe argues that the sermons circu-lated in smaller groups before being gathered into their present form and that they did not circulate as a collection prior to the episcopacy of Caesarius of Arles (502–542).[20]

Leroy's case for Faustus, however, is far from conclusive. Other Gallic bishops were known for their preaching, had ties to Lérins, preached to both monks and laity, and espoused what has been char-acterised as a "semi-pelagian" theology.[21] Leroy's argument chiefly consists in demonstrating that these other candidates are less likely than Faustus. The only positive argument Leroy can offer, linking the bishop of Riez to the sermons on stylistic grounds, has not been decisive. As Morin and Wilhelm Bergmann note, challenging the earlier attempt by Engelbrecht to establish a "control" of Faustian style, such efforts inevitably stumble against the barriers of genre and the plagiaristic nature of late antique homiletics.[22] The extensive tex-tual borrowing of the Eusebius Gallicanus sermons make a mockery of "stylistic parallel" lists such as the one Leroy has painstakingly compiled. As Glorie points out, a similar exhaustive trawl through the writings of other authors from the same milieu as Faustus would find as many echoes in the Eusebian sermons.[23] To search for an iso-latable and original voice in the Eusebius Gallicanus is to misunder-stand their nature and their process of formation.

Most scholars agree that some of the sermons in the Eusebius Gallicanus are the work of Faustus of Riez,[24] but Leroy's insistence that all of them are his work has been contested. Jill Harries, Weiss, and Ralph Mathisen argue that the sermons on Blandina and on Epipodius and Alexander were most likely the work of a bishop of Lyon, perhaps Eucherius (d. ca. 449/55) or Patiens (d. ca. 480).[25] A good case could be made that the sermon on Genesius of Arles should be attributed to a bishop of that city, perhaps Hilary (ca. 401–449).[26] Rivet doubts that the litany described in sermon twenty-five had been instituted in Riez by the time of Faustus' episcopate.[27] Kasper argues that twelve sermons in the collection are either not by Faustus or do not contain sufficient material for a definite attribu-tion.[28] These arguments constitute a serious challenge to Leroy's case that the Eusebius Gallicanus sermons are all and only the work of Faustus of Riez.

Ironically, given that Glorie's edition of the Eusebius Gallicanus is based on Leroy's work, Glorie has been the most vocal opponent of the "only Faustus" theory. He attacks Leroy's claim of authorial unity and maintains that the sermons in the collection were originally by a number of different authors, including, but not limited to, Zeno of Verona, Ambrose of Milan, Augustine of Hippo, Hilary of Arles, Faustus of Riez, and "Eusebius of Alexandria."[29] These sermons, he argues, were collected, rewritten, and circulated in the sixth century by Caesarius of Arles, and from Caesarius' small compilations a later hand put together the Eusebius Gallicanus collection, perhaps in the seventh century.[30] Glorie sees this line of transmission as explaining the many parallels between the Eusebius Gallicanus texts and Caesarius' sermons. In contrast to Leroy, Glorie emphasises the stylistic disunity of the collection, and maintains that any coherence it now possesses can be attributed to the editing and reworking of a compiler.[31] Glorie's argument has not gained widespread acceptance for several reasons. First, although the words and phrases of the authors he cites appear in the Eusebius Gallicanus, this is a result of their plagiaristic character, not a consequence of the wholesale importation of sermons by non-Gallic authors. Second, establishing the chronology of textual borrowings is notoriously difficult.[32] Several scholars have studied the same texts and concluded the opposite of Glorie: they see the parallels as showing that the collection must have existed *before* Caesarius.[33] Finally, as subsequent chapters will make clear, there are substantial differences in the pastoral styles of the Eusebius Gallicanus sermons and the sermons of Caesarius of Arles.[34] Morin, the foremost expert on Caesarius, concluded that the Eusebius Gallicanus sermons were neither written nor edited by him, but that he had access to the texts.[35] Morin's argument is supported by the conclusions of my study.

Though Caesarius has not replaced Faustus as the guiding hand perceived to be behind the collection, a number of scholars have shared Glorie's view that the sermons do not have a single author. As early as 1898, Bergmann attacked any arguments for stylistic unity

in the Eusebius Gallicanus collection, maintaining that the plagiaristic nature of the sermons makes authorship claims difficult, if not
impossible, to sustain.[36] More recently, Kasper has delineated in
great detail which sermons he thinks are by Faustus, which are revised versions of Faustian sermons and which are not by the bishop
of Riez at all.[37] Weiss and Weigel share this scepticism about Leroy's
theory, both arguing for some form of multiple authorship.[38]

These differences over provenance have paralysed scholarship.
Both sides have talked themselves to a standstill, while those seeking
to use the collection as evidence have been disheartened by the confusion. This outcome is understandable but unnecessary. It is possible to pluck points of common ground from the disagreements and
to suggest plausible solutions to some of the issues. Most importantly, however, it is essential to recognise the scholarly dissensus as
arising from an approach which is ill-suited to the character of the
source. Once this point is appreciated, the usefulness of the Eusebian evidence becomes apparent.

Despite their disagreements, almost all scholars date the Eusebius Gallicanus sermons in their original form to the mid- to late
fifth century and locate them in south-eastern Gaul. Though they
have been denuded of much specific detail in the compilation and
copying process, their style, their stance on issues of grace and free
will, their accounts of local saints' cults in Arles, Lyon, and Riez, and
their references to the monastery at Lérins and to barbarian "troubles" are sufficient to convince.[39] At least some of them were the work
of Faustus, bishop of Riez during this period. The collection was
very popular, and copies of it were circulating widely by the seventh
century at the latest.[40]

From this common ground it is possible to offer a plausible reconstruction of the Eusebius Gallicanus' origins. As Morin and Stancliffe suggested, the collection may have been compiled chiefly out of
the archives of the church of Riez. Copies of Faustus' sermons would
have been kept there, but so too, perhaps, were sermons of his colleagues, friends, and predecessors, of which he had received or commissioned copies.[41] The epistolary networks of late antique Gaul are
well documented for this period—sustained not only by exchange of

letters but also by the circulation of works such as treatises and sermons.[42] This kind of exchange was particularly established among the alumni of Lérins, among whom can be counted a number of names mentioned as possible Eusebian authors: Hilary of Arles, Eucherius and Patiens of Lyon, Maximus of Riez, and Faustus himself.[43] These kinds of exchanges would have resulted in impressive episcopal libraries, ripe for subsequent plundering.[44] If the Eusebian compiler was working out of such a library or archive in Riez, this would explain the prominence of Faustus' works and the collection's lingering association with him. The compiler was probably working in the early to mid-sixth century, around the same time as Caesarius of Arles. Caesarius may have known the collection in the form we have it, or the sermons may have circulated in other forms as well. There are interesting points of both connection and conscious divergence between Caesarius' sermons and the Eusebius Gallicanus collection, which I will explore in the course of this study.

The Eusebian compiler had specific pastoral goals in mind, so he chose sermons in a common style, edited them of specific content, reworked them, and undoubtedly added phrases of his own.[45] The extent of such a reediting process is no longer recoverable, but would both account for what coherence the collection possesses and the observable disjunctures and differences between individual sermons which remain. The compiler included whatever he found useful, because he was not putting together a collection of the sermons of Faustus of Riez, but a preaching guide or resource—a series of "models" to be followed. This is clear from the way the collection follows the liturgical year, provides examples for all major feasts, and even includes "sample introductions" to suit various situations and audiences.[46] This was a preaching handbook.[47] The sermons were not examples of amazing rhetoric and composition, or the famous words of famous men, but were solid, simple, reliable examples of the main subjects on which a Gallic pastor would have to preach. The collection may have been commissioned by a sixth-century bishop of Riez seeking to support and facilitate the preaching of his clergy. We know that such handbooks were being produced in this period and the Eusebius Gallicanus has all the characteristics we would expect

in such a work: coverage of the liturgical year, generic topical sermons, and model introductions. Caesarius was engaged in the same
kind of endeavour, gathering groups of sermons and circulating them
among his contacts.[48] His accompanying correspondence makes it
clear that the goal was to enable preaching, not just to provide inspirational reading.[49] The structure and usage of the Eusebius Gallicanus collection suggest a similar intent.

Some form of multiple authorship seems the best explanation for
the current form of the Eusebius Gallicanus. I will therefore always
refer to the "preachers" and "authors" of the collection. The compiler
is always a presence, too, but unfortunately his contribution or influence is impossible to separate from the work of the original authors.
As Dolbeau has shown in regard to Augustine's sermons, it is extremely difficult to disentangle authentic from apocryphal elements
in homilies which have undergone extensive editing. Indeed, even
approaching sermons with such categories in mind is much too sim-
plistic.[50] Rather than trying to tease out earlier and later elements in
the transmission of individual sermons, this study treats them as integral texts in and of themselves. Where the nature of the collection
as a whole is considered, on the other hand, the voice of the compiler
will be assumed to be the guide.

Overall, however, the question of authorship is less important
than the debates have made it appear. It is possible to write about
the Eusebius Gallicanus, to use it as a source, to study its contents,
and to examine its nature as a collection without knowing or agree-
ing on which fifth-century preacher(s) in south-eastern Gaul are responsible for its contents. The works of Kasper, Nürnberg, Bruzzone, Weiss, and Brigitte Beaujard point the way forward in this
respect. These authors do not agree on the collection's origins, yet all
use it in ways which provide insight into the development of the late
antique Church. As the manuscript tradition shows, our obsession
with authorship was not shared by medieval scribes. The sermons
were copied and used not because they were the work of a famous individual, but because they were useful. Attribution gave a text the
stamp of authority and was freely manipulated to provide it when
necessary. Moreover, just as the authors of the Eusebian sermons "cut

and pasted" the Bible, Ambrose, Augustine, Jerome, and the words of their friends and colleagues to build the final product they wanted, so subsequent scribes and compilers did the same to them. These were words to be cannibalized, rephrased, reworked, edited, and plagiarised. The orthodox textual tradition was available for all. Not knowing the authors of the Eusebian sermons did not prevent medieval preachers and scribes from using them. It should not prevent us either.

It is therefore both possible and important to move past the still unresolved debates over authorship and begin using the Eusebius Gallicanus as a source. Its pastoral style not only reveals the goals, strategies, and aspirations of the fifth-century Gallic episcopate, but also which of their ideas had resonance in the sixth century and beyond. It lays bare the canonisation of ideas and arguments within the Christian tradition and the development of a cultural fund of sanctioned words. It illustrates the centrality of pastoral care in the Gallic Church and the lasting influence of its fifth-century formulations. It deserves, in other words, far more attention than scholars have so far given it.

CHAPTER THREE

Building Community

The first priority of Gallic pastors was to build Christian communities. Communities were there already, of course, but they were not necessarily Christian in identity or focused on the Church. Christianity was not indigenous to Gaul. It was an imported religion, laid over preexisting structures and relationships.[1] If the Christian Church was to succeed in Gaul, it needed to integrate itself into these communities and to change their sense of themselves, perhaps even their very nature. In each individual community, clergy were faced with a small version of the big challenge. They needed to find a place for themselves within their own town or city and to make their authority felt, their instructions respected, and their position supported. While this integration was never an explicit goal, immediate pressures and needs pushed pastors towards it, and it was advanced by their individual, uncoordinated efforts in their own interests.

The efforts of clergy to build and maintain the ties of community have been the subject of extensive scholarly discussion and analysis. Attention has focused on three main mechanisms of community formation: the cult of the saints, the fusion of secular and religious models of leadership in the figure of the bishop, and the creation of community boundaries through the exclusion of some members and the enforcement of more uniform behaviour upon others.[2] The Eusebius Gallicanus sermons provide some further substantiation of these strategies, but they also challenge aspects of the picture as it has been understood up to now. The collection makes clear that not all pastors went about building community in the same way and that not all had the same vision of the ideal community. For example, although the Eusebius Gallicanus collection contains sermons exalting saints, each works slightly differently depending on specific local pressures. The style of leadership found in the Eusebian sermons, meanwhile, is markedly distinct from that of some other contemporary visions: salvation is conceived of as a community project rather than an individual one, and the enforcement of boundaries was rejected as a strategy in favour of a looser and more inclusive community model. In all of this, the Eusebius Gallicanus preachers were very influenced by monastic models of community building, but the result was not necessarily what we might expect.[3]

Concord and consensus were established ideals of community relations. Paul's first letter to the Corinthians provided an early Christian archetype for exhortations to unity.[4] His use of the metaphor of the body for human society, in which all parts must work together for the whole to thrive, served as a template for subsequent Christian understandings of how communities should ideally function.[5] His conception of the church as "a family or household in need of harmony," meanwhile, became standard.[6] These aspects of the early Christian intellectual tradition melded with Stoic notions of the communality of humankind and concomitant duties to mutual care and sociability.[7] Love, mutuality, and the sharing of burdens were presented to late antique Christians as the goals towards which they should jointly strive. Consensus became the mark of a successful community, but its achievement in practice was so rare, so contrary to human nature, that it was seen not only as a triumph of human virtue, but also as a signal of the working of the Holy Spirit. It was especially lauded in the election of bishops and the decision making of church councils, notoriously fractious events, out of which unity was a result both necessary and miraculous.[8] It came to be seen as the definitive characteristic of orthodoxy and was used to browbeat dissident religious movements or to canonise the status quo.[9] Consensus could, therefore, be a tool of coercion as well as incorporation. Its very importance sometimes required the exclusion of inconvenient dissent, thus operating as a mechanism to negate difference.[10] Notions of consensus, however, were not uniform. Not everyone envisaged the same kind of unity or drew the same kind of implications from the rhetoric of mutuality. These varied notions served as persuasive tools, not stable ideals. We will gain a fuller sense of the diverse forms and ideals of Christian community in late antique Gaul if we examine the strategies employed in any particular text.

Like a number of other Gallic pastors, the authors of the Eusebius Gallicanus sermons saw the cult of the saints as a useful mechanism by which to build community. The Eusebius Gallicanus sermons on local saints are unlike others in the collection. This is because they can be fixed in certain locations, whereas most of the Eusebius Gallicanus sermons float untethered by geography.[11] Their fixity enables a more precise analysis of the pressures behind their particular strategies. We find in these sermons the most explicit and familiar efforts at community building which the collection has to offer, and they shed important light on the rest of the collection.

The sermons on local saints also remind us how much context we are missing. They were very likely only one part of the celebration of the saint, accompanying perhaps a procession to an associated holy site, the veneration of a tomb or of relics, or a feast in the saint's honour.[12] These could be highly charged occasions on which some people expected miracles.[13] These ritualized acts were intended to build community and consensus, and the rhetoric of the sermons we have was therefore bolstered by the surrounding events which are now largely invisible to us.[14] They connected the cult of their saints to the landscape of the cities in which they were preached and established a correlation between Christian and civic identities. They were clearly part of the pastors' efforts to integrate themselves into Gallic communities.

The most striking feature of the Eusebius Gallicanus sermons on local saints is their sometimes intense parochialism.[15] This is most evident in the two sermons from Lyon, both of which celebrate the martyrs killed there in 177/8.[16] Sermon fifty-five, for example, expounded at length the virtues of two of them, Epipodius and Alexander, and recommended their veneration to the citizens of Lyon by evoking local pride and connections.[17] It may be a great thing, the preacher conceded, to join in general Christian celebrations, but it is greater still to celebrate the virtues of our alumni. For "just as the cult of our native martyrs and the honour of our special patrons give their own particular joy, so they demand their own special devotion."[18] The connection between the people of Lyon and their martyrs was partly one of "civic fellowship" with "fellow citizens," but it was also a familial bond. "We are related" to the saints, the preacher told his audience, "by right of birth, because we sat on the lap of the one parent."[19] Their story of persecution is a call to action on behalf of the family. "Does it not cry to our hearts, the living voice of the blood of our kin?"[20] The preacher of this sermon repeatedly emphasised the native status of Epipodius and Alexander, and made this the basis for their claims upon the citizens of Lyon. "So it is, dearly beloved, that in order to hold fast to our faith, in order to cultivate religion, we should not await some examples from far away: we are instructed by the tutors of our fatherland, and we are admonished by examples from our household."[21] The rivalry with other, more prestigious Christian cities was explicit. "The faith of our Church celebrates together the double victories of Epipodius and Alexander . . . not festivals with relics which come from abroad, but festivals with inviolate memorials of the bosom of the *patria*."[22] "What could suffice for the entire world, we hold enclosed exclusively within the bosom of this city and we raise up those twin palms of triumph rivaling the apostolic city, and, having also our own Peter and Paul, we vie with our two supporters against that exalted see."[23] The repeated first person plural forms testify to the attempt to build local pride into a common, local, Christian identity.[24] This emphasis combined with imagery of kinship and family to provide what the preacher clearly hoped would be a potent bond. He was not trying to build a universal Church, but rather to establish a central place for himself in Lyon.

The same highly localised conception of community can be found in sermon eleven, the other Eusebius Gallicanus sermon known to have been preached in Lyon. Ostensibly it celebrates Blandina, one of the more famous of the Christians killed in the persecution of 177/8, but in fact the entire group of martyrs is glorified.[25] In a long speech, the personified city of Lyon exclaims upon the superiority of its own martyrs to those of Bethlehem, that is, the children killed by Herod. "The innocence of the dead crowned you, the glory of the triumphant crowned me; yours arrived at the reward of the kingdom without consciousness of martyrdom, mine, however, reached it afflicted by torments, confirmed by prayers, cooked in the manner of a sacrifice by savage flames."[26] These virtues were translated into a powerful local pride. "The people of a city exult even if they are defended by the relics of one martyr; and behold, we possess an entire populace of martyrs. Our land should rejoice to be the nurse of heavenly soldiers and fertile parent of such virtues."[27] Once again the images of citizenship and family served as the interconnected bonds tying the community to the saints, and community members to one another. Their deaths were linked to the geography of the town, and its landscape served in the sermon to support the theological points the preacher wished to make. The waters of the Rhône may have swallowed their dust, but could not deny their resurrection.[28] In Eusebian sermon eleven, as in sermon fifty-five, the language of possession, and exclusion, and the extensive use of first person plural forms acted almost to break down the possibility of a universal Christian identity and to replace it with one focused solely on the immediate community.

This strategy made sense in Lyon. Lyon's position within the Roman empire of the fifth century was nothing to celebrate. The Christian community there dated back to the mid-second century, but after the bloodbath of 177/8 there was little further certain trace of Christianity until the fourth century.[29] Hit hard by the crises of the period and by new political arrangements, Lyon and its church were alike on the downward slide from former preeminence during the fifth and sixth centuries.[30] This sharp decline in power, prestige, and prosperity meant that the city had to be increasingly inward-looking and self-reliant. To rekindle civic pride and to do so in a way which aided the Church, the preacher reached back to a past moment of Christian heroism. He sought to evoke continuity of community from that persecuted group of martyrs to the current citizens of Lyon, their heirs, and their descendants. He evoked local pride in deliberate contrast to a broader community which was doing Lyon no favours. Although his rhetoric was standard, it was tailored precisely to the pastoral pressures he faced.

The situation in Arles was different. Arles enjoyed a position of thriving prominence in the late Roman empire.[31] Newly promoted to capital of the praetorian prefecture, Arles added to this secular status a claim to metropolitan rights over many of the bishoprics of the south.[32] Although it suffered in the military struggles of the late fifth century, it remained an important administrative centre for the Church, reflected in the fact that its bishop Caesarius (ca. 502–542) obtained confirmation of his metropolitan powers, was appointed papal vicar in Gaul, and presided over a series of important Church councils.[33] The preacher of the sermon on Genesius of Arles therefore felt no pressure to evoke such intense localism or to claim superiority over a broader, more universal vision of Christian community.[34] The challenge here was to build civic unity. Arles was a city wracked by divisions, especially between the inhabitants of the separate banks of the Rhône river.[35] The preacher therefore emphasized the ways in which Genesius connected the two sections of the community.[36] In the course of his martyrdom, the preacher told the city's inhabitants, Genesius crossed the dividing river. He died on one side, was buried on the other, and had commemorative buildings on both.[37] Each side of Arles was sanctified—one because it possessed his body, the other because it was where he spilt his blood.[38]

To this argument the preacher added the rhetoric of familial and civic imagery. On the day of their martyrdom, the preacher told his congregation, "sons of man," the saints, "ascend into the adoption of divine paternity, and those who a short time before were brothers and sisters of mortals, suddenly begin to be fellow-citizens of an-gels."[39] As a result of their veneration, the faithful people of this "most fortunate city" exult in "the assistance of their very own per-petual defender."[40] Possessiveness of and common identification with the saint were the bases of the preacher's attempt to build communal unity.

In Eusebius Gallicanus sermon thirty-five, the same vocabulary of citizenship, family, and belonging can be seen employed in a dif-ferent way in response to yet a different situation. This sermon, al-most certainly by Faustus, commemorated a more recent hero of the Church, Maximus of Riez, Faustus' predecessor as bishop.[41] The purpose of this sermon was thus different from those celebrating already legendary martyrs. Maximus was not a martyr, and was in fact only recently dead. The sermon reads as a *vita,* providing the story of the saint's journey through life and his achievements as bishop of Riez. It constituted an appeal to the community of Riez to accept Maximus as a saint, and as a local focus of Christian identity in a city which lacked an illustrious martyrial history. Christianity seems to have arrived relatively late in Riez. Its bishopric was prob-ably not created until the beginning of the fifth century and Maxi-mus is the first bishop we can name.[42] This perhaps explains the compacted sense of historical time which the sermon displays, as well as its concern to establish the bishop as a central figure in the community. The fifth century seems to have been a period of relative prosperity and prestige for Riez, marked by the construction of the episcopal group in the centre of the city, and by the episcopates of two well-known and active bishops.[43] The sermon on Maximus re-flects some of this optimism as it attempts to build a central Chris-tian position in the city's identity.

Unlike the sermons on the saints of Lyon, that on Maximus did not rely on an explicit contrast with the wider Christian community—the preacher perhaps lacked comparable confidence in his community's importance. Even so, it contained an implicit contrast with universality through its repeated tying of Maximus to Riez by stressing his indigenous status. The preacher told how, after rejecting family and homeland to become an ascetic, Maximus was sought as a bishop by the town of Fréjus, "which embraced him as if he were their own—a native inhabitant of their territory."[44] Fréjus was not his true homeland, however, and Maximus fled the honour, an act applauded by the preacher; the hero is "chastised," however, for similar behaviour when he sought to avoid his responsibilities to the town of Riez.[45] "Wherever you hide, you deny yourself in vain to your homeland through your flight."[46] According to the preacher, the claim of his *patria* upon him was just.[47] All Maximus' time at the monastery in Lérins had been but preparation for his role as bishop in Riez. He was like a merchant, gathering treasures from across the sea to bring back to his homeland.[48] He had an obligation to return.

The emphasis in this sermon on Maximus' status as a native appears pointed in the light of the controversy over foreign bishops in Gaul at this time. Tensions had particularly surrounded bishops coming, as both Maximus and Faustus did, from the Lérins monastery.[49] In this context, the preacher's evocations of family, locality, and belonging take on a defensive light. The preacher, probably himself a foreigner, was seeking to build community identity around the Church, and around himself, by highlighting the example of his native predecessor and colleague, with whom he identified strongly.[50] In a place where the church may have been a relatively young institution, the preacher's priority was to use civic imagery to create a vision of a community bound tightly to its bishop.

The sermons on local saints make clear the degree of variation and specificity at work in pastoral care. It is unfortunately not possible to be as precise about other sermons in the Eusebius Gallicanus, because they cannot be as confidently pinned down to particular cities or probable authors. The focus on community building which dominates these sermons can, however, be found in less explicit forms through the rest of the collection. The sermons on local saints draw our attention to three strategies: the evocation of civic bonds, the use of familial imagery, and an emphasis on concord and unity. Other Eusebian sermons make more explicit how these communal bonds should work in practice. We also get a more specific sense from the rest of the collection of the ideal form of Christian community, and particularly the model of the relationship between a pastor and his flock. These visions of community were also strategies for creating it, but they have been less studied than the cult of the saints and they reveal some interesting divergences from other contemporary approaches.

Attention to the specific forms of imagery is once again rewarding. Family was a standard model of the ideal community, and not just in a Christian context;[51] family was a useful metaphor because of the strength of connection and the bonds of affection it implied, and because of the opportunity it afforded to evoke a "naturalised" hierarchy.[52] Leaders who depicted themselves as fathers were conveying a sense of great power, exercised from a position of superior knowledge, in the interests of those under its sway.[53] This was not, however, the only form which kinship imagery could take. In Eusebian sermon fifty-four, for example, the kinship image employed was the relationship between siblings, a relationship also strong and affectionate, but more egalitarian and reciprocal in nature.[54] The preacher of this sermon used fraternal imagery to evoke the ideal bonds between community members, himself included. "For we are all brothers, begot from the one creator, and descended from the same flesh, from the first man, tied together by the double binds of Christ and the Church, joined by nature and the power of grace, called into one faith, restored by one price. We are brothers, I say . . . and, if we deserve, we are joined in the fraternity of angels as heirs to the one father . . . We are brothers, born of the same mother through the bath of one font, we are blood-brothers through the one salvific transaction."[55] This rhetoric evoked not hierarchy, but a community governed by mutual responsibility and common interest.

The author of Eusebian sermon fifty presented the same communitarian ideal, but he chose a series of images from the natural world as his vehicle. When birds travel long distances, he told his audience, they arrange themselves such that "the stronger ones successively support the weaker, and it is as if the journey itself teaches diligent mutual care to each of them."[56] Likewise, when deer swim, they support the weight of their horns by resting their heads on each other's backs, taking turns to be in the front of a line, and then going to the back, sharing the labour among them.[57] This passage was drawn almost word for word from one of Augustine's sermons on the Psalms, which was itself drawn from Pliny's *Natural History.*[58] In his take on the passage, Augustine had drawn a link between the story of the deer and Galatians 6.2: "Bear ye one another's burdens." This theme was not Augustine's pastoral priority in this sermon, and he had quickly returned to his main topic of longing for God.[59] The Eusebian preacher, however, took Augustine's side remark and built upon it to make the passage a model of ideal Christian relations. "And thus brute animals, who do not know charity, assist one after another through their labours, and render a mutual service to themselves. What should we do, to whom the author of reason has given understanding, to whom the redeemer has offered an example of love?"[60] To this argument the preacher added further scriptural authority. "Humbly reckon others better than yourselves," he instructed, paraphrasing Philippians 2.3–4, "considering not your own interests, but those of others."[61] "That is," he explained, "consulting with others over mutual needs."[62] We should beware, he told his congregants, "lest, like the reeds which are tossed about by every wind, and collide against each other with light blows, so we, by the inconstancy of our souls, are led to inflict injuries on our neighbours, and there should be in us an inability to help and an ability to hinder. But rather, considering our mutual advantage, we should attend to the good of others and take turns to carry our labours and burdens."[63]

Concord, mutuality, and reciprocity governed the ideal of community presented in these two sermons, and the preachers' choice of imagery reveals the specific ideal they had in mind. In contrast to the standard Christian metaphors of the body and the hierarchical family unit, the imagery chosen for both Eusebian sermons fifty-four and fifty was strikingly egalitarian. The birds and the deer epitomised relationships in which individuals took turns to lead and to follow, while siblings possessed coequal status within a family.[64] These models of community were based on close and affectionate bonds among members who owed service to one another; they were communities of equals.

We should not conclude, however, that the cooperative model of community was noncoercive in intent: rather, a choice was being made about how best to pressure and persuade a congregation. Those Eusebius Gallicanus sermons which gave practical advice on community relations make this dynamic clear. Communality, the author of sermon fifty-three argued, meant that congregants should never claim religious or spiritual superiority over each other. His hero was the humble publican, contrasted with the smug condemnation of his companion offered by the Pharisee.[65] Even if our brother delights in sinning, we should turn our minds' eyes inward. We should ask if we are really any better. This tone was reflected in the collection as a whole. Among the sins most frequently condemned by the Eusebian preachers were detraction, hypocrisy, and the denigration of others.[66] These were identified as dangerous because they threatened the harmony of the community. The author of sermon fifty-three developed this emphasis into an argument that the strength and progress of the Christian community required the contribution of all its members. Every individual, he argued, shares in the common debt owed to God. "One does not therefore owe less, if another should owe the same."[67] The individual is obliged to contribute to the group since the group debt can be paid only if all take their part equally. The preacher of Eusebian sermon forty-eight shaped his argument to make the point that no Christian had the right to withdraw from the community, and he berated congregants who remained at home to work their land rather than going to town to attend church. "But perhaps someone says to himself: 'I should take care of my body, I should be concerned about the necessities of life.'" "Can it really be, dearly beloved," the preacher rejoined, "that man, made in the image of God, should think this his primary care, rather than that which he sees he has in common with the flock?"[68] Thus the notion of obligation to others could be an effective coercive tool.

In these sermons, salvation was portrayed as a community task, a joint undertaking requiring the commitment of all community members. This theme emerged most clearly in sermon twenty-five, which described a penitential litany. This litany was similar to the communal processions and prayer offerings recounted in other late antique Gallic sources, and often referred to as the Rogations.[69] We know of such ceremonies taking place in Clermont and Vienne in response to threats to the consensus of those communities. At moments when the cities were riven by class-based divisions and beset by disasters, the bishops sought to unite their congregants through a common ritual action which reduced all to the level of penitents and thereby obviated social difference.[70]

The penitential litany described in Eusebian sermon twenty-five was expected to function in this way. According to the preacher, the community had been engaged in three days of fasting, supplications, and labours of contrition in an attempt to ward off natural and human catastrophe and to ensure that their prayers were heard. "For we are about to obtain through prayer that the Lord forbids infirmities, plagues, and tribulations: that he drives away the evils of pestilence, of hostility, of hail and of drought; that he brings together the proper mixture of weather for the safety of the body and for the fertility of the earth, that he grants the peace of the elements and the tranquility of the times, that he dismisses sins, and withdraws the scourges."[71]

There were those, however, the preacher claimed, who were sceptical about the effectiveness of communal prayer, and who questioned what it had achieved in the past. "What good did it do us to have laboured before, and to have exhausted the strength of our hearts in groans and tears? . . . What good did it do us to have prayed and to have laboured with total contrition of the spirit?"[72] According to the preacher, those who thought this way, and did not participate in the communal penance, were stealing from the community. "He who does not feel that he is obligated by these dangers, takes unto himself the property of another, out of the communal offering."[73] This intransigence endangered the good of the community. It was due only to such communal offerings of prayer that the town had so far been spared from the ravages of danger and destruction. The salvation of the community both in this world and the next required that each member should participate, and consider their own good as linked to that of their fellow congregants. Such an ideal contained an inherent or potential coerciveness. Dissent or withdrawal could not be tolerated when the good of all was at stake.

This model of community required the erasure of individual and class differences. Congregants were instructed to see themselves as a single whole, working together for salvation. The sermons in the Eusebius Gallicanus collection are silent on the constitution of their audiences. Social historians never cite them because they have nothing to tell in this regard. Either the original preachers, the compiler, or both, have elided the diversity of their communities. Other late antique preachers dwelt on difference, even developing sophisticated pastoral strategies predicated on catering to it.[74] They clearly described and distinguished the duties of the rich and the social role of the poor, the separate sins of men and women, the characteristics of "good" and "bad" Christians, the "wheat" and the "chaff," the "sheep" and the "goats."[75] The Eusebian preachers never addressed these groups and never used these metaphors. They did not want to divide their audiences, and thus they nullified difference. It was far more important to them to establish the unity of the community than to point up the reality of its diversity.

These choices had implications for forms of leadership. The model of the Christian community as a community of equals extended, in the Eusebian collection, to the position of clergy. The model of clerical leadership which the Eusebius Gallicanus preachers advanced was based on mutuality and consensus. In their sermons, pastors were positioned at the centre of the Christian community rather than above it, and the laity shared an equal responsibility for their salvation which required common labour for common rewards.

These sermons highlighted the importance of consensus and unity around the pastor, as well as the pastor's indebtedness to the congregation. They avoided any and all confrontation, combativeness, or controversy in their exhortations, seeking instead to establish respect for and obedience to pastoral authority by advancing a reciprocal, service-oriented ideal of the relationship. Clergy were still in control of the terms, but they evinced none of the fear, anxiety, or profound sense of responsibility which marked, for example, Caesarius' vision of the pastorate.[76]

Pastoral care was a central concern of a good leader, according to the Eusebian preachers. Sermon fifty-one, for example, written for the occasion of a bishop's burial, lauded the fact that its subject restored the sight of truth to those blinded by sin, filled ears deafened by disobedience with divine commands, cleansed those leprous with vices, and resurrected those dead to God.[77] The upshot, however, was a "service" model of religious leadership, rather than an authoritarian one. In sermon thirty-five, Faustus presented Maximus' time in the monastery of Lérins as preparation for service to his congregation in Riez. "For you, indeed, this athlete of Christ sweated in his struggle . . . Sowing for himself there, he gathered for you; searching for himself there, he unknowingly acquired for you; preparing wealth for himself he released you from usury."[78] All of Maximus' ascetic achievements were recast as pastoral training. "That distinguished man was taught there, so that he might teach here; was enriched there, so that he might lend here; was illuminated there, so that he might shine here; was purified there so that he might sanctify here; and, so that he could work here at the making of cures, he sought there the spices and pigments of virtue."[79]

The Eusebian preachers evoked kinship models for leadership, but emphasised their ideal reciprocity. "Enrich him" with your progress, the preacher of sermon sixty-five instructed the flock of a newly ordained bishop, "because your fruits are his treasures, and, although as the apostle said: 'Parents should enrich their children,' now the children should enrich their father. And since his life should be your glory: by mutual commerce your salvation should be his crown: so that he who is given by the Lord, according to your wishes, is commended to the Lord by your merits."[80] Although the imagery was that of father and children, the relationship was inverted. In this model, the children bore as much responsibility for their father's salvation as he did for theirs. The congregation were active participants in a common effort. "Relieve the burden of [your new bishop's] honour, support through obedience the one whom you deserve to raise up through grace."[81] The preacher urged his audience to love the vows their pastor had made, to honour his judgement, to gladden him with their deeds, and to decorate him with their good practices.

Sermon sixty-one sent a similar message. If you do something good, taught by me, the preacher informed his audience, we are both rewarded. "The application of the instructor is to the benefit of those obeying; the zeal of the encourager serves to the advantage of those listening, but also acts to the good of the encourager."[82] As the sermon continued, the preacher reiterated this theme of mutuality. "Recognise the merit of your works also through my feeling of exultation; understand how much you should rejoice about the gift of salvation acquired, if I rejoice so much about the wages of the sermon."[83] In these exhortations, the laity were urged to be not passive recipients of their pastor's benefactions, but active participants in their own salvation, bearing responsibility also for that of their leader. It was a markedly interdependent model of the Christian community.

For the Eusebius Gallicanus preachers, therefore, the place of the pastor within the Christian community was at its centre: providing an example, in service to his flock and aiding them in their struggle for salvation, but also benefiting from their efforts on his behalf. The ideal result of this mutually advantageous relationship was harmony and consensus. Such unity was a reflection of the will of God for the Christian community, argued the preacher of sermon sixty-five when describing the election of a new bishop. "There was one voice in so many voices and one will in so many hearts; and, that, which the apostolic words celebrated at the sacred origins of the nascent Church: 'There was in them,' he said, 'one heart and soul' . . . we see fulfilled here in the single accord of so many people, induced by

Christ. Therefore we give thanks to the Lord: that he passed the concord of one assembly into innumerous multitudes, into clamourous
and discrepant hearts, through the magnificent and eminent character of one man."[84] Thus this consensus was as miraculous as it was
necessary.

All the emphasis on mutuality did not mean, however, that the
laity might usurp the place of their religious leaders. God instructs
you, the preacher of sermon sixty-one informed his congregation, to
listen to the ministers of the word who speak in his name.[85] "No
one should think that he surpasses the priests, if he is obedient to
them."[86] The pastor was still directing the terms of the relationship,
but the form was not a hierarchical one. While paternal imagery was
used in very specific ways in the Eusebius Gallicanus collection—for
example, to refer to God or sometimes to express respect for other
pastors—it was seldom used to describe the self-identity of the
preacher.[87]

Sermon fifty-one contains one instance in which the paternal
model was used of another pastor, in this case to commemorate his
burial. "The Lord gave him to this our land," the preacher said of
his subject, "to this region, so that we might mould all the acts of
our lives to his example, so that we might arrange the shape of our
souls, looking to him as if to a mirror, and, like good sons, we might
cultivate in ourselves a similarity to our father."[88] The preacher continued, however, by shifting the focus to God, as the *magnus paterfamilias*.[89] God, he argued, had provided the deceased bishop as a
model for imitation, much as a man wishing to embellish his home
might provide models for a painter.[90] "Following him, therefore, we
should paint the hues of each of the virtues of that man over the vis-
ages of our soul, as if they were precious gems. This one lays ahold
for himself of the pleasing form of remorse, the other the most daz-
zling pigment of shining chastity, this one seizes the pallor of abstinence, that one the blush of shame."[91] In this way the whole Church
will be remade in the holy pastor's image, and he will recognise us
as his own in the world to come.[92] This metaphor placed the onus
of action upon the congregants, with the leader serving as an inert
model. A similar conceptualisation of the relationship emerged in

another sermon celebrating a dead pastor—that of Faustus of Riez on his predecessor Maximus. "Each one should seize what we can from the goods of the intestate parent: he should take from his inheritance the most precious silk garment of deeds; he should take possession of the coin of mildness and simplicity; he should lay claim for himself to the ornament of the benevolence of the heart and the necklace of wisdom; he should seize the pearl of compunction and the treasure of chastity . . . Thus we should act, imitating his good deeds: so that he, who has been raised up into eternal glory, now might appear again, restored to his Church through the renewal in the merits of his sons."[93] Thanks to the example of Maximus, "those who want to come to the road of health can, and those who neglect it cannot find an excuse."[94] The only pastoral "father" to be found here was deceased and his children had to find their own way.

Taking a fraternal rather than paternal approach, the Eusebian preachers encouraged more often than they chastised. They were optimistic about the human capacity for achieving salvation. "We can all have within ourselves the keys to the kingdom of heaven."[95] They were generally tolerant of doubt, uncertainty and failure. "Charity should be inclined to compassion, not insulting sinners but consoling them, for it is easy to lapse into sin and the human condition is fragile."[96] They did not regard virtue as a difficult path. "I do not know, dearly beloved, why the rough and uneven ways of sins and pride are more pleasing to us, when the road of humility is more pleasant, level and direct. Where there is humility, there is peace, there is tranquility, there is serenity of all things . . . But truly, on the contrary, the paths of pride are filled with obstacles, are filled with steep precipices; because, where there is pride, there is indignity, there is animosity, there is labour, there is tribulation."[97] If you find the yoke of Christ a heavy burden, the preacher went on to claim, you have made it so yourself, and need only turn from your previous ways to make it light and pleasant.[98] Virtue was presented to the Eusebian audiences as within their grasp. While the burden of salvation was thus placed upon the laity, the pressure was indirect and non-confrontational.

Once again, the purpose of the Eusebius Gallicanus preachers is clarified by understanding what they were *not* doing. Caesarius of Arles, who was roughly contemporary with the Eusebian compiler, makes clear the pastoral path which he was rejecting. Caesarius relied heavily upon patriarchal models of authority and inequality to describe the relationship between pastor and community—father to his congregational sons, watchman for the citizens, ship's pilot for the passengers, doctor to the sick, and head of the body of the Church.[99] In his vision, the clergy were "a chosen race," set apart from other Christians.[100] This office, he argued, placed a "grave responsibility and immense burden" upon pastors and put them in great danger.[101] We must stand before God on judgment day, Caesarius warned his colleagues, and account not just for our own souls but for the souls of all our flock. If we are negligent, and do not warn the members of our congregations of the consequences of sin, "the blood of their souls will be required at our hands."[102] As a result, Caesarius repeatedly argued, pastors must never cease to teach, to terrify and to threaten, to proclaim the rewards of the just and the punishment of sinners.[103] He urged the clergy to be like Phineas, who killed the sinners and was rewarded by God, rather than Eli, whose failure to admonish his sons severely enough resulted not only in his own death, but the destruction of his community.[104] "The word of God," Caesarius warned, "must be offered to those who are willing to listen; it must be forced upon those who are averse to it."[105] Pastors must fear the judgment of God more than the ill will of their congregants.[106] Caesarius' model was John the Baptist, who "preferred to suffer injustice rather than fail to say what was right."[107]

Caesarius borrowed much of this last sermon from one in the Eusebius Gallicanus collection, but the praise of John the Baptist was entirely his own. The Eusebian sermon from which Caesarius drew his exegesis offered no such conclusion.[108] Indeed, we can contrast Caesarius' stern pastoral approach with the warning delivered by the preacher of Eusebian sermon sixty-three to his congregation. In this sermon the preacher apologised for his delayed return from a trip, but noted that the congregation ought to be able to look after themselves while he was away. "Even when the pastor is absent, fear of the future judgment should be there, a very sharp anxiety about the eternal necessities should be there, and even if he, who can urge you on to fulfilling the act of daily redemption, is absent, man, who stands alone before the tribunal of God with his deeds, should urge himself on."[109] Salvation cannot be forced upon another and we will have no one to blame but ourselves in the end.[110] We should not expect to be urged to perfection by someone else, the preacher warned, since we will not be content to be crowned by anyone else on judgment day.[111]

Caesarius attempted to build community by drawing clear and nonnegotiable lines around it. His sermons are filled with statements of what was and was not acceptable Christian behaviour. Those who engaged in pagan practices, who had sex with the wrong people, at the wrong time, or with the wrong intent, who got drunk, or who consulted a doctor when sick, were not Christians.[112] Those who violated these regulations, Caesarius emphasised, should be excluded from the community.[113] Congregants were responsible for the correction of their neighbours and should use violence if appropriate.[114] Far from emphasising good relations and mutual support, Caesarius envisaged the ideal Christian community as one in which morality was enforced through mutual recrimination and the report of misdeeds to the bishop.[115]

The Eusebian preachers never urged such an enforcement approach to the moral welfare of the community. Their priority was, as we have seen, to ease community relations, not exacerbate tensions. Nor did they rail against any of the practices Caesarius condemned. One sermon ridiculed "Jove and Minerva" and poked fun at foolish customs, but never identified these as a threat.[116] Sexual sins were mentioned only in passing, doctors and fertility controls not at all.[117] Drunkenness was denounced in general terms, without any suggestion that congregants might be guilty of it.[118] Given the level of Caesarius' apparent concern with controlling his flock, the Eusebian silence is striking.

There is no reason to believe that the audiences of the Eusebian sermons were any more chaste, sober, or pious than those of Caesarius. The difference derives solely from pastoral strategy. Whereas

Caesarius gave priority to "right action" and expended a great deal of energy in urging his congregants to it, other preachers, including those whose work survives in the Eusebius Gallicanus collection, were more concerned with building consensus within the community. This may have required turning a blind eye to some practices, if the condemnation of them would have been potentially divisive.

Caesarius himself admitted that many of the practices he condemned were accepted, or at least widely tolerated, in Christian communities. He complained that men openly boasted of their affairs, saw no sin in having sex with their wives on forbidden days, and expected to take a concubine before settling into marriage.[119] He lamented that drinking was an acceptable social activity, that many Christians, including the clergy, incorporated pagan practices into their worship and that it was common to visit a doctor or healer when ill, instead of praying for a cure.[120] Caesarius' views on the limits of acceptable Christian behaviour were far from universal—other sources show support or toleration for the practices he condemned so long as they were performed under the aegis of the Church.[121]

Confrontational attacks on common practices required a charismatic preacher with a strong position in his community. Caesarius was such a preacher, and yet his hard-line approach may have been the cause of the dissent he faced from within and beyond his congregation.[122] He was accused of treason three times, put on trial, and sent into exile. He alienated members of the clergy and members of the nobility, and had to lock the doors of his church at one point to stop congregants who did not want to listen to his sermon from walking out.[123] Caesarius knew that his tirades against common practices did not make him popular, but he risked the chance of opposition and managed to marshal others to his defense.[124] He was a prominent figure and could call upon substantial religious and secular resources. Not all pastors were prepared, or perhaps able, to take Caesarius' approach. We should remember that the Eusebius Gallicanus collection was designed as an aid for clergy who lacked the confidence, ability, or resources to compose their own sermons. They were unlikely to be charismatic rhetors or to enjoy the uncompromising self-belief of Caesarius. They were unlikely, too, to have his status and connections. For them, attacking popular or common practices in their communities may not have been a feasible option. More subtle methods of approach may have been more attractive.

The Eusebius Gallicanus is a collection of sermons by a variety of different authors. We would not necessarily expect it to offer a consistent model of pastoral technique, but in fact, clear common themes emerge from the sermons considered as a whole. Certain key notes are struck again and again: harmony, mutuality, consensus. These are taken to imply concrete behavioural ideals: respectful relations between congregants, leadership from among rather than from above, and obedience to the overriding common good. Many of these were central themes of monastic community, and the parallels are very clear in the Eusebius Gallicanus sermons to monks. All of these values would have been urged in the midst of ritualised acts which themselves articulated and enacted the same ideals. The combination was potentially potent.

We cannot, however, track its success beyond noting the spread and popularity of the sermons themselves. As the sermons on local saints reveal, moreover, there was no single recipe for building community. In each of the sermons which we can locate, preachers can be seen responding to very specific pastoral demands. Doubtless the preachers of the other Eusebius Gallicanus sermons were doing the same, in ways which we are no longer able to perceive. Doubtless, too, the users of the collection adapted the sermons at will to suit their own needs and conditions. Community building in late antique Gaul was a precise and demanding exercise.

CHAPTER FOUR

Explaining the Faith

Building community was a fundamental, but not a sufficient, aim for the authors of the Eusebius Gallicanus sermons. Unless the faithful were bound by a clear understanding of and appreciation for the articles of their faith, any community would be vulnerable to misguidance. Moreover, correct belief was a prerequisite for salvation, and it was the job of the clergy to make sure their congregants achieved it. Finally, full and accessible public teaching was central to the Church's self-understanding of Christianity as a religion available to all. For all of these reasons, explaining the Christian faith was an imperative task of preachers in late antique Gaul. Yet as they sought to explain the faith, preachers were also conscious that explanation must stay within carefully controlled and directed limits. Questions must be posed within frameworks which provided correct answers, a strategy that created the illusion of access while it actually sought to make disagreement unthinkable. Explanatory preaching did not usually take the form of an obvious or direct assertion of pastoral power over the community, but it served, at least potentially, as a subtly coercive reminder of that power. Explanation was therefore an essential part of the process by which the Christian Church found a place for itself in the world of late antique Gaul.

By the fifth century the Church had developed an immensely complicated and precise theology. It had established a canon of foundational texts and had refined its answers to the major metaphysical questions. Scholars have queried, however, how much of this system was communicated to the laity and, indeed, how much the laity cared about such detailed explications of the faith. Discussing the situation in late Roman Cappadocia, Raymond Van Dam has recently argued that scholars "often ignore the precipitous obstacles to communicating with ordinary people. Educated theologians used the techniques of formal logic, the jargon of classical philosophy, and the vocabulary of an archaic, literary Greek, and still struggled to articulate their ideas. In contrast, their audiences typically included illiterate country-folk who spoke only common Greek or some local language, and whose overriding obsessions were their poverty-stricken agrarian livelihoods and their back-breaking efforts to survive from week to week. Bishops were offering the crumbs of erudition to ordinary people who were more concerned with obtaining their daily bread."[1] As we have already seen, however, Gallic preachers worked hard to overcome these obstacles, delivering their sermons in simple, accessible Latin rather than the "archaic, literary" language which Van Dam observes in the Eastern context.[2] They felt compelled to communicate with their congregants and laboured to ensure that their explanations were understood. The extent and delicacy of their labours will become clear in the course of this chapter. Furthermore, the "ordinary people" they addressed probably cared more about theology than we tend to give them credit for. The questions the Eusebius Gallicanus preachers raised and sought to answer were fundamental ones. Why do the good suffer? Why do the bad flourish? Are the Bible passages read in Church true? How can we believe seemingly impossible things? What do we need to know to get to heaven? It would be strange indeed to presume that such questions did not matter to ordinary Christians as much as they did to the elites. Theology in the late antique Church was not purely the preserve of intellectuals arguing over excruciatingly nuanced doctrines. For both lay congregations and pastors alike, there was a great deal at stake in understanding and explaining the elements of their religion.

It was fundamental to Christian self-perception that the truth was, and must be made, available to all.[3] God's truth was given to fishermen and was constructed as self-evident to all who encountered it.[4] It is important not to underestimate the practical force of this self-perception, even as we recognise its rhetorical function. It shaped the rejection of Gnostic arguments for a secret or hidden truth and it defined the developing character of the "Catholic" Church.[5] Universalism was an explicit goal; exclusiveness thus became a marker of heresy and demands for extraordinary "purity" were a cause of suspicion.[6] Pastors were committed, compelled even, to make their faith accessible and comprehensible. Their publicly articulated identity depended on it.

Averil Cameron has identified this relative "inclusivity" of Christianity as one of its major advantages over paganism and has argued that it was a quality keenly exploited by leaders of the faith.[7] Accessibility and explanation were not without their problems, however. Successful instruction increased the chances of independent interpretation and consequent diversity, and this was an outcome the late antique Church had learnt not to tolerate. From its inception, the Church had been suffused with anxiety about misinterpretation and false teaching, and hard-fought battles over theology and practice through the fourth and fifth centuries had confirmed these fears.[8] The still visible Arian and Donatist churches were reminders that diversity could lead to permanent fissures in the community of the faithful. Moreover, the problem was not confined to dissenting intellectuals. As Peter Brown points out, "non-literate and half-literate believers who were convinced of their own essential orthodoxy" posed just as serious a threat.[9] A little bit of knowledge could lead people in dangerous directions. The faithful needed to be guided along the path of theological orthodoxy, and explanation of the faith thus needed to be given in such a way that interpretation was kept under control.

Maurice Bloch's ideas take this point further. Bloch argues that religious explanation does not in fact explain at all.[10] He maintains that formalised religious language, of which he identifies sermons as an example, is nonlogical and denies the possibility of contradiction.[11] Certainly the Eusebius Gallicanus preachers hoped for such an effect, using rhetorical techniques to coerce the responses of their audiences without an open exercise of power. They used what Bloch would term a deliberately "impoverished" code of language and reason, which greatly reduced its susceptibility to argument.[12] The formality of their speech would have been accentuated by the even more ritualised language which surrounded it—prayers, chanting, and song. The usefulness of Bloch's analysis, however, ends here. The Eusebius Gallicanus sermons still had "a job to do."[13] They could not be a closed system which simply stated, reiterated, and repeated received truths, but rather had to engage with their audiences. This pressure to engage is characteristic of pastoral care. The resulting picture is therefore far less static and assured than Bloch suggests: consent and acceptance of the explanation were not guaranteed. Explanations were formal and deliberately circumscribed, but must still be meaningful to their audience.

The solution to this dilemma, for the preachers, was to stage what Murray Edelman has called "dramas of problem solving."[14] That is to say, preachers articulated questions and concerns in ways which acknowledged them, yet at the same time set up the answers they wanted.[15] Preachers engaged and explained, but always on their own terms. This was a subtle insinuation of power—not direct, not obvious, not overt—and thus difficult to challenge. This approach suited the kind of preacher who produced and, especially, who used, the Eusebius Gallicanus collection. Pastors who relied on a preaching guide were unlikely to be highly educated, rhetorically skilled, or confident in their ability to persuade. This picture fits with our earlier observation that the Eusebius Gallicanus preachers did not offer,

perhaps did not feel able to offer, a dominating style of clerical leadership.[16] This clerical uncertainty made the prospect of differing interpretations a genuine threat, and the explanations of the faith
offered in the Eusebius Gallicanus sermons were therefore fashioned
to be conservative and singular. Although they took care to make
the faith accessible, they allowed little space for individual, independent exploration of the Christian mysteries. They avoided controversial issues and uncompromising answers. In this regard, their
approach differed from that of Augustine of Hippo and Caesarius of
Arles, who were prepared to adopt more authoritative and authoritarian leadership positions. The Eusebius Gallicanus model relied
instead on basic and well-established rhetorical mechanisms to guide
the thinking and reasoning of the faithful and to try to preclude the
possibility of contradiction or argument.

The strategies which the Eusebius Gallicanus preachers used to
control and direct explanation in ways which suited them can be divided into two main categories: "circle of faith" reasoning and the
rhetoric of paradox. Neither was unique to them. Both were established mechanisms for controlling and directing interpretation. In
the Eusebian collection, however, we see these strategies employed in
a practical context and in response to specific needs. The sermons illustrate the potential power of rhetorical strategies as pastoral tools,
but also the delicacy required in employing them.

The "circle of faith" refers to the self-contained reasoning used
by preachers when explaining Christianity.[17] It describes the fact that
certain principles were treated by the speakers as though they were
accepted by the audience prior to any explanation. These points were
never treated as debatable in themselves, but as starting points from
which explanation should proceed, and included principles such as
that God exists, that God is infallible, that scripture is God's word,
and that God has revealed his doctrines to the faithful. They began,
in other words, from a point already within the circle of faith. This
strategy was workable because the preachers were not missionaries or
apologists trying to convince unbelievers of Christian truth. Instead,
they were addressing believers sitting before them in church, where a

different logic could be applied.[18] The preachers could act as though certain things were givens—accepted by all Christians—and by treating them as givens could encourage the laity to embrace them as such. Any challenge to these principles could then easily be explained away as the result of imperfect human understanding. It was necessary, as Augustine liked to put it, to believe in order to understand.[19] In other words, the circle of faith functioned not only as a starting ground, but as a delimitation of how far it was possible for inquiry to go. It enclosed the reasoning and understanding of congregants and aimed to be a self-fulfilling prophecy of belief. As such it was an extremely useful explanatory strategy.

The second strategy the Eusebius Gallicanus preachers employed was what Averil Cameron has described as the "rhetoric of paradox," or the Christian tradition of embracing paradox as a characteristic of the faith.[20] As Cameron points out, although the Christian doctrines and texts were constructed as clear and straightforward, they were, at the same time, mysteries which transcended the limits of human intelligence and comprehension. While most theological and homiletic interpretations from this period present Jesus' parables, for instance, both as simple statements and as mysteries containing hidden depths, the rhetoric of paradox went further. As Cameron puts it: "Christianity itself, not just Christian language, is sometimes seen as resting on impossible opposites."[21] Impossibility was treated as a characteristic of divinity. Where doctrine seemed to contradict itself, or the laws of nature, the rhetoric of paradox permitted preachers to argue that this was proof of divine power. Thus God could be three and one, Jesus could be God and man, and Mary could be a virgin and a mother at the same time. Preachers could argue that the impossibility of Christian doctrine or the apparent self-contradictions in Christian scripture were not only not negations of the faith, but were rather confirmations of its truth. They held, as Kierkegaard later would, that it was unreasonable to hold religion to "normal" standards of reason.[22] This explanatory strategy worked, however, only if one stood already within the circle of faith. Preachers had to act as though audiences had already accepted the premise that Christianity must be true. By treating this acceptance as a given, they headed off any possibility of negation and were able, using the rhetoric of paradox, to answer almost any challenge.

The rhetoric of paradox, like the circle of faith, functioned to place limits upon necessary or possible explanation. Certain parts of the divine truth were constructed as simply unexplainable, and were therefore cordoned off from criticism. Since complete understanding of God is impossible, we should, Augustine argued, limit ourselves to what we are presently able to digest.[23] It is enough, Peter Chrysologus stated with his typical bluntness, to believe in God. You should not rashly try to fathom him or inquire whence, how great, or exactly what he is.[24] Caesarius agreed. There are limits, he argued, to what people have a right to discuss.[25] You should not want to know what God has hidden from you.[26] The rhetoric of paradox therefore had a gatekeeping function. It kept access to the ultimate mysteries of the faith closed to most Christians and could be employed by pastors to end explanation at the point they saw fit. Like the circle of faith, the rhetoric of paradox was subtle in its operation and difficult to challenge—seeming to explain while effectively precluding further questioning. Both rhetorical strategies were mechanisms for insinuating the power of pastors without provoking dissent.

Given the nature of the Eusebius Gallicanus collection, these rhetorical strategies emerge piecemeal from various sermons, rather than appearing in any neat, single articulation. I will therefore examine them in depth by means of four case studies: we will look at how the Eusebian preachers explained the creed, the virgin birth, the meaning of scripture, and the justice of God. This approach will enable us to see how the two strategies worked together to control and delimit explanations of the faith, and also how one sometimes suited the needs of a particular preacher or topic better than the other. Each of these case studies represents an essential element of Christian knowledge—part of what the faithful needed to know to get to heaven—but each was also a potential source of anxiety. At the same time that these topics were of immediate relevance to all Christians, they had been and would continue to be the subjects of high-level theological debate. They were therefore the repeated focus of explanation not only in the Eusebius Gallicanus collection, but also in the sermons of other late antique preachers, and thus provide us a useful taste of how the rhetorical strategies worked in practice.

The first case study concerns the explanation of the creed. This topic was treated in slightly different versions in two sermons in the Eusebius Gallicanus collection—evidence not only of the diverse authorship of the collection, but also of the fact that the creed was still not fixed in Gaul, and that this lack of fixity caused no especial concern to the compiler.[27] Both of these sermons were designed for preaching during Lent, the traditional time for teaching the fundamentals of the faith to those who were to receive baptism at Easter.[28] In communities where child baptism was the norm, however, the exposition of the creed served primarily to remind the already baptised of the fundamental theological statements of their religion. The creed functioned in these sermons, as in the Christian Church generally, as a minimum statement of faith. It contained the basic definitional doctrines of Christianity which all Christians should know and believe. Augustine had described it as a "password" by which a faithful Christian could be recognised.[29] Caesarius of Arles echoed this idea and added that if anyone wanted to be saved, he should learn the creed, firmly adhere to it, and preserve it inviolate.[30] As the foundation stone of Christian identity and hope for salvation, therefore, the creed was an important beginning point for theological explanation. Yet it was difficult to understand and to expound: its form by this time was the result of centuries of theological argument, and so its deceptively simple wording carried enormous and precise freight. The Eusebius Gallicanus preachers took great care both to enable and to limit understanding of it.

In the first place, the creed had to be given and congregants had to be instructed to learn it. The preacher of sermon ten urged his congregants to imprint those teachings, "so few but so precious," in the depths of their souls, "so that faith might believe, hope might increase, memory might retain, and life might guard this eternal treasure of your hope in all places and at all times."[31] Learning the creed, the preacher emphasised, was a command "which naked poverty, contemptible insignificance, and unlearned simplicity can easily fulfill."[32] It was simple and memorisable. The preacher of sermon nine depicted it as a convenient distillation of Christian faith—"brief and fixed words, unencumbered with sentences but full of mysteries . . . confined in its expression, but varied in its meanings."[33] This distillation made the enormity of the Christian tradition manageable. "From both testaments the *uirtus* of the whole body was poured into a few sentences, so that the treasure of the soul might be easily carried not in a chest, but in the memory."[34] The Christian faith was thereby rendered so accessible that even the simplest of the faithful could grasp what was required.

This access was made possible, however, by those who controlled interpretation. The preacher of sermon nine emphasised that the creed was the result of the efforts of people described in one place as the "fathers" of the Churches, in another place as the "masters," who "divided the greatest from the great in the holy writings . . . so that the knowledge of truth could be easily acquired by any heart, however narrow, however rustic, without the impediment of any difficulty, so that the vital lyrics, wholesomeness, and brevity might invite people to hold and acquire heavenly wisdom."[35] In other words, the Christian faith had been predigested and simplified before being offered to the people. Importantly, the Eusebian preachers did not claim for themselves this gatekeeping power. It was attributed to anonymous Church leaders whose authority was unquestionable and therefore unchallengeable. The preachers merely presented themselves as heirs to this tradition, even as they made full use of the controls it placed upon explanation of theology.

At times, however, this control is rendered more explicit by how preachers used the rhetoric of paradox to limit interpretation of the creed. The author of sermon nine employed it to put an end to investigation of creedal mysteries at the point he saw fit. "When some deeds of God are set forth to you, do not think or say to yourself: 'How or in what way can this have been done?' Divine works should not be discussed, but believed. Do not disturb yourself, nor let the novelty of the deeds make you anxious, but let the power of omnipotence suffice for you."[36] Christians should not expect to understand the divine fully, the preacher told them. "Do not subject the greatness of heaven to the regulation of your understanding—the dignity of the divine maker goes beyond the narrowness of the human mind."[37] Far from instilling doubt, the preacher argued, incomprehensibility should increase faith. "The more difficult it seems to you to investigate the divine dispensations, the more you should reverentially admire them."[38] Impossibility was evidence of divinity. The preacher of sermon ten made a similar argument, although in less explicit terms, warning that anyone who thought they could penetrate the heavenly mysteries through their own wisdom was like a man who built a house without a foundation, searched for a doorway in a roof, or went out into the night without a light.[39] Access to the faith was provided, but only within strictly controlled limits.

The approach of the Eusebius Gallicanus preachers to the creed was quite simple: present it clearly, make it accessible, but use the rhetoric of paradox to limit investigation of it. Their approach to the explanation of the next case study, the virgin birth, was more complex.[40] In part, this was because the subject itself both needed more explanation and was acutely vulnerable to incorrect interpretation. The Eusebian preachers expected, or recognised, congregational unease about a doctrine contrary to all empirical experience and vulnerable to particularly unflattering alternative explanations. "But 'how,' you say, 'can she be a virgin after a child?' . . . 'how can this have been done?'"[41] Do not ponder its novelty, the author of sermon ten warned, nor say, "'That is impossible, that cannot be done.'"[42] The Eusebian preachers were not alone in such expectations. As Augustine framed it: "The virgin conceived; you're astonished; the virgin gave birth; you're more astonished still."[43] "Do not be disturbed at this conception," Peter Chrysologus counseled his congregation, "or confused when you hear of this birth."[44] The subject could not, however, be easily side-stepped. The virgin birth lay at the heart of the doctrine of the incarnation, which a series of Church councils had painstakingly hammered out.[45] Jesus was man, but without sin. He occupied the flesh, but without the taint of carnality. Preachers needed to explain this article of faith to their congregants and wanted them to understand how it worked. Furthermore, Mary's virginity was a highly visible issue. Partly as a result of the debates over the incarnation, she had become central to Christian doctrine and her role had been highlighted.[46] In 431 the council of Ephesus accorded her the title of *Theotokos,* Mother of God, and veneration of her figure began to increase.[47] Her status as virgin and mother needed to be addressed and defended. To do so, the preachers combined the rhetoric of paradox with the circle of faith.

As the first step in this dual strategy, questions concerning the virgin birth were framed in ways which appeared to articulate congregational anxieties, but which actually shaped them into answerable form. As we have just seen, focusing on the issue of impossibility enabled preachers to employ the rhetoric of paradox to good effect. The author of sermon two, for example, reveled in the miracle of a plant, without any seed, flourishing in "untouched and untilled earth." He delighted in the very conundrum itself, in the internal contradictions which confirmed the mystery. "The creator is born from his creature, and the virgin mother marvels at the fruits of her womb, and a woman is made the author of her author!"[48] According to the preacher of sermon seventy-six, not *ratio,* but *admiratio,* is the more appropriate faculty to employ when contemplating this paradox.[49] This argument provided a transition to the second step in the combination strategy, allowing the preacher to situate the debate within the circle of faith. If you believe in the omnipotence of God, the preacher of sermon ten told his audience, you must believe that he is capable of being born to a virgin. "If you doubt his deeds, you allege the powerlessness of omnipotence."[50] The author of sermon seventy-six reminded his audience that the virgin birth is the work of one "whom you confessed to be omnipotent in your first confession."[51] A virgin birth is no less than we should expect from the true God.[52] If Jesus can enter through the closed doors and stand among the apostles, argued the preacher of sermon twenty-seven, then he can enter through the closed doors of his mother's womb.[53] Within the circle of faith, such arguments were self-supporting and incontrovertible. They explained at the same time that they shut down further questioning. "Why do we seek reason here? Why do we wear out human understanding? . . . Why are we astounded at the novelty, where we perceive majesty? We are amazed that our Lord accomplished man without the seed of any man in the virginal uterus, whom we know fashioned the immensity of heaven and earth from nothing?"[54] Once we have accepted that God created the universe, nothing else he does should surprise or astonish us, the preacher of sermon two argued. Preachers thus began with the dual premises that impossibility was a divine characteristic and that God was capable of all things. Unsurprisingly, therefore, they were able to provide reassuring answers to their congregations' questions, for they had shaped the entire "dialogue" to that end.

The Eusebius Gallicanus preachers were hardly alone in employing this strategy. Augustine of Hippo had also delighted in the paradox of the virgin birth as a characteristic of divinity. "Born in a wonderful way; what could be more wonderful than a virgin giving birth? She conceives, and is a virgin; she gives birth, and is a virgin."[55] "Who can grasp this new, unheard of novelty, unique in the history of the world, something unbelievable that has become believable and is unbelievably believed throughout the whole world; that a virgin should conceive, a virgin should give birth, and a virgin she should remain in giving birth? Faith grasps what human reason cannot work out; and where reason falls back, faith marches on."[56] Furthermore, Augustine relied on one biblical miracle to confirm the possibility of another, and "explained" entirely within the circle of faith.[57] "And when we say he was born of a virgin, it's a great thing, you're astonished. He's God, don't be astonished; let astonishment give way to thanksgiving and praise."[58] Similar reasoning can be found in the sermons of Peter Chrysologus, who made the limits of appropriate explanation explicit. The fact that the virgin gives birth is a mystery of God, not an activity of marriage.[59] No one should try to penetrate this heavenly mystery with earthly reasoning: we should not pry into it, but simply believe it, knowing that everything is possible for God.[60] The virgin birth invited, perhaps even required, such explanatory approaches.

Explanations of scripture, our third case study, had a far more variegated history within the Christian tradition. The early Church had famously produced two major schools of exegesis, often associated with the cities of Antioch and Alexandria, which differed in the degree to which they advocated allegorical readings of the scriptures.[61] Their divergence was symptomatic of the challenge which scripture posed to the Church. Debates over interpretation were ongoing and important.

Explanation of the scriptures was essential because these texts provided the justifications for all the practices and teachings of the late antique Church, and they formed the foundation for common Christian identity.[62] Christians attending church were exposed to their contents in readings, but they needed explanation and elucidation as well. This was necessary because scripture was, in many ways, problematic—a series of writings which addressed very different cultural contexts, most of which had originally been formulated in the service of another religion, and which were, in many places, either too opaque or too straightforward to suit Christian understandings. Readers of the same texts could, and had, come away with very different understandings of God's message, and the correct forms of devotion.[63] To some, such as Augustine, they had been a barrier to overcome on the path to Christian belief.[64] For others, they were a puzzle and source of anxiety. Explanation of scripture was therefore both a vital and a delicate undertaking.

Scripture had already proved itself amenable to explanation using the rhetoric of paradox and the circle of faith. An established Christian tradition viewed the words of scripture as paradoxical—a *sermo humilis* with a sublime meaning.[65] This meant that scripture operated on at least two levels. On one level it was accessible to all— written in simple language, filled with straightforward moral commands. At the same time, however, it was a system of signs—a representation of divine mystery whose true meanings were beyond the grasp of human intelligence.[66] The contradiction could be cited as evidence of divinity at work. Furthermore, exegetes traditionally operated from within the circle of faith. They began with the premise that scripture was the word of God, and that it must be true and make sense. From this they reasoned that whenever the meaning of scripture seemed obscure, inconsistent, or contrary to accepted doctrine, the fault must lie with human understanding, or from a failure to perceive the hidden depths of the paradox. By employing these two rhetorical mechanisms, pastors explained the words of the Bible to their congregations, but kept interpretations under their control.

Both mechanisms can be found in the Eusebius Gallicanus treatments of scripture. In particular, preachers interpreted both Old and New Testament events as *mysteria* for the sacraments which they administered. The crossing of the Red Sea was thus a prefiguration of baptism,[67] and reference to wine or bread was a symbol of the Eucharist.[68] Jesus' transformation of water into wine was both an actual event and a symbol of the transformation which the baptismal sacrament worked. "For if we look at them properly, in a certain way these very waters set forth a likeness of baptism and regeneration. For when something is changed within itself from one thing into another, when the inferior creature is transformed into a better form through a secret *conuersatio,* the mystery of the second birth is described. Suddenly the water is changed, just as men will change afterwards."[69] The story of the creation of Eve from Adam's side was used to link the Old Testament to the New Testament and the present, as it prefigured both the crucifixion and the sacrament of baptism.[70] Each of these scriptural passages was interpreted by the Eusebian preachers as a paradox which from within the circle of faith pointed at once to itself and to the Church. On the assumption that true meaning was present, true meaning was found.

What is striking about the Eusebius Gallicanus collection in relation to scriptural explanation, however, is not what the preachers did, but what they did not do. The exegesis outlined above was standard and well established.[71] It was controlled, safe, and simple. Compared to the explanatory styles of Augustine, Peter Chrysologus, and Caesarius of Arles, it was extremely conservative. The Eusebius Gallicanus collection contains nothing comparable to Augustine's *Enarrationes in Psalmos,* where the entire point was the line-by-line analysis and interpretation of scriptural passages, linking them with other parts of scripture and other commentaries to provide a vast intertextual, exegetical compendium. It contains nothing to compare with Caesarius' deliriously multiplied interpretations of the Samson and Delilah story, or his joyful explications of "true meaning" in obscure Old Testament details.[72] Nor does it contain anything analogous to Peter Chrysologus' dense mystical interpretations of numbers in scripture.[73] In their preaching, Augustine, Caesarius, and Chrysologus all devoted far more time to exegesis of scripture than did the Eusebius Gallicanus preachers, treating it not just as a support for particular practices, but as an end in itself—God's message to the faithful.[74] All three delighted in the complex veils of meaning within the texts, produced multiple possible interpretations of the same passages, and were willing to admit that there were some parts of scripture which they did not understand.[75] The Eusebian interpretation, by contrast, was always directed to a specific end and was always singular.

The Eusebius Gallicanus preachers were also more controlling in the access which they provided to scriptural interpretation. Whereas Augustine and Caesarius were willing to engage in controversy and tackle difficult scriptural passages head on, the Eusebius Gallicanus preachers simply ignored or avoided them. They did not seek to explain to their congregants how God could justly harden Pharoah's heart, why the Old Testament prophets were justified in their extreme acts, or why the polygamy, incest, and promiscuity of the patriarchs was acceptable. They did not present passages which seemed to contradict each other in order to explain how they did not.[76] The noncombative, nonconfrontational style of the Eusebian preachers would have been ill-suited to such an approach, and indeed, such issues simply did not surface in the collection.

The Eusebian preachers were also far less willing than the expert theologians to encourage their congregants to access scripture on their own. Augustine of Hippo and Caesarius of Arles each attempted to equip their audiences with the tools of understanding and interpretation and then urged them to read the scriptures for themselves, forearmed with a way of doing so which should ensure that they remain on the right path.[77] They both believed that it was important for congregants to access scripture directly and as often as possible. Nothing comparable can be found in the sermons of the Eusebius Gallicanus collection. Members of their lay congregations were never encouraged to read for themselves. They were seldom even given systematic directions on how scripture should be read or understood. The right of interpretation and the skills to do so remained in the hands of their pastors.

The variety in Christian practices of scriptural exegesis therefore allowed the Eusebius Gallicanus preachers to choose the explanatory style which best suited their needs and which differed from that of some contemporaries. The Eusebius Gallicanus authors prioritised harmony, consensus, and the construction of community. Since scripture could be interpreted to provide different understandings of Church structures and practices, and since knowledge of scripture could be the foundation for alternative claims to authority, the Eusebian preachers were very careful to keep it under their control. They did not do so overtly, but used established rhetorical mechanisms to guide interpretation along safe paths, keeping explanations simple and singular, and restricting lay access, especially to difficult or controversial passages.

The greatest amount of explanatory energy in the Eusebius Gallicanus collection, however, was directed towards our final case study: the justice of God. As Kevin Uhalde has demonstrated, lay Christians had consistent, if often disappointed, expectations of secular justice.[78] Their expectations of divine justice were even higher, and the contrast with the injustice which surrounded them was thus even greater. If God was all-powerful and all-good, people wondered, why was there still evil in the world? Why did the virtuous suffer while the sinful prospered? How could the fall of man and the possibility of damnation be defended? These issues constituted then, as they do now, one of the most fundamental theological challenges faced by the Christian Church, and one which required satisfying explanations.[79] Augustine summarised the challenge it posed to the pastor: "In this world the prosperity of evil men is the pit for sinners. People are habitually upset by this, and often religious people too, people who wouldn't dream of blaming the Lord and yet wonder to themselves why bad people are so often successful. And such people are supremely upset when they themselves are beset by miseries and disasters though they are well aware that they live better lives than the others. They see evil people prevailing successfully all along the line in all their business which is admittedly earthly and temporal, but is still good. And they sigh in their miseries, and can hardly restrain their thoughts from blaming God."[80]

In response to this challenge, the author of Eusebius Gallicanus sermon fifty-five employed the rhetoric of paradox, beginning by articulating his congregation's concerns in an answerable form and coercing the direction of explanation. He depicted a congregation in despair of God's justice. When they see that "good and holy people are suffering so many bad things," they assume that God does not care for them, and pays no attention to human affairs. "Either he ignores sins if he does not damn them, or he promotes sins if he pretends to damn them." "Why," the preacher presented his congregants as asking, "does he not punish immediately those guilty of sin?"[81] This framing of congregational anxiety enabled the preacher to address it. Immediacy, he answered, reasoning from the circle of faith, is not the be-all of justice. What matters is that justice will come in time and that we know that God will bring it about, in the next world if not in this. The crux of the preacher's response, however, was that the Christian experience should be understood in paradoxical terms. The evils you experience, he told his audience, are not misfortunes, but blessings. You are being given an opportunity to earn your eternal reward. You are not being deserted, but tested. In fact, the preacher contended, turning the argument on its head, the felicity of the wicked is evidence of God's justice, since it would not be fair to condemn sinners before they have had a chance to repent. Explanation was thereby achieved through inversion, and paradox was cited as characteristic of the divine plan.

This method of explanation was well established in the tradition of Christian pastoral care, with Augustine of Hippo its most enthusiastic exponent. The good and bad things of this world are only apparently so, he reassured his congregations: punishments on earth are kinder than rewards, and the absence of judgment on earth should compel us to believe in judgment in heaven.[82] We are just sheep, Augustine argued, and we must recognise the greater knowledge of the shepherd.[83] We are children being punished for our own good, although we cannot presently see why.[84] God has created order. "Let it not be doubted by religious piety, even if it is not understood by human infirmity." We should believe in a hidden and inscrutable order in human affairs which we are incapable of comprehending or inspecting.[85] When we arrive to the sight of God, all will be made clear, including the reasons for the apparent injustices of this world.[86] In the meantime, Augustine counseled his congregants to have patience and to submit to their travails.

This approach was, however, pastorally problematic. It was one thing for preachers to claim that Christians should not expect rewards in this world, but quite another to wean people from the expectation that their virtue would pay off and that their prayers would be answered.[87] The preachers themselves were inconsistent on the topic, and emphasised reward on earth when it suited them.[88] Augustine's position entailed a helplessness and passivity in the face of the divine dispensation which was difficult to preach. Even the bishop of Hippo shied away from its more extreme implications unless he thought that audiences could handle them, and there is a marked difference in how Augustine approached these issues in his preaching, as compared to his treatises.[89] The hesitation of pastors is understandable. Without the carrot of reward and the stick of punishment, there seemed no basis for urging congregants to virtuous effort. Predestined grace, at least one Eusebian preacher objected, seemed to violate natural justice. In such a world, the author of Eusebian sermon fifteen pointed out, damnation would be decided by the chance of birth, and some of the faithful would descend into the baptismal font "as if into a grave."[90] Since God could not be unjust, the preacher reasoned from within the circle of faith, this could not be the case.[91] Indeed, most of the Eusebian preachers who addressed the problem of divine justice did not urge patience or encourage their congregants to view their misfortunes as blessings. Instead, they contended that the true injustice would be for God to coerce virtue. Since human beings had chosen sin, the preachers argued, they must also choose virtue to ensure salvation. This view retained, albeit in ambiguous and carefully blurred terms, some room for individual action in mer- iting grace, and it placed responsibility for ensuring their salvation firmly back upon the faithful.

Instead of lamenting God's injustice, the Eusebian preachers ar- gued, the faithful should act to make themselves righteous. The au- thor of sermon nineteen, for example, focused on the issue of why God did not simply save man from damnation through his omni- potent power. The preacher explained that the present struggle was necessary to ensure justice—if man was "seduced by the devil through the fault of disobedience and the assent of a free mind, not coerced," he should be "invited" back, "not dragged by force." It would, the preacher noted, "seem most unjust that he who fell of his own free will would be raised unwillingly. You see that the zeal of the most worthy physician requires the assent of his patient. Captiv- ity was taken up through free will, liberty should have been restored back again through free will, for the Lord, who opens the door, still waits for us to knock."[92] If God had acted otherwise, the preacher made clear, the devil could accuse him of injustice, an unacceptable scenario within the circle of faith. "If man were carried out of the power of the devil through the power of God, by force," the devil could rightly say to God: "Justly be a judge of the matters: man is in- deed yours through the creation, but he began to be mine through fault, he is yours through nature, but mine through disobedience, because he preferred to listen to my seduction than to law . . . He is yours by deeds, but mine by will, because he could have observed your command but he did not want to."[93] Circle-of-faith reasoning made this an impossible scenario. God must be just, therefore he could not act unjustly—the devil had to have his chance. In answer to those who questioned why God had to humiliate himself in the flesh, the preacher of sermon eighteen responded that it was for the sake of justice. "The first man had sinned through his own fault, the lapse of disobedience and the impulse of his own will, seduced by the devil, not forced . . . and therefore he could be redeemed through mercy, like a guilty man, and should not be liberated through power, as though he were innocent."[94] Justice required that human beings take the necessary steps to ensure their own salvation.

A similar explanation of God's justice can be found in Eusebian sermon twenty-two. "Indeed, dearly beloved, our Lord could have destroyed the enemy of the human race solely by his majesty, without the humility of the incarnation, without the struggle of the passion, but man was held liable to punishment through his own crime of transgression. He who incurred servitude through his own fault had to be freed, not through violence, but through compassion."[95] Justice, the preacher implied, required that God obey his own laws, and since man acted freely, it would be unjust to raise him up unwillingly. "It was more fair and salutary that he who had been led by the devil to death through pride, should be induced to life by God through humility. Therefore it was justly ordained that he who had not been driven but seduced to perdition through the cunning of the malevolent serpent, in return should not have been compelled, but led to salvation through the wisdom of the benevolent redeemer." The preacher concluded that even the zeal of the most worthy doctor requires the assent of his patient.[96] The justice of God required that the punishment (and the reward) be the consequence of choice, not of predestined compulsion.

The preachers of these sermons treated divine justice as an issue requiring a different level of explanation than was sufficient for, say, the virgin birth. Whereas the virgin birth could be taken on faith, offered as a paradox, as evidence of God's transcendence, the truth of divine justice needed to be felt. It was so important, such a burning and ever-present issue, that pastoral comfort was required. Explanation therefore appealed to categories which made intuitive sense. The preachers did not wish to insist that God's justice was incomprehensible, but precisely that it was perfectly comprehensible, consistent, and predictable. The rhetoric of paradox, most of the Eusebian preachers seem to have felt, was actively unhelpful here. In this they differed in approach from Augustine, who was always far more willing to challenge his congregants and tell them what they did not necessarily want to hear.

A divergence in emphasis on grace and free will between Augustine and the Eusebius Gallicanus preachers clearly also played a role in the preachers' approach to human salvation. The latter were consistently more prepared to see a space for human activity within the scheme of salvation and to encourage their congregants accordingly. It should be noted, however, that this divergence was not a consequence of any "semi-pelagian controversy." This point is made clear by striking parallels between the Eusebius Gallicanus explanations of God's justice and those of Caesarius of Arles, who is famed as one of the chief proponents of Augustine's views on grace in sixth-century Gaul.[97] In his sermon eleven, the bishop of Arles borrowed extensively from Eusebius Gallicanus sermons eighteen, nineteen, and twenty-two. "This idea affects many people, dearly beloved; such a thought sends many men of little learning into anxiety. For people say: Why did our Lord Jesus Christ, the power and wisdom of the Father, effect the salvation of man, not by His divine power and sole might, but by physical humiliation and human struggle?"[98] In response to such concerns, Caesarius also reasoned from within the circle of faith that God would not have acted in a manner which could be construed as unjust. God could have used his divine power to triumph over the devil, but "justice did not allow it." If he had, the devil could have complained that "man united himself to me by his own will; he estranged himself from you with the same will, not unwillingly."[99] Because God is just, Caesarius concluded, he had no choice but to let mankind struggle.[100] Caesarius indeed made almost no reference at all to the role of divine grace in his large collection of sermons. Instead he preached a straightforward moral equation: do good and go to heaven, do bad and go to hell. He even adapted Augustine's sermons to imply that salvation was achievable through human effort,[101] and preached as though he believed that salvation was entirely dependent upon merit, because any other position was pastorally untenable. Without the carrot and the stick a preacher lacked any weapons to ensure good congregational behaviour and to maintain his own authority.[102]

This is not to say that there are no differences between the Eusebius Gallicanus sermons and those of Caesarius of Arles in the explanation of divine justice. In accordance with his more hard-line position, and with the Augustinian emphasis on human sinfulness,

Caesarius was far more likely than the Eusebius Gallicanus preachers to emphasise that Christians deserved the evil they suffered. The evil in this world, he argued, was the fault of man, not of God, and the tribulations of the times, including the incursions of the barbarians, were the just deserts of their sins.[103] The less combative Eusebian preachers shied away from any such conclusions, but their reticence was a nuance of style rather than a difference of substance. Caesarius of Arles' explanations of God's justice were thoroughly consistent with those found in the sermons of the Eusebius Gallicanus collection.

Preachers faced common problems when attempting to explain theology in a pastoral context, and for us to see them as participating in high-level controversy would be to ignore the low-level immediacy of their responses to community concerns.[104] The challenge, after all, was a genuinely difficult one. To be effective, explanation had to be offered to just the right degree and in just the right way. In achieving these aims, the Eusebian preachers tended to turn to circle-of-faith reasoning and the rhetoric of paradox, but they did not do so in a consistent or singular fashion. Approaches differed from one sermon to another, and especially in relation to different topics. These variations reveal not only how careful and responsive preachers could be in formulating their pastoral approaches, but also how they perceived different questions as posing different kinds of challenges. The final image is not of theologians struggling to convey abstract ideas to disinterested lay audiences, but of both parties striving to understand and explain their world in ways which made sense to them. The answers mattered a great deal to everyone.

CHAPTER FIVE

Dealing with Sin

The third pastoral challenge facing late antique clergy was what to do about sin. The presence of sin in the community threatened its coherence and identity. Some Christians argued, indeed, that sinners needed to be excluded from the Church so as to keep its pure character, while others argued that excommunication of sinners would soon result in there being no community left.[1] The issue of how to handle sin provoked deep divisions in the late antique Church and proved an ongoing headache for pastors, but as we have already seen, the Eusebius Gallicanus preachers were inclined to be understanding: "for it is easy to lapse into sin and the human condition is fragile."[2] They therefore did not cast out the erring, but sought to bring them back into the Church and show them how to stay there. Sometimes, when sins were grave, the sinners were prominent, and the good of the community was threatened, dramatic, public penance was required. Far more often, however, penance involved the quiet, regular, repeated expiation of ordinary, unavoidable sins. In this respect, the Eusebius Gallicanus preachers did not substantially differ from most other pastors in the Western Church; but here, as with other challenges, the preachers also made choices.[3] Their emphases, priorities, and strategies arose from their ideals of Christian community and of proper pastoral leadership, as well as from their conception of the relationship between God and humanity. The preachers showed the faithful the path to heaven, and told them how to expiate their sins, but emphasised that they were finally responsible for their own salvation or damnation. God, the Eusebian preachers argued, would not be tolerant on judgment day.

This sense of a looming limit to tolerance and understanding created an indirect pressure. The Eusebius Gallicanus preachers urged lay Christians to judge and punish themselves. The sermons presented an ideal of internalised compunction and expiation which preempted intervention by either pastor or God, emphasised the role of individuals in ensuring their own salvation, and appeared to limit clerical control over the penitential process. This apportioning of responsibility did not represent a relinquishment of pastoral power, but rather a reshaping of it. It was less overt, less open to challenge, but potentially no less effective. If the Christian faithful could be convinced to be their own "most severe" judges and to circumscribe their own lives, the strength of the Gallic church would be increased, not diminished.[4]

Here, as elsewhere, the spectre of the semi-pelagian controversy has distorted discussion of the issues, as has an overly rigid view of the lay-ascetic divide. Scholars have contrasted the hard-line ascetic approaches to penance promoted by Provençal monks with Augustine's more forgiving defence of "Christian mediocrity."[5] Yet, as Kevin Uhalde's recent work on penance has shown, ascetic perspectives underlay some of the most sympathetic and flexible penitential schemes for the laity in this period.[6] The Eusebius Gallicanus sermons provide just such an example of how the demands of pastoral care interacted with ascetic traditions and theological beliefs to create a nuanced response to the problem of sin.

How Christian writers, pastors, and theologians treated sin was a litmus test for their view of the nature of the Church.[7] Baptism wiped the slate clean: on that they all agreed. But what then? From the beginning of the Christian tradition, expectations of postbaptismal purity and future punishment for sin warred against the realities of human behaviour, including the natural, powerful impulse towards forgiveness. This tension became more acute over time. The widespread practice of infant baptism and the rapid growth of the religion combined to make baptism a beginning, rather than an end, for most spiritual journeys. If the Church was to grow and flourish, it had to find a way to incorporate sinners within its folds. Over time those Christian traditions which claimed that there was no place for sin within the Church fell by the wayside. The focus of Christian pastoral care became dealing with sin in the Church and finding ways to cleanse it while keeping the sinner within.[8]

Augustine of Hippo was a central theorist of this incorporative Church. His position evolved in response to the rigorist challenges posed by the Donatists and the Pelagians, both of whom were intolerant of sin within the Christian community. He was not the only one to offer new understandings of baptism, sin, expiation, and the nature of the Church, but his formulations were profoundly influential and he is often considered by scholars to mark a definitive break with early Christian treatments of sin.[9] Scholarship on the issue has, indeed, been dominated by discussion of Augustine's doctrines. The comparison between the treatment of sin in the sermons of Augustine and those of the Eusebius Gallicanus collection is therefore an interesting one. It enables us to track Augustine's influence in tangible ways, but it also pinpoints limits to it. The points of disconnect, where the Eusebius Gallicanus preachers differed with Augustine, show how other ideas and other pressures played an important role. The comparison provides a far more complex picture of pastoral responses to sin than any schema of theological controversy would allow.

In order to appreciate the pastoral care of late fifth-century Gaul, therefore, it is first necessary to appreciate the peculiar tensions in late fourth- and early fifth-century Africa. The Donatist schism which cleaved the African Church in this period had arisen precisely over the treatment of sin. After the end of the persecutions, some in North Africa argued that sinners who had failed the test of persecution had no place in the Christian Church.[10] No penance could cleanse such grave sin—only a new baptism might suffice.[11] Over time these hard-liners, who became known as Donatists, justified this stance by arguing that the Church should be a pure entity, untouched by stain or blemish; sinners in the Church constituted a pollution of it.[12] Faced with this rigorist, exclusive view, Augustine argued for a tolerant, inclusive Church.[13] Only God, Augustine maintained, can separate good Christians from bad, and he will do so only in the final judgment.[14] "Why be in such a hurry?" he asked. "You see the weeds among the wheat, you see bad Christians among the good ones; you want to pull out the bad ones; take it easy, it isn't harvest time yet."[15] To separate good from bad before the last judgment would be to deny God's patience and mercy. "It can well happen that those who are weeds today are wheat tomorrow."[16] For Augustine, baptism was not a singular moment of divine mercy. God's forgiveness was available to sinners so long as they lived, and no sin was so great that it could not be forgiven. Through penance Augustine allowed the sinner a second chance and provided the imperfect with a way to stay within the Church.

This allowance was essential due to Augustine's argument, *contra* the Pelagians, that perfection was impossible. In accordance with a long Christian tradition, Pelagius and his followers had maintained that it was possible, after baptism, to live without sin.[17] Failure to do so was a failure of human free will, which was able to choose good, but could also choose evil.[18] To sin was therefore to fall out of the Christian community. Augustine, however, argued that sin was an unavoidable part of the human condition.[19] For him it was not a question of insufficient effort, since salvation was always only achieved through the unmerited mercy of divine grace. Baptism removed the stain of original sin, but it did not remove human infirmity, and if Christians lived beyond the moment of baptism, they inevitably engaged in sinful thoughts and deeds.[20] These deeds might be only small ones, but, as Augustine put it in his sermons, enough drops of water can cause a flood and enough grains of sand can form an avalanche.[21] These small sins thus needed to be expiated. Augustine summed up this view in his sermon fifty-six: "Those who are baptized and depart this life come up from the font without any debts and go off on their way without any debts. But those who are baptized and held in this life pick up something through the weakness of their mortal flesh, which even if it doesn't lead to their being shipwrecked, still needs to be pumped out; because if it isn't pumped out, the level in the bilges gradually rises until the whole ship is swamped."[22] At least partly in response to Pelagian pressure, therefore, Augustine articulated a view of Christian life as a state of constant penance and expiation for inevitably committed sins.[23] "Until we come to that peace, where we shall have no enemies, we must go on fighting long and faithfully and strenuously, in order to earn the victor's crown from the Lord God."[24] "Don't just ignore even minor sins . . . pump your bilges every day."[25]

Augustine's arguments that baptism was only a beginning, that sin was inevitable, and that sinners could remain within the Church if they treated their lives on earth as an opportunity for expiation, were part of a fundamental shift in the pastoral care of the late antique Church. His influence can be traced in the works of a number of late antique preachers. Following Augustine's lead, Peter Chrysologus maintained that no victory over original sin would be possible in this life, so almsgiving and compassion were a necessary basis for continual penance.[26] Avitus of Vienne told his audience that they were deceiving themselves if they thought that they had no sin.[27] Caesarius of Arles, too, made Augustine's point repeatedly. He informed his congregants that no man could live without sin, but that, with the Lord's help, they could redeem themselves.[28] "Since we cannot spend a day without sin, what is the sense of gradually piling up slight offenses and thus making endless streams out of tiny drops?"[29] We are all sinners, he told his audience, and must do penance all our lives if we are to ensure salvation. Those who thought that baptism made them safe were fools.[30]

Augustine's influence is also clear in the Eusebius Gallicanus sermons. Like him, the Eusebian preachers presented baptism as the beginning of a lifelong struggle, rather than the culmination of it. Baptism did not guarantee salvation, the author of sermon twenty-nine warned. It got you into the fortress, but the fortress must then be defended against attack. The soldier must do more than join the army; he must be armed and equipped for the fight. "In baptism we are brought forth to life, after baptism we are confirmed for the fight; in baptism we are purified, after baptism we are strengthened. And thus, although the gift of baptism is sufficient for immediately crossing over, the assistance of confirmation is necessary for victory. Baptism in itself instantly saves those who receive it in the peace of the blessed realm; confirmation arms and instructs those who are kept back for the contests and battles of this world."[31] Like Augustine, the Eusebius Gallicanus preachers used the same imagery to describe both baptism and penance, signaling that one was the continuation of the other. Just as baptism washed away the dirt of sin, so did penitential tears. Just as baptism healed the wounds of crime, so did reparational almsgiving. Just as baptism purified the pollution of evil, so did expiatory fasting.[32] In sermon fifty-one, penance even appeared as a rebirth and as a restoration to life, imagery normally reserved for baptism. The preacher celebrated a bishop who applied the "medicine of penance" and raised those who were as good as dead in sin. Through rebuking and emendation, "he restored to life through a temporary resurrection those whom he had plucked from the deceitful jaws of death."[33]

Yet Augustine's views were not uncontroversial. We have already seen that his insistence that divine grace alone was responsible for salvation caused discomfort among many Gallic monks and pastors alike. So too did the related argument that forgiveness for sin would always be available, and that it did not depend upon human expiatory action. The lifelong recalcitrant sinner who begged for penance on his deathbed should be granted it, Augustine argued. However, when Paulinus of Bordeaux wrote to Faustus of Riez asking whether deathbed penance was sufficient for salvation, Faustus replied unflinchingly that it was not. Simple confession and contrition, he argued, were not enough to erase a lifetime of deliberate sin. Long and arduous penance was necessary for expiation.[34] As a result, Faustus, the only certainly identifiable contributor to the Eusebius Gallicanus collection, has been cited by some scholars as a prime example of a rigorist and ascetic current within the Gallic Church. This current was supposedly resisted by more pastorally-minded bishops such as Avitus of Vienne and Caesarius of Arles, following the example of Augustine. This division reflects the two sides which scholars have perceived to be at odds in the semi-pelagian controversy, and Faustus' views have been assumed to reflect his insistence that Christians earn their salvation.[35] In effect, he has been accused of being a blunt and unsympathetic pastor, driven solely by theological concerns.

The Eusebius Gallicanus sermons make clear, however, that such dichotomies between "pastoral" and "ascetic" or "pastoral and "theological" are simply untenable. They do not do justice to the nuanced pastoral approaches of *any* ecclesiastics.[36] As Uhalde and Demacopoulos have demonstrated, the ascetic John Cassian had an enormous impact on the development of Gallic pastoral techniques, and his influence is tangible in the sermons of both the Eusebius Gallicanus collection and Caesarius of Arles.[37] The preaching in these sermons was just as pastorally responsive as that of Augustine, but it reflects some different priorities. These points of divergence are all the more revealing given the general commonality among views of sin within the late antique Church.

Much modern scholarship on penance has been concerned with issues of definition and distinction between forms.[38] For the Eusebian preachers, however, as for many other late antique and early medieval pastors, expiation worked on a sliding scale. For the author of sermon forty-five, it was primarily important that the expiation fit the crime.

> If perhaps the transgressions are slight, for example, if man either in conversation or in some reprehensible desire has sinned with the eyes or with the heart, the stains of words and thoughts should be cured through daily prayer and cleansed through private remorse. If anyone, however, examining his own conscience from within, has committed some capital crime, or if he has subdued and betrayed his faith through false testimony, and violated the

sacred name of truth through the temerity of perjury, if anyone has corrupted the snow-white tunic of baptism and the shining silk of virginity through the filth of defiled shame, if anyone has killed the new person in himself through murder, if he has given himself up to the captivity of the devil through augurers and diviners and enchanters, crimes of this kind cannot be expiated inwardly through common, ordinary or secret satisfaction. Grave faults require more weighty, more severe and public cures.[39]

Expiation, in other words, was a flexible procedure. It had to be sufficient to atone and it had to be in the best interests of the whole community. Mayke de Jong and Rob Meens have illustrated that this late antique distinction between public and private expiation was not the same as our own. Private penances would still have been visible to all in the community, public penances did not mean social ostracism, and the line between the two was less clear than historians would like to think.[40] However, as the author of sermon forty-five concluded: "He who has ruined himself with the destruction of many should in the same way redeem himself with the edification of many."[41] The serious sinner needed to be made an example of, and also to redeem the damage caused to the virtue of the group. For this reason, shame played a large role in the expiation of grave sins. "He should not be ashamed to do penance," the author of Eusebian sermon fifty-eight maintained, "who was not ashamed to sin."[42] The author of sermon forty-five reminded his congregation that even David, one of the greatest of the Old Testament kings, undertook the humility of penitence.[43] Severe penance of this kind was extreme and unusual. De Jong has argued that it was only brought to bear upon those who had power and status to lose and regain—in other words, the elites.[44] It was a dramatic, singular, unrepeatable act, implying a permanent change of lifestyle and orientation.[45]

Only one sermon in the Eusebius Gallicanus collection addressed in detail the expiation of such serious sins. The tone of sermon fifty-eight was bleak and uncompromising, at odds with the rest of the collection. It began with a series of short, stark sentences. "Penance is an excellent but last-ditch remedy. You have arrived at it.

Seize it as if it were the first, guard it as if it were the only. Just as another baptism cannot now heal one reborn in Christ, except through the medicine of penance; so, after penance, nothing heals."[46] The sermon then launched into a series of sustained metaphors, first comparing penance to a plank to which sinners must cling in the shipwreck of their lives, and then insisting that sinners must think of themselves as now dead to the world.[47] Act, the preacher instructed the penitents, as if you are suspended from the cross, so that the pleasures of the world no longer mean anything to you, and all your thoughts are fixed upon the world to come.[48] "Offer emendation every day as if you are about to cross over from this world."[49] This penance was a preparation for death.

Severe penance was, however, unusual. Like Augustine, the Eusebian preachers were far more concerned with the expiation of the small, ordinary sins of everyday life and it is these which were the focus of most of their preaching on penance. Formal penance, public shaming, and permanent conversion to a penitential state were neither appropriate nor necessary for such sins. Indeed, the distinction between grave and ordinary sin was important to pastors in general. Caesarius went out of his way to reassure congregants that penance was appropriate to the sin. When he called on the faithful to atone for small sins, he told them, he was not expecting young married men to cut their hair and assume the religious habit.[50] There were numerous other methods of expiation available and these could be both administered by the laity themselves and finely calibrated to suit their own sense of sinfulness.

The four methods for the expiation of small sins which were most commonly recommended by late antique pastors were prayer, lamentation, fasting, and almsgiving. All of these methods had scriptural basis and patristic precedent,[51] and all can be found amidst the exhortations of the Eusebius Gallicanus preachers. The author of sermon sixty-four, for example, noted that the publican made a cure for his sins through his tears, and according to the preacher of sermon fifty-three, sighing for sins with tears was the best medicine for wounds.[52] For the preacher of sermon seventy-four, prayers and tears were the best internal medicine; in sermon twenty-six, it was tears and fasting.[53] The author of sermon seventy-four also dwelt at length on the example of the apostle Paul, controlling his flesh through abstinence and following the example of the fasting Christ.[54] We should castigate our members with fasting, instructed the author of Eusebian sermon sixty, and defeat our hearts with prayers.[55] The preacher of sermon forty-five told his audience to follow the example of Zacchaeus who gave half of his goods to the poor.[56] Sermon eight, which was directed to monks, described the power of almsgiving to purge or redeem sins and linked it to prayer, urging that both things be done in harmony.[57] These exhortations did not amount to a standardised expiatory "programme." They constituted a menu of acts, out of which both pastor and congregation could choose how to cleanse souls and ease the way to heaven. The approach was nuanced and flexible, and it differed from one sermon to another.

Expiation was not only an individual matter; it could also be undertaken by the group. Two sermons in the Eusebius Gallicanus collection exhorted penance on a communal level. Sermon twenty-five described a three-day-long communal litany involving supplications and fasting, intended to ward off unspecified disaster. Sermon twenty-six used the story of the Ninevites as a basis for the justification and defense of such practices.[58] The expiatory acts urged upon the community in these sermons, and other late antique sermons on communal penance, did not differ significantly from those urged upon individual penitents—the congregants were instructed to lament their sins, to fast, and to pray. The chief difference was the sense of corporate responsibility which the preachers conveyed. Withdrawal from the communal efforts, the author of Eusebian sermon twenty-five argued, was tantamount to stealing from the community. Since the benefits would be shared by all, the burden should likewise be shared, and nonparticipation threatened the group as a whole.[59] This reflected the same ideal of community that we have already found in the Eusebius Gallicanus collection—one in which congregants worked together and strove for a Christian consensus.

The pastoral approach to expiation found in the Eusebius Gallicanus had a great deal in common with that of other late antique preachers. Communal penitence loomed large in their exhortations, also, and was defended on similar grounds. Caesarius of Arles likened nonparticipation in communal penance to deserting an army on the eve of battle.[60] Both Caesarius and Avitus of Vienne argued that the penitence of the Ninevites was effective only because of the participation of all.[61] Individual struggle could be dangerous, Avitus informed his congregation, and could leave us vulnerable to attack, "but truly, when the assent of the multitudes fights against the common enemy, the strength of another draws along even the timid soldier."[62] For Maximus of Turin, communal penance constituted, rhetorically at least, a more important defense of the community than military efforts. The best way to conquer our enemies, he urged his congregants, was through fasting.[63] This fasting must, however, be undertaken by the community as a whole, equally and together. "Therefore, in the time of tribulation the whole city of the Ninevites fasted . . . Whence we too, brothers, should all fast together, bearing the difficulties of the times and through the abstinence of all, weeping for the compassion of God."[64] Much of this preaching on penance was marked by a common approach to the challenge.

This did not mean, however, that there was uniformity. Within the ambit of staple expiatory injunctions, pastors made choices which revealed their priorities and their views of the Christian community. Almsgiving is one such example, and several preachers made almsgiving the centre of their expiatory exhortations. Ambrose of Milan likened almsgiving to baptism in its power to cleanse—alms can extinguish sins, he claimed, like water extinguishes fire.[65] Maximus of Turin echoed Ambrose's ideas. "Almsgiving is like another bath for the soul, so that if perhaps, after baptism, anyone is strained by human frailty, there remains to them the opportunity to be emended again by almsgiving."[66] "There is no sin so grave," Maximus averred, "that it is not purged by abstinence or extinguished by almsgiving."[67] "However much you are polluted or enclosed by sins, if you give alms, you have begun to be innocent."[68] Peter Chrysologus told his congregation that there was no benefit in fasting if they did not give alms, as well as no benefit in giving alms if they did not fast. A fast without charitable compassion, he said, was "hypocrisy."[69] It was good to fast, Caesarius told his congregants, but it was better to give alms. If you could do both, then do, but if you could only do one, give alms. Fasting without almsgiving was like a lamp without oil.[70] For each of these preachers, almsgiving was the preeminent penitential act, around which other measures coalesced. In contrast, the Eusebius Gallicanus preachers treated almsgiving as less important than fasting, lamentation, and prayer. It appeared less frequently and with less emphasis.[71] The author of sermon fifty-eight even seemed to regard it with suspicion. For the sake of our redemption, he argued, God does not require gold or silver, but weeping and tears of affliction and contrition.[72] Expiation, he seemed to imply, could not be bought, but must be earnt. On this point, indeed, the Eusebius Gallicanus preachers came closest of anyone to Augustine of Hippo, who had been similarly circumspect in praise of the penitential value of almsgiving.[73]

The great deal that the Eusebius Gallicanus preachers had in common with Augustine makes their differences with him all the more striking. Influential though Augustine's approach to penance clearly was, Gallic preachers did not follow it in all particulars. They instead responded to the specific pastoral demands they faced and adapted their message according to their own view of the best way to expiate sin.

Augustine, as we have already seen, focused on the operation of divine grace. He believed that salvation was brought about by unmerited grace rather than by human action. Following this logic, penance could not expiate sin. Augustine urged his congregants to penance not in order to perform reparation, but merely to show awareness of their own sinfulness and demonstrate their hope for redemption. The main penitential action which Augustine therefore urged upon his congregants was prayer—in particular, the recitation of the *pater noster* and its plea for forgiveness. "You are cleansed every day from light and minor sins through your prayers, if you say from the heart, if you say truthfully, if you say in faith, 'Forgive us our debts, as we too forgive our debtors.'"[74] "There is one forgiveness of sins which is given only once in holy baptism; another which, as long as we live here, is given in the Lord's Prayer. That is why we say, 'Forgive us our debts.'"[75] For Augustine this prayer, representing a mental state as much as an actual action, was the key to the penitential life-style. He gave it far more attention than any of the other traditional expiatory acts such as fasting, almsgiving, or lamentation. For Augustine the ideal posture of the Christian, as Carole Straw points out, could only be one of "active passivity": placing hope in the grace of God.[76]

Like a number of other Gallic clergy, however, the Eusebius Gallicanus preachers appear to have found Augustine's approach unsatisfactory as a pastoral strategy. Their exhortations to expiation placed far more emphasis on human action; they urged their audiences to earn their salvation. Anyone who died immediately after receiving baptism, the preacher of sermon twenty-nine told his audience, would go to the last judgment with unstained innocence. All others required continued effort to ensure their victory.[77] God banishes the blemishes on our hearts through baptism, the preacher of sermon twenty noted, "but it is necessary that we exert ourselves, lest we should pollute again that which he purified, lest we should tear open the wounds which he healed, lest he should have to boil out of us again in the fires of hell that which he once washed away in the waters of baptism."[78] Virtue was an exercise that required work; according to this approach, prayer was not the central penitential act in such an approach and the *pater noster* scarcely featured. Instead of urging congregants to pray for mercy, the Eusebian preachers instructed them to take part of the responsibility for their own salvation. The preacher of sermon twenty-six emphasised how the Ninevites deflected God's punishment through their acts of penance, and then imagined God speaking to the sinner. "What you admit is grave in yourself, I will kindly forgive; what you sadly accuse yourself of, I will gladly absolve; what you recall in public, I will disregard in eternity. And because you have anticipated my sentence through your penance, I will resheath my sword."[79] "Anticipation of the sentence" was the key to the Eusebian penitential approach. It involved enacting the last judgment in this life, rather than waiting for the next. If you accuse yourself, the author of Eusebian sermon sixty-four informed his congregants, "justice is born out of sins . . . Here, therefore, we should condemn our faults and offenses through daily emendation and contrition; we should be our own most severe judges and we should anticipate the judgment of the future examination through full satisfaction. Here, daily tears and daily weeping should blot out what would otherwise be consumed by the eternal fire."[80] The sermons were filled with imagery of judgment and punishment, but ordinary Christians were responsible for enacting both. The author of sermon twenty-six instructed that he who would "be pleasing to God" should be "his own witness, accuser and judge, under the judgment of a private examination."[81] Two sermons in the Eusebian collection, in variations on the same passage, urged members of their community to "condemn ourselves" and "accuse ourselves daily to our judge."[82] The author of sermon sixty-four approvingly offered the example of the publican who was his own accuser and judge, and beat his breast in the form of his own punishment.[83] The sinner must preempt the role of God in presiding at the last judgment. Other Eusebian preachers used metaphors of introspection and medical examination to convey the same idea. We must inspect ourselves inwardly, the preacher of sermon fourteen urged, and gauge our own deficiencies.[84] We should do within ourselves, the author of sermon forty-five told his audience, what doctors do externally.[85] In the sermons of Augustine of Hippo the image of the doctor was used only of the pastor or of God, never of the sinner.[86] Augustine did use judicial imagery at times. In sermon twenty he urged his congregants to "let your sin have you as its judge, not as its defending counsel."[87] He did not come close, however, to matching the enthusiasm of the Eusebian preachers for forensic imagery.

The difference between Augustine and the Eusebius Gallicanus preachers in their view of the operation of divine grace was clearly important, but this was only one factor at work in their departure from his views. Another was the willingness of the Eusebius Gallicanus preachers to urge supposedly "ascetic" penitential techniques upon their lay congregations. These sermons embraced introspection and compunction, which were not seen as monastic "specialities," but as common Christian "instruments of repentence."[88] Augustine, by contrast, had shown himself ambivalent about the value of such techniques.[89] Another factor at work was the practical position in which clergy found themselves. Augustine was a figure of enormous charisma. He had built up, over his lifetime, a network of powerful supporters and a reservoir of moral authority. Even he, however, struggled at times to assert his pastoral power.[90] Most clergy had far less behind them when they spoke. When they emphasised the role of the laity as their own judges, therefore, the Eusebius Gallicanus preachers shifted a pastoral burden from their own shoulders. Congregants were instructed to internalise judgment and circumscribe their own lives, thus enjoining sinners to be their own judges, their own doctors, their own "inspectors of the heart."[91] This is not to say that the clergy held no power according to such a model of expiation. Preachers set the parameters, defined the grounds, and exerted considerable pressure. All of this power, however, was indirect. It did not rest upon the charisma of the pastor, nor did it emphasise his role as a mediator. It was difficult to challenge and it suited the kinds of preachers who relied upon prepared sermon texts to get them through the liturgical year.

How this difference played out in practice becomes clear as we further compare the pastoral directions of Augustine and the Eusebius Gallicanus preachers. Because Augustine argued that sin was inevitable, and that human beings were entirely dependent upon the unmerited mercy of God to achieve salvation, he focused his pastoral energies on combating despair. For him, penance was a sign that forgiveness was always possible. So long as the sinner lived, no matter how wicked his or her crimes, God could grant absolution. "It wasn't so much the crime that Judas the traitor committed, as his despair of pardon that brought him to total destruction."[92] It was to combat such despair that God offered the "haven of repentance."[93] No one should assume that damnation is certain, and indulge in sin thinking that all is lost anyway.[94] "Now is the time of mercy, for us to correct ourselves," the bishop of Hippo told his congregation in sermon seventeen. "The time of judgment has not yet come . . . The journey is not yet over, the day has not yet drawn to a close, we haven't yet breathed our last. There is no need to despair, which is worse than anything, because on account of those human and pardonable sins . . . God has established in the Church set times for requesting mercy, a daily medicine that we might say: 'Forgive us our debts, as we too forgive our debtors.'"[95] The wages of the worker, Augustine assured his congregation, will not be dependent on how long he has worked.[96]

Augustine recognised the danger of complacency. He knew that some Christians might interpret his reassurances as a license to sin and delay penance deliberately until death was near.[97] In sermon twenty, Augustine struggled to reason with such thinking. "Now God has promised to pardon all who turn away from their sins," he pictured sinners thinking to themselves. "The very day they are converted he will forget all their iniquities. So I will do whatever I want, and whenever I want to I will have a conversion, and what I have done will be blotted out." The pastor did not deny that the claims of the sinner were true. "What are we to say to that? That God does *not* heal the repentant whenever they turn back to him? God does forgive everything that has gone before. If we deny it, we contradict the divine indulgence, we clash head on with the words of the prophets, and we are struggling against the utterances of God. This is not the way of a faithful steward."[98] All Augustine could respond with was a threat that time may run out. "Why not today? Why not now? 'Tomorrow,' he says. 'God promised me indulgence.' Do you promise yourself tomorrow?"[99] Do not rely on deathbed penance, he warned his congregation in sermon seventeen. "Haven't many people gone to sleep in good health, and been stiffs in the morning?"[100] "No one has promised you that you are going to be alive tomorrow."[101] Nonetheless, Augustine insisted that even a deliberately delayed penance or confession could be sufficient to ensure the expiation of sin.[102] Despair was a more pressing pastoral threat to the bishop of Hippo than excessive confidence.

The Eusebius Gallicanus preachers, who emphasised the power and responsibility of congregants to expiate sin themselves, were far more worried about combating an undue sense of security on the part of believers. We need to beware, warned the author of sermon thirty-three, "lest either pernicious relaxation should trip us up on the left, or ruinous pride on the right, lest either perverseness arising from negligence or vanity from merits should begin to contaminate us, because in the one case sin arises from infirmity, in the other, error arises from virtue."[103] Repentance should happen now, the preachers repeatedly urged, while there is still time and in case of sudden death. Penance will not be possible in the afterlife, and the sinner will regret not having taken the opportunity easily within his grasp. "And therefore, dearly beloved, let us convert ourselves to the better while the remedies are still within our power."[104] Whatever we do not redeem here, deceived by a fatal security, the preacher of sermon twenty-seven insisted, we will carry with us into the presence of the saints and of the judge.[105] "And thus, through present mortification, the sentence of future death is anticipated."[106] In the time to come, it will no longer be possible to perform good works or redeem sin.[107] "No emendation will be possible there, no prayer will have any force."[108] Those sinners would want to return, if they could, not to joys, not to lusts, not to sins, but to penance and the labours of emendation and salubrious lamentation. We are granted a period of unknown brevity "to cure stains, wash faults, heal the things of the past, consider the things of the future and make undone the things which are done."[109] The pressure of this responsibility was intense. Furthermore, the Eusebian preachers made clear what was at stake by emphasising the horrors awaiting the damned. In sermon six, for example, the flames of hell licked the bones of sinners, tortured their thoughts and entered into their very marrow.[110] The "unquenchable fire," the preacher warned, will extinguish in hell whatever penance has failed to correct on earth. "The burning pit of hell will be opened and there will be a descent, but no return."[111] "Too late," sinners will lament their failure to repent and to avert these horrors through alms and tears.[112] There was no comparable theme in the sermons of Augustine.[113] The laity might be granted some degree of agency in their chance of salvation, but the Eusebian preachers tried to make sure that they felt its full weight. Responsibility could be coercive as well as liberating.

These two pastoral styles were not in conflict: both were orthodox and both had precedent within the Christian tradition. They reveal, however, different priorities in the care offered to Christian congregations. Two case studies clarify the nuances of emphasis in the Eusebius Gallicanus collection. The stories of the good thief (Luke 23.39–43) and the Ninevites (Jonah 3–4) were standard penitential *exempla*. They could be spun, however, to support a variety of pastoral points. The story of the conversion of the thief on the cross and his immediate salvation was used by preachers who followed Augustine's lead to rebut both despair of redemption and the Pelagian position that grace must be merited by human action. In the telling of these preachers, the story demonstrated that sincere deathbed repentance could be sufficient to expiate sin. Maximus of Turin, for example, noted that the thief had been promised paradise swiftly, even though many others laboured to attain pardon through tears and fasts.[114] It was the hope and faith of the thief which gained him pardon, in Maximus' telling, not any good deeds or penitential acts which he undertook.[115] Peter Chrysologus likewise used the example of the thief to restore hope—he "broke into paradise" at the last moment, when there no longer seemed time—and to recommend that all Christians likewise undertake penance on their deathbeds.[116] Avitus of Vienne used the story as the centrepiece in his defense of last-minute repentance, arguing that in the thief's case faith was sufficient for salvation.[117]

The Eusebius Gallicanus sermon which treated the good thief began with a similar point. His absolution, the preacher argued, "was done for the consolation and hope of all the people."[118] His sudden salvation was "a cause of our hope and advancement; for the immense goodness of our God freely gave that which he foreknew to be generally beneficial."[119] However, the preacher of this sermon also implied that this grace was not wholly unmerited. "But not without reason did he merit so much."[120] The thief believed in Jesus with a praiseworthy faith, even as the apostle Peter denied him.[121] God filled him with the Holy Spirit, and "thus he joined grace to merit."[122] The thief earned salvation, according to the Eusebian preacher, through the rapidity and utter perfection of his belief. This was not quite Augustine's view of unmerited grace.

Moreover, whereas other late antique preachers used the good thief as an argument against despair, the author of the Eusebian sermon focused on ensuring that he would not be an excuse for confidence. He expressed his anxiety that hearing this story might make someone feel so "secure" or "relaxed" that they might say to themselves: "I see in what a short space of time the crimes of the thief were remitted, and so they will also be cancelled for me."[123] The devil introduces such security, the preacher warned, in order to bring you to ruin. "He misleads himself and fools around with his own death who thinks, 'Indulgence can heal me at the last moment.'"[124] Against such security the preacher offered a standard pastoral rebuttal. "We should daily be expecting our passing and the uncertainties of the migration, which are now either unexpected or sudden." "Remedies," the preacher reminded his audience, "will be lacking in eternity."[125] The stakes were too high to risk such calculations. He went still further. "It is hateful to God when man sins freely, relying on a penance reserved for old age." "Artifice," he warned, "is not admitted to salvation."[126] The good thief did not deliberately put off redemption, but grasped at it the moment he knew of it. "He neither delayed knowing the time of salvation, nor deceitfully arranged the remedies for his condition at the last unhappy moment, nor saved up the hope of his redemption until the desperate end."[127] The Eusebian preacher did not deny the possibility of deathbed remission, but he cast serious doubt upon its efficacy. The story of the good thief was therefore spun as a warning against the last-minute unmerited penance which it seemed to support.

The story of the Ninevites, who repented and were spared their threatened destruction, was more problematic for preachers following in Augustine's wake. The wording of the passage, suggesting that the Ninevites' penance caused God to change his mind, was difficult to reconcile with a model in which salvation and damnation were both predestined and unmerited. Augustine himself chose to use them as an example of God's mercy and an argument against despair. "They didn't despair of God's mercy," Augustine observed. "They turned to repenting and God did spare them."[128] He did not otherwise dwell on the Ninevites in his preaching.[129] Other preachers, too, struggled with how to spin the episode. Maximus of Turin noted that the Ninevites merited mercy and conquered God through humility, but mostly used them as an example of citizens who stuck together and conquered their enemies through abstinence and prayer.[130] This message suited a pastor seeking to keep his community together in the face of barbarian threat.[131] Peter Chrysologus observed that the Ninevites anticipated the judge and thus revoked their sentence, but focused on them as contrasts to the "obstinacy" of the Jews, concerned as he was to promulgate an anti-Jewish message.[132] For none of these preachers were the Ninevites a perfect penitential model.

In the Eusebius Gallicanus sermon which treated them, however, they served as a central vehicle of the pastoral message: an optimistic defense of the power of communal penance and an example of how Christians could effect their own redemption. The preacher began by characterising the penance of the Ninevites as a "conversion to the better." The city was indeed "overthrown," since purple was changed into sackcloth, affluence into fasting, and joy into tears.[133] This reading might suggest that the preacher would go on to emphasise that Nineveh's conversion had been God's plan all along, but he instead immediately emphasised the power of the citizens to secure their own salvation. "Where are those who deny the remedy of penitence, who do not believe it should either be accepted or that the community should be rewarded after worthy labours?"[134] The example of the Ninevites, he went on to claim, ought to remove any doubt that God hearkens to human supplication. "Therefore, every one of the faithful should not doubt that the sacrifice of requests, the burnt offering of prayers and the sacrifice of tears can immediately rise up to the divine presence; behold, even the lamentations of brute animals reaches the ears of the Lord."[135] When God rebuked Jonah for his anger, the preacher maintained, he was also rebuking those who refuse to believe in the redemptive power of penitence. "Therefore the Ninevites, through penance and abstinence, caused the ruin of imminent anger from above to be suspended, and with children and cattle abstaining equally, they turned back, as I said, the blow coming forth from the Lord and the judgment about to fall upon them."[136]

The emphasis of the preacher in all of these passages was upon the action of the citizens. It was their penitence which brought about their redemption. He did not claim that these deeds forced God's hand, but he told his congregants that through the actions of the Ninevites, severity was "strongly urged" towards divine clemency.[137] The preacher then used the story as a basis on which to set a more general discussion of penance, urging congregants to restore themselves to baptismal purity, and be their own witnesses, accusers, and judges, thereby anticipating and deflecting, like the Ninevites, the punishment to be meted out in the next life. The Eusebian preacher used the Ninevites as an *exemplum* of penitential behaviour. He took the opportunity which the story provided to emphasise the role of human action and responsibility for salvation and to exhort his lay audience to feel the consequent pressure in their daily lives.

The Eusebius Gallicanus preachers did not try to preach "active passivity." Even Augustine found it difficult to motivate a congregation while maintaining that their efforts were irrelevant. The gap between the working theology of Augustine's sermons and the programmatic statements of his treatises and letters demonstrate his own awareness of the problem.[138] Augustine also recognised the benefit in preaching the value of human effort and did so when he felt it was pastorally necessary.[139] What we see in Gaul in the fifth and sixth centuries, therefore, was not so much a disagreement with Augustine as a different response to some of the same challenges.

This response cut across the supposed lines of the semi-pelagian debate. Caesarius of Arles, otherwise generally seen as residing in the "moderate Augustinian" camp, in fact closely imitated the stance of the Eusebius Gallicanus preachers on the expiation of sin.[140] Several of the bishop of Arles' sermons on penance were little more than expanded and rewritten plagiarisms of Eusebian sermons, and a quick scan through the endnotes of this chapter will illustrate the extent of the textual parallels.[141] The tone of Caesarius' rewritings did not differ substantially from the Eusebian originals. Caesarius, too, was far more worried about security than despair, and he fretted over a congregation confident that penance could always be deferred. He railed against those who sinned now with the intention of redeeming themselves afterwards.[142] He followed the Eusebian preachers in expressing doubts about the efficacy of deathbed penance and the ability of the calculating sinner to achieve forgiveness in this fashion. "Merely the word of the penitent does not suffice to wipe out sins, because in satisfaction for great sins not only words but actions are sought. Of course, even at the very last moment penance is given because it cannot be denied. However, we cannot be a guarantee that one who has thus sought it deserves to be absolved." The penance which is sought by a man only when he is weak, Caesarius told his audience, is itself weak.[143] Caesarius thus sought to puncture the security of the faithful. "If a man repents and is reconciled at the last moment, I am not sure whether he will die secure. I can give penance, but not assurance."[144] God, he warned them in another sermon, "knows with what faith and intention of soul [each man] has sought repentance."[145] Clearly, there was no theological rift that determined the treatment of penance by these Gallic pastors.

The pastoral care which the Eusebius Gallicanus preachers offered to sinners gave them a way to be in the Church on this earth and after death to join the Christian community in heaven. They built on Augustine's argument that baptism was only the beginning of a commitment, and that the whole of Christian life could and should be spent in expiation of unavoidable sins. The Eusebian preachers were optimistic about the human capacity to do this, but worried correspondingly that their congregants might relax too far. Virtue is a constant effort, they told their audiences, and hellfire is the punishment for those who do not sustain it. This view of penance fit well with the Eusebian models of leadership and community. The pastor showed his congregants the path, but it was up to them to walk it. Hence, although the Eusebian preachers and those who used the collection appeared to shift power into the hands of the laity, that appearance could be deceptive. In removing some of the pastoral burden from themselves, they also increased the pressure on their congregants. They hoped that the laity would control themselves, and by acting as their own "most severe judges" would pre-empt both clerical and divine judgment. This may have been a more realistic option for many clergy than attempting to shoulder the burden undertaken by Augustine. Christians must choose to expiate their own sins, the preachers argued, or these would bear witness against them on judgment day.

CHAPTER SIX

Sermons to Monks

Our attention has so far been on the sermons to the laity, but at least ten sermons in the collection were directed to monks.[1] The inclusion of these sermons in the collection by the compiler clearly troubled some subsequent users of it. Most medieval copyists preferred to lift these sermons out and treat them as a discrete group.[2] Modern scholars have largely done the same, looking to these sermons for evidence of the nature of ascetic life at Lérins, their probable setting.[3] These sermons have consequently been the most examined in the Eusebius Gallicanus, yet the context in which they appear is ignored. Our discomfort with the coexistence of sermons to monks and laity in the same collection should, however, cause us to pay more attention to the conjunction, not less. The different treatment given by scholars to the Eusebian sermons to monks has, in fact, created the perception of a division between monastic and lay forms of Christian community which the Eusebian compiler, and perhaps also the sermons' preachers, did not seem to feel.

Modern scholarship has long been fascinated by late antique models of ascetic-episcopal authority and by the connections between ascetic and lay Christian communities. As Demacopoulos puts it, what happened when monks became bishops?[4] The Eusebius Gallicanus collection offers an invaluable opportunity to answer this question. It demonstrates, moreover, that we should not assume a unidirectional "invasion" of one community by the values and practices of another.[5] Instead, the collection shows us the development of a common vision of Christian community among people who did not see divisions as clearly as we do. When examined from a pastoral perspective, the sermons to the monks and to the laity are surprisingly congruous, especially in their common concern for community and their similar perception of the role of individuals in their own salvation. The collection reveals that for at least some late antique Christians the borders between monastery and world were not strictly drawn. They saw themselves as participants in a common endeavour.[6]

Determining which of the Eusebius Gallicanus sermons were directed to monks has not been a completely straightforward task. In Glorie's edition, sermons thirty-six through forty-five have the title *ad monachos*. This reflects their most frequent designation in the manuscripts, and although manuscript titles are hardly conclusive evidence of the original audiences, most of these were undoubtedly directed to monks. Sermons thirty-eight, thirty-nine, forty, forty-two, and forty-four urged their audiences to hold to their pious professions, live in religious community, and obey their abbot. Preachers described those they addressed as being in the desert, outside of the world, and on the island of the monks. They detailed monastic abstinence, vigils, and temptations. Sermons thirty-seven, forty-one, and forty-three were less explicit, but described practices consistent with monastic profession and a community gathered to live together in the service of God. Clearly all of these sermons were written for an ascetic audience. A title is not, however, always reliable. Sermon forty-five, despite appearing in the *ad monachos* series in some manuscripts, and in the Glorie edition, was in fact originally directed to the laity.[7] It seems to be a Lenten sermon, chiefly concerned with fasting, vigils, penance, and the appropriate role of charitable giving in the Christian community. The preacher focuses his attention on worldly issues and makes no reference to any ascetic or monastic context for his audience. In previous chapters, we have treated this sermon as a work preached to the laity, and we will not discuss it further here. Nor is it clear whether sermon thirty-six should be treated as a sermon to monks. It contains no explicit references to an ascetic profession and is entitled *ad monachos* in some but not all of the surviving manuscripts.[8] Both Kasper and Glorie have expressed doubts over whether its audience was originally ascetic.[9] The sermon is very distinctive as it is written in a high style and contains an unusual number of learned references to pagan Roman authors.[10] Clearly the audience was an elite of some kind, and a group of which the preacher had high behavioural expectations; professed monks are a possibility, but the question is at best unsettled. We will treat it in this chapter, but with some caution.

Three sermons outside the *ad monachos* series were, however, also directed to monks. Sermon seventy-two, an encomium of Honoratus of Arles, was delivered to the monks at Lérins—it is concerned with Honoratus' time there, with his ascetic virtues, and with the attempts of the audience to follow his precepts. Arles may have his body, the preacher said, but we have his spirit and teachings, and it was here that he laid the foundations for what he achieved when he went on to become bishop. Sermon seven contains a number of standard injunctions to monks, including the warning to guard their profession and not think of themselves as outside the world when they hold it within.[11] Ascetics were also among the audience for sermon eight, which contains instructions for religious and emphasises that the professed must set a good example for the rest of the Christian community. Whether other members of that community were present is not known. The sermon's exhortations were delivered in the third person, which suggests that it was preached by a visiting bishop and was not the internal product of a monastery. This makes for some differences in pastoral style and focus from the rest of the series.

Sermons thirty-seven through forty-four share a common style and form a coherent group. They were probably the work of a single preacher, whom most scholars have assumed to be Faustus of Riez.[12] This is plausible, but not provable, for reasons we have already outlined in chapter 2. Reference to an "island" suggests the monastery of Lérins as the place of composition for these sermons.[13] Sermon seventy-two was certainly delivered to the monks of Lérins, and was probably also the work of Faustus.[14] Sermon eight, however, is the work of a visiting preacher addressing a monastery of which he is not and has never been a part. Faustus would not have preached in this way to the monks of Lérins. The tone of sermon thirty-six likewise diverges markedly from any others in the collection: it is either addressed to a different community from the rest of the series, or is the work of a different author. The Eusebian sermons to monks, therefore, probably reflect a diversity of authorial voices and preaching contexts, just like the rest of the collection.

The collected works of Augustine of Hippo and Caesarius of Arles contain sermons both to monks and to the laity, just as the Eusebius Gallicanus does, but these sermons were preached to monks by bishops who were visiting the monasteries under their care. Despite their previous ascetic experiences, both Augustine and Caesarius therefore preached as outsiders.[15] They expressed admiration for a lifestyle of which they were no longer a part, even as they critiqued and challenged the foibles of their monastic audiences. With the exception of sermon eight and possibly sermon thirty-six, however, the Eusebius Gallicanus sermons to monks were preached by insiders. The preachers focused on internal problems faced by the community, treated tasks as a joint struggle, and made extensive use of first person plural pronoun and verb forms. The Eusebian sermons may have been preached by the abbot (his absence as a referent point in the sermons supports this view) or another senior member of the community. They were probably delivered in much the same context as those to lay congregations—during the regular church service, or to mark particular occasions.[16] They were, in fact, very similar to the sermons to the laity in goals and functions, since both sets of sermons were part of ongoing efforts at community formation and leadership modelling. Just like the rest of the sermons in the collection, they were instruments of exhortation, of instruction, and of excoriation. Pastoral care and spiritual direction were just as important and necessary in a monastic community as in a lay one.

The connection of at least some of these sermons to Lérins has burdened them with a great deal of scholarly baggage. This island monastery has been extensively studied, and there is no need to review here the well-known narrative of its foundation and development, only simply to note that it has long been recognised as one of the most important forces in the religious landscape of late antique Gaul.[17] Lérins has been variously acclaimed as the pilot project for Western coenobitism, a fortress of Latin culture in the encroaching Dark Ages, a refuge for aristocrats fleeing chaos and invasions, the mediator of Eastern ascetic ideas to the West, the heart of the "ascetic invasion" of secular society, and the stronghold of anti-Augustinian sentiment and ascetic triumphalism in Gaul.[18]

One common thread running through almost all of these representations is commentary upon what Nouailhat called "la fécundité épiscopale de Lérins."[19] In short, despite the fact that the monastery was founded upon a fundamental desire to leave the world, it kept sending its members back into it.[20] An astonishing number of the most prominent bishops of fifth- and sixth-century Gaul had first passed through the gates of the island monastery.[21] As a result, Lérins is seen to stand at the heart of one of the most striking phenomena of the Gallic Church—the combining of the ascetic and the episcopal charismas in the "monk-bishop."[22] Whether depicted in an idealist light as the introduction of new spirituality to the Gallic episcopate, in a cynical light as a machination of careerist bishops, or in a more neutral light as the transformation and reorientation of the upper classes into a new social leadership role, the force of the Lérinian engagement with the world is undeniable.[23]

As the hagiographical trope had it, these men remained monks even after they had become bishops. It has been difficult, however, to establish what this meant in practice. The commonalities between the sermons to monks and to the laity in the Eusebius Gallicanus collection are therefore especially interesting, as is the smooth and uncomplicated relationship between monastery and world which they envisage. Both monasteries and lay communities were treated by the Eusebian preachers as forms of Christian community which faced the same problems and could be approached with the same pastoral strategies. Although there was some adaptation to the needs of specific audiences, the fundamental approach did not differ.[24]

The first element of similarity is the concern with community. The same emphases on harmony, mutuality, and consensus which emerged in chapter 3 dominate the sermons to monks as well, and the same models of common identity, respectful relations, erasure of dissent, and nondisruptive leadership characterise homilies to monks as well as to the laity. This development was far from automatic. Asceticism was not inherently a communal enterprise: renunciation of the world began with an individual decision and might involve a rejection of all forms of social organisation and engagement. The first heroes of the ascetic movement had been ostentatiously solitary and their stories were still read and studied for inspiration.[25] In the West, the ascetic movement had been channelled from an early stage into communal expressions, but this trend was not always quiescently accepted.[26] The Eusebian sermons to monks found preachers having to justify the many restrictions which communal life placed upon an ascetic: obedience to an abbot, and perhaps to a rule, the renunciation of personal property, prescribed daily routines, and an end to freedom of movement.[27] The author of sermon thirty-eight articulated the tensions these restrictions could provoke among the aristocratic men who joined Lérins. Such people, the preacher complained, rejected correction and discipline and wallowed in impudence, saying, "I give up and I depart, I will not suffer to bear this; I am a free man! . . . I am a free man, I owe you nothing!" Faced with the restrictions of communal life they balked and demanded to know: "Are we your slaves?"[28] Monastic communities were vulnerable to such discontent and some did not long survive because of it.[29]

Defending the monastic community against such threats required emphasising the bonds of affection and mutual advantage among its members. The preacher of sermon thirty-eight reminded all those who wished to leave the monastery of the reasons why they had joined it. You are leaving a place to which your God has called you, he lamented, where you were first illuminated, where you found shelter from the storm. Suddenly you have forgotten "fraternal fellowship and comfort."[30] Birds love their own nests, he exclaimed, and wild beasts the place where they were raised, their beds and their pastures, and no matter what freedom is offered, they always return to the place that they love. Too late, if you leave, will you realise your error, repent of your ruin, and weep.[31] The community was depicted as the monk's home, his family, the place to which he belonged. Moreover, its restrictions were recast as comforts. The ascetic's natural place, the preacher maintained, was in a community. To those who threatened to leave, the preacher also offered the pointed reminder that they were not free at all—they were slaves to sin and debtors to God.[32] "Such ones do not know what they vowed. They have forgotten for what reason they came here."[33] It will do you no good to leave, he told them. "What use is it, I say, that you flee? You carry yourself with you wherever you go . . . Let no one deceive themselves—one does not flee the enemy from place to place, from sin to virtue, from passion to emendation. For if you flee him in this way, he follows you."[34] Instead the sinner should emend himself, and the devil would flee from him. Leaving the community, the preacher emphasised, would bring the deserter no peace, only further punishment. He who leaves the monastery "may seem to guard the name and the appearance of his profession, but actually his soul languishes and is lost through negligence."[35] "Look to your calling," was the Eusebian preachers' refrain.[36]

Individualism was consistently linked in the sermons to pride. God has called you to this place, "and you, endowed with understanding, fortified with reason, meanwhile will become such a stranger to good sense that you prefer your wishes or efforts to the benefactions of God, and you follow your own thoughts."[37] Against such an attitude the author of sermon thirty-eight marshalled a fusillade of biblical quotations. "A fool's conduct is right in his own eyes," he told his audience. "A road may seem straightforward to men and yet end in the depths of hell." "All who hear my word and do it not are like the foolish man who built his house upon the sand."[38] Nor were these dangers restricted to newcomers. Senior monks who thought that they had moved beyond the training wheels of community were, according to the author of sermon forty-two, particularly susceptible to the sin of pride. The devil will try to conquer such monks "by means of their very success and through their own merits, so that while they pile up time and merits, they also cast out the humility of their hearts through most impure vanity."[39] No monk should be so prideful as to think that he was better than the community, and no monk should be so lacking in humility as to think that he could leave it and prosper.

The community was the most advantageous place for a monk to be, according to the Eusebius Gallicanus preachers. It was fruitful to live with others, the author of sermon thirty-nine argued, and it was dangerous to lack distraction.[40] The greatest manifestations of virtue, according to the preacher of sermon forty-two, were to be found in the company of others. "That soul is blessed by God, whose humility confounds the pride of another, whose patience extinguishes the anger of a neighbour, whose obedience silently rebukes the sloth of another, whose fervour awakens the idleness of another's tepidity!"[41] "That soul is happy," the preacher went on, "which, while living well in company, is the joy of many, and many are either instructed or illuminated by it: for when its goods are shared with many, they are increased."[42]

Community could also, however, be an important test of moral character. The soul which, through its disobedience or pride, compels those around it to sin, incurs damnation for as many as it destroys.[43] "Therefore, dearly beloved, we should strive to do those things which pertain to edification when we are in the midst of a community, lest our sins should do harm to the virtues of others."[44] Dissension was repeatedly identified by the Eusebian preachers as the greatest threat to communal harmony, and considerable pastoral effort was devoted to suppressing it. The author of sermon forty, for example, warned monks that when "we are agitated by diverse wicked and unseemly thoughts of the heart or we are wounded by the poisoned sword of the tongue, tempted to evil on account of small and unimportant things, bursting forth in quarrels and disputes . . . we violate our profession through the transgression of the rule."[45] The author of sermon forty-three castigated those monks who detracted, spoke ill of, or allowed themselves to be angered by their brothers.[46] There was no point in abstaining from wine, according to the preacher of sermon forty-four, if you were drunk with bitter discord.[47] Such dissension, the preachers maintained, was the work of the devil. He tried to destroy the monastery from within, instigating "pretexts and causes," making "those things which are small and light seem intolerable and impossible" and arousing "the passion of disobedience which always accompanies communal unhappiness."[48] The devil has taken up arms against us with our own tongues, the author of sermon forty-two warned, making us speak with anger and passion in the false belief that others have done us harm.[49] To maintain communal harmony was to fight the devil. Not to obey the communal rule, and still more to desert the monastery, was doubly to do his will.[50]

Humility was therefore yoked to obedience as the virtue which would keep monastic community intact. Disobedience hardens the soul, the preacher of sermon thirty-eight warned, "so that it is persuaded to accept rules neither by authority nor by reason, but, what is worst, believes only in itself and follows its own aims instead of all reason and thinks only that is right which it conceives in its own hardened heart."[51] Humble and obedient souls, on the other hand, overcome all tribulations and difficulties. "To the extent to which we shall have been humble and obedient, so much more sweetly will we feel the yoke of the Lord and alleviate [the burden] on us; to the extent to which we shall have been obedient to our leaders and to our fathers, so much also will God hearken to our prayers."[52] True humility for the Eusebian preacher meant never becoming an expert, never rising above others within the community. "For he advances well, he finishes well, who daily behaves as though he is always beginning."[53] This was the only way to ensure spiritual progress.[54] The ultimate goal was renunciation of the individual will and its replacement with the will of the community, which itself represented the will of God. "I have not come to do my own will," the preacher of sermon thirty-eight reminded the monks, "but the will of him who sent me to my home."[55]

This view of community triumphing over individualism was but a more sharply articulated version of the model found in the Eusebius Gallicanus sermons to the laity. In both, the protection of the group's coherence and harmony was paramount. It is not surprising, therefore, that the model of leadership found in the Eusebius Gallicanus sermons to monks is congruous with that offered to the laity. Leaders stood amidst rather than over their communities. In the Eusebian sermons to monks, the abbot did not play a central role. Obedience was demanded, but it was obedience to the community, to its customs and practices, rather than discipleship to an individual. The one sermon which described a monastic leader, that concerning Honoratus of Arles, told the story of his domestication from a wandering charismatic to a safe and stable coenobite.[56] His greatest virtue, according to the preacher, was that he never trusted in himself alone—that "whenever anything had to be either arranged or done by him, he considered the discussion and judgment of [his companion Caprasius], as the fairest means of examination."[57] Honoratus' qualification as a leader resided in the fact that he perfectly fulfilled the same obligations of obedience and humility which he imposed upon others.[58] He was styled as a *paterfamilias,* but of a family consisting of brothers.[59] Greatest praise was reserved for Honoratus' pastoral care. He was styled as a "magnificent pastor," "vigilant" and "solicitous" in this office, an "ever-watchful guardian of souls," devoted to the improvement of his flock.[60] This care could take a parental form, as when the preacher claimed that Honoratus licked his congregants into shape as mother animals lick their formless newborn young, creating in them the image of Christ, turning beasts into men and men into angels.[61] This was a parenthood of maternal solicitude, not paternal authority. It was the good of the community and of the group as a whole which mattered, not the charismatic action of an individual.[62]

There were in fact points of difference in the approach to monks and to the laity. The Eusebius Gallicanus preachers to monks worried about ascetic superiority and elitism. This was understandable. At its heart, asceticism was a response to the feeling that ordinary expressions of Christianity were insufficient. It was adopted by those who wanted their religion to be not just a part of their life, but the defining feature of it, calling for full-time, professional commitment. The implication that secular Christians did not do enough was always close to the surface. Witness the vituperative debate between Jerome and Jovinian, as well as the challenge of the Manichees, for evidence that such suggestions provoked a profound disquiet.[63] Pelagius' insistence that perfection was both possible and necessary for salvation simply took ascetic ideas to the logical next step, earning him both a wide following and, eventually, condemnation as a heretic.[64]

The Eusebius Gallicanus preachers were far from alone in this concern. Combat against ascetic elitism was the central focus of Augustine's pastoral care for monks.[65] His concern emerged sharply, for example, in his sermon 354, preached to an unknown group of religious, in which he attempted to break down, or at least moderate, such elitism. "You have a higher goal set before you," he told them, "that is to say, you have a more honourable place in the body of Christ," but this is through the grace of God, not your own merits.[66] Moreover, "the first thing for you to realise, dearly beloved, is that in the body of Christ, the more excellent members are not the only ones. After all, married life too is something to be admired, and has its place in the body of Christ."[67] Just as married Christians honour and respect you, Augustine warned his ascetic audience, so you should honour and respect them. It is better to be married and humble, than chaste and proud.[68] The bishop of Hippo went on to attack those religious who considered themselves superior even to their own parents by virtue of their chastity.[69] Although ascetic renunciation was the better course, both were essentially good. "The mother will have a lower place in the kingdom of heaven, since she is married, than the daughter, since she is a virgin. The virgin daughter, you see, will have a higher place, the married mother a lower place, but still both will be there; just as one star is bright, another star dim, but still both are in the sky."[70] Augustine's concern with spiritual pride derived from and motivated his combat against such elitists as the Donatists and, especially, the Pelagians. To him it seemed that Pelagius and his followers wanted to make the whole world into a monastery.[71] He strove to ensure that there would still be a place for the ordinary, lay Christian within the Church and within his vision of heaven—ascetics could not be allowed to set the agenda or to flaunt their superior commitment.[72] As a result, he was inherently suspicious of the monk-bishop and of the role of ascetics in the broader Christian community.[73]

While the Eusebius Gallicanus preachers, like Augustine, were concerned to break down any monastic pretensions to superiority over the laity, they took a different approach. Their sermons treated monks as no better than the laity in practice. Sermon after sermon informed the monks that far from being superior to lay Christians, they were simply more exposed. "Indeed, to come to the desert is the greatest perfection," the author of sermon forty-four noted, but "to live imperfectly in the desert is the greatest damnation."[74] Far better to stay in the secular world than to relax in a monastery.[75] The preacher of sermon forty made the point repeatedly. "We should not think that it is sufficient for us to achieve salvation that we are either assessed by habitation or reckoned by name to be among the servants of God; that we are seen to live on the island and sing psalms among the monks."[76] No one should foolishly flatter himself into thinking that he is safe from sin. To relax once we reach the monastery would be like putting down our arms in the middle of the battle.[77] "To some extent we think that is sufficient for us, that we have embarked upon that solitude, that we have changed our place and our clothes, that we have spent some time here, investing all hope in the number of years . . . But it is not so." God remembers all our sins, even as we strive to forget them.[78]

The author of sermon thirty-nine concurred. We are not gathered in this place so that the world may serve us, he warned his audience. We came here not for rest and security, but for a fight.[79] The preacher of sermon forty-two advanced a similar attack on negligence and overconfidence. "I do not know what sins they can feel secure about—they will have to be judged even for sins of ignorance, and reckoning will be extracted for idle words and thoughts. I do not know what sins they can neglect, since the Lord himself declared in an authoritative statement: 'Amen I say unto you: if anyone should say to his brother, "fool," he will be liable to the fires of hell.'"[80] There can be no respite from the storm, or relaxation in its face, until we reach the safe harbour of death.[81]

Simply by joining the monastery, the monks were informed, they had increased the the spiritual stakes. "We should not think that it is sufficient for us to have joined together in this school, unless our professed perfection condemns our faults even more than if we had not taken it up."[82] The more opportunity we have, the more is expected of us, the preacher informed his audience, and nowhere are there such great opportunities as here.[83] Joining the monastery had made them more exposed, rather than more secure. "In the middle of the fight," the preacher of sermon forty-two exclaimed, "we surrender to the enemy, whom we have provoked through our conversion, and we do not persevere in the fervour in which we began, but submit in tepidity, bringing the war to an end." As a result, we are "worse off than we were in the world."[84] Here, the enemy stands directly against us. "But truly now, after we have broken off from his wishes . . . he 'draws up his forces of sin against them, bringing with him seven spirits more wicked than himself.'" If he finds the house of our minds empty and not occupied by spiritual goods, the preacher warned, he will fill it with sins, and make it into a mansion for himself.[85] The more successful we become, the author of sermon forty told his audience, the more careful we need to be—the devil sets his mind to destroying a place where sin does not prosper.[86] "It is certain, dearly beloved, that unless we daily restrain ourselves and our passions here it is much worse for us to have done this than when we lived in the secular world."[87] The Eusebian response to ascetic elitism was therefore to turn it on its head. The preachers depicted the monastery not as a haven from the battle with sin, but rather as the centre of it. "Here we are, and we are not safe."[88]

The Eusebian preachers added to this atmosphere of vulnerability by emphasising the necessity of constant effort. The sermons convey a powerful sense that to be a monk was to be in a permanent state of anxious striving. "The wise man," the author of sermon forty maintained, "is always in a state of remorse, always in a state of fear."[89] We should not think that seeds of sin can be easily removed or the deep wounds in our souls easily cured. "It should not be that those debts for which eternal death is owed are repaid in light contrition, nor that a momentary satisfaction is an adequate return for those sins on account of which the eternal fire is prepared."[90] Our efforts, the preacher told his audience, are but a drop which cannot hope to purify an ocean of sin.[91] A similar tone was set in sermon forty-three. The simplest of slips can lose you all the benefit of your difficult labours. "If, returning from vigils, the passion of disobedience or the spirit of envy or the habit of detraction should capture me, if clandestine presumption should induce me to transgress the rules . . . in one moment I have wasted the labour of the whole night."[92] Consistently, the pastoral care offered to these monks involved unsettling them, challenging them, keeping them on their toes.

To underscore what would happen if the monks should relax, the preachers made frequent reference to the horrors of hell. They described the physical pain, the mental anguish, the shame, and the fear which awaited recalcitrant sinners. They lingered over gruesome details of their tortures and emphasised the depths of the coming misery.[93] All this suffering, they pointed out, could be avoided, but the monks had to make the appropriate effort.[94] This approach contrasts with sermons to the laity, which focused on encouraging congregants rather than filling them with fear. A Eusebian sermon to monks described the path of virtue as narrow and difficult, while the laity were assured of its breadth and ease.[95]

Still, this difference was more one of style rather than of substance. Both audiences were assured that salvation was possible and that effort was required to achieve it.[96] Preachers to both audiences rejected Augustine's "active passivity" in the face of an unchangeable divine dispensation in favour of "an assisting, cooperating, responding grace."[97] "And when God has seen more ardent devotion of the soul," the preacher of sermon thirty-eight assured the monks before him, "he will insinuate the right disposition of mind, and as much as we have added to our zeal, so much he adds to our support; as much as we have increased our diligence, so much he augments our glory: 'He who has will be given more and he will abound.'"[98] In other words, grace operates by the snowball effect. "Therefore grace springs forth from grace and successes assist in further successes. Profit makes a place for profit and merit for merit: so that, the more one begins to acquire, so much more one should try to seek."[99] Sermon thirty-eight is an extensive invocation of the importance of effort. "'Ask,' [God] says, 'and you will receive, seek and you will find, knock and it will be opened to you.' That is, we ask by praying, we seek by striving, we knock by longing, we knock by accomplishing, we knock by persevering. We are urged forward by such zeal in the hope of the promised heavenly things, and we burn with such desire that the magnitude of the longing is in accordance with the greatness of the rewards."[100] God does not want us to come by his benefaction too easily, "for to seek the grace of the divine gift slowly and with little gratitude is the greatest injustice to the rewarder."[101] Therefore we should strive as much as we are capable, with all of our strength, so that we might be worthy of the reward.[102] We knock as hard as we can, because we cannot knock as much as we should.[103] The remainder of the sermon explores this theme and details how to go about it, before ending on the same note. "Therefore we should keep to our course, dearly beloved, so that our life might increase in distinction until the end; we should seek continuously until the end, at which point we may merit to rejoice without end."[104] Other Eusebian sermons to monks were likewise saturated with the language of effort.[105]

To the monks, the preachers advanced a more sophisticated notion of what it meant to win the battle against sin, using Cassian's purity of heart as a goal.[106] Fasting, vigils, prayer, and chastity, though important features of the monastic lifestyle, were depicted as possessing no value unto themselves.[107] What would be the point of such actions, the preachers repeatedly challenged their audiences, if they were only acts? "What use is it," the author of sermon forty-one argued, "that we wear ourselves out in extravagant vigils and labours, when we lack that which our Lord most desires in us—that is, 'a pure heart'?"[108] We are God's farmers, the author of sermon forty-three informed his audience, and we must tear up the thorns from the earth before we plant our harvest. "We should not think that it suffices for us to conquer the territory of our body through the exercises of vigils or to wear it out through the labours of fasting, but rather we should try to clean our minds through the extirpation of sins."[109] The author of sermon thirty-nine chimed in on the same theme. It profits us nothing to afflict our flesh with fasting and vigils if we do not amend our minds and take care of that which is inside us. "What use is it that you ruin your body, when nothing profits your heart?"[110] Again and again the Eusebian preachers told the monks before them that the sole use of physical labour was to produce spiritual fruits—otherwise, work brought them no profit in its own right.[111] In fact, the author of sermon forty-three concluded, it is better to concentrate on your mind than your flesh, since where the former leads, the latter will follow.[112] Any other approach, they argued, was hypocrisy. "What use is it," asked the preacher of sermon forty-three, "if we fight the war outside the city, and inside we have been overthrown?" If the fortress of the mind has been conquered, the whole is lost.[113] "What use is it," asked the author of sermon forty-four, "if a quiet place is thus grasped for the body, but disquietude abides in the heart; if there is silence in the home, but tumult and passionate struggle in the dwelling places of the sins; if serenity is the master of our exterior, but storms of our interior?"[114] Such a person is like a house, according to the author of sermon thirty-nine, which seems to be beautifully constructed and decorated, and yet which, when you enter, is filled with serpents and scorpions.[115] We should take care, the author of sermon forty-four admonished his audience, that our life agrees and harmonises with "the obedience of our tongue," for when the cupidity, malice, and anger of the world reigns within us, we might believe that we are "praiseworthy hermits who are outside the world," while in fact we hold the world enclosed within us.[116]

The Eusebian preachers were not trying to make the whole world into a monastery, as Augustine feared the Pelagians would do. However, many of them may well have come to their role as pastors from a monastic background and naturally extended into their new roles the patterns of association and pastoral styles which they had already absorbed. They did so because for them, the monastery was another form of the Christian community, not a locale utterly divorced from and antagonistic towards the world. For them, asceticism naturally translated, as Rosemarie Nürnberg puts it, into a "social impulse."[117]

This is particularly clear in sermon eight, which may have been preached by a visiting bishop, and probably to a mixed audience of lay and religious. According to the author of this sermon, the ascetic's chief role was to be a good example for the rest of the Church. Sometimes, he noted, even those who have been consecrated since adolescence seek out public penance. "We should know that God inspires this for the sake of the progress of our Church . . . when that person, who perhaps hardly needs penance, faithfully does something worthy and remorseful before the eyes of the Church, his reward multiplies due to the edification of others and his merit piles up due to the gain achieved, so that when the life of another is amended through the perfection of that man, the profit of the good works returns to him as spiritual interest."[118] Those who provide such an example, the preacher argued, will redound in merit. "He is a fortunate man, whose merits overflow into the salvation of others! He is a fortunate man into whose mind the salvation of others pours back!"[119] Sin can creep through the members of the Church like a contagion, but whenever a son of the Church freely offers some good in public, "the devotion of good works increases in the crowd of marvellers."[120] The communicable effect of virtue extended beyond the monastery's walls.

The potential for this kind of reaching out is latent in the other Eusebian sermons "to the monks" and explicit in those "to the people." As detailed in chapter 3, when Faustus preached about Maximus, who had been both abbot of Lérins and bishop of Riez, he presented the former phase of Maximus' life as essential preparation for the latter. "That distinguished man was taught there, so that he might teach here; was enriched there, so that he might lend here; was illuminated there, so that he might shine here; was purified there so that he might sanctify here; and, so that he could work here at the making of cures, he sought there the spices and pigments of virtue."[121] It is a common motif, and one found in a number of other hagiographical works, but it is surrounded in the Eusebius

Gallicanus sermon collection by practical examples of how models of monastic pastoral care and community could extend to the world beyond.[122]

Gallic monasticism has sometimes been depicted as torn between two ascetic models: that of Augustine of Hippo and that of John Cassian, both of whom were concerned with the implications of monastic morality for the entire Church.[123] There is a danger, however, of setting up a false dichotomy between the two. Cassian and Augustine agreed on much more than they differed on.[124] Their influence was not mutually exclusive—the inspiration of both can be traced, for example, in the works of Pomerius and Caesarius.[125] The Eusebius Gallicanus collection provides another example of how preachers could draw from both thinkers in the formulation of their pastoral care. For example, the centrality of community which defines the collection echoes the approach of Augustine, as do the anxiety over ascetic elitism and the model of communal equality.[126] The Eusebius Gallicanus preachers do not blindly borrow, however. Ascetic elitism was attacked from an angle which suited the different sense of the operation of divine grace and the role of individual effort which is found in the collection. The influence of Cassian, meanwhile, is discernable in the style of community leadership and in the strong conviction that authority resided within the structure of the community rather than in the individual. The Eusebius Gallicanus model, like the Cassian one, presented leaders simply as those who best knew the ways of the community and who ensured the maintenance of its habits and regulations.[127] Cassian, too, focused on sin as a threat to community, saw community as an answer to sin—the best place for a monk to reach his potential[128]—and emphasised that the ascetic was responsible to the broader Christian community.[129] The Eusebian sermons implemented in practice many of the ideas that Cassian expounded in theory. They realised Cassian's broader potential and established strong connections between the monastery and the world beyond.

Gallic pastors did not occupy set or oppositional camps, but they did display nuanced and differentiated approaches on how best to interconnect ascetic and lay communities. Caesarius of Arles was composing and circulating his sermons in the same region and around the same time as the Eusebius Gallicanus compiler, and he relied on many of the same source texts. He drew on both Augustine and John Cassian and extended monastic models learnt at Lérins to his lay congregation in Arles.[130] His focus, however, was not on community, but on the behaviour of individuals. He sought to impose monastic practices upon his lay congregants: urging biblical reading, fasting, and participation in the offices of the monastic liturgy.[131] His emphasis on moral discipline, strict regulation of sexuality, condemnation of drunkenness, and attacks on pagan practices have all also been attributed to his ascetic mentality.[132] As we have seen in chapter 3, Caesarius was less interested in unity and harmony than in combat with sin, and he was prepared to divide the community into good and bad Christians, to enlist the former against the latter, and to urge the pious to rebuke the reprobate and refuse to associate with them.[133] We have also already seen how Caesarius' view of pastoral authority diverged from that of the Eusebius Gallicanus preachers.[134] In his view of the pastoral relationship, there was no joint task, no mutual support, no communal responsibility on the part of the laity. What mattered to Caesarius was not that the community assist each other, but that they obey him. Caesarius used his monastic background and drew from patristic tradition to create a model of lay pastoral care which was starkly different from that of the Eusebian preachers. A possible origin of this difference may lie in Caesarius' approach to the monastic life. There was no room in the Eusebian sermons to monks for the kind of bravura ascetic displays credited to Caesarius of Arles by the authors of his *vita*. In that text Caesarius was depicted as creating hostility by imposing his own levels of abstinence upon others and as disrupting the monastic equilibrium by wrecking his body through an excess of asceticism.[135] He was praised in the *vita* for acting in ways which Cassian explicitly and the Eusebian preachers implicitly condemned, that is, for elevating himself above the community and indulging in vainglorious displays.[136] Caesarius was forced to leave Lérins—for the sake of his health, the authors claimed, but perhaps also because he had proved himself ill suited to the coenobitic lifestyle.[137] In the account of his hagiographers at least, Caesarius was a charismatic individualist—an ascetic of an entirely different stamp from the ideal fostered by Cassian and the preachers of the Eusebius Gallicanus sermons.

It is tempting to draw a clear line from Caesarius' disruptive stance in the monastery to his disruptive role as a pastor in Arles. It is tempting also to compare his case with that of Faustus of Riez, who clearly found in Lérins an amenable home and who reigned as its abbot for around thirty years before going on to contribute heavily to the sermons of the Eusebius Gallicanus collection. As a caution, it is worth noting that in his sermons to monks Caesarius painted a somewhat different picture of ideal ascetic community than that provided by his hagiographers. He, too, made humility and obedience the cardinal monastic virtues and urged the monks whom he addressed to persevere in their profession.[138] Yet while he instructed monks to remain consistently humble towards their superiors, their equals, and their inferiors, Caesarius was more likely than the Eusebian preachers to observe and comment upon social differences within the monastic community.[139] He was also more likely than the Eusebian preachers to urge the castigation of others, even though he recognised that this process must begin with oneself.[140] Caesarius interpreted the monastic responsibility to the "outside world" differently than did the Eusebian preachers. It was incumbent upon ascetics to set a good example and to live up to the world's expectations. "Now since the whole world both admires and loves your deeds because of your holy and spotless obedience," he told the monks of Lérins, "it is necessary that you repay the honour and love which you receive from everyone by your continuous prayers and spotless life."[141] Even more important, however, was the role of monks as intercessors. They must pray, Caesarius repeatedly insisted, for those who have not had their opportunities, and earn pardon for sinners as well as themselves.[142] Caesarius was not interested in fostering the institution of the monk-bishop.[143] His monks remained within their community.

Robert Markus has argued that in the fifth and sixth centuries, "ascetic norms came to penetrate wide sections of Christian society and to colour aspirations far beyond the walls of the cloister."[144] For

Markus, the fullest expression of this process was in Gaul, where "the invasion of the City by the Desert was achieved through the confluence of aristocratic and ascetic traditions in its episcopate" and where bishops with monastic sympathies brought ascetic ideology "from the fringes of society to its centre." "From institutionalised alienation," Markus concludes, "the monastery had turned into focused representation of the community's social ideal."[145] In his account, Lérins stood at the very heart of this change.[146] As this chapter has demonstrated, the Eusebius Gallicanus sermons support the argument that there were substantial and important connections between monasteries and lay Christian communities in late antique Gaul. The picture they provide, however, is not exactly that which Markus points to as emblematic of the "ascetic invasion."[147] Relying heavily on Caesarius of Arles for his Gallic evidence, Markus traces the export of scriptural reading practices, monastic liturgy, and ascetic morality to the lay congregation in Arles.[148] He interprets Caesarius' strict limitations on behaviour and his unambiguous delineation of the boundaries between pagan and Christian as enactments of a worldview formulated in Lérins.[149] None of these supposedly ascetic characteristics can be found in the pastoral care of the Lérinian Eusebius Gallicanus sermons; instead, we find something which Markus refers to only in passing: the "infection" of the model of the Christian community by the model of the monastic life.[150]

The stress placed by the Eusebian sermons to monks on the centrality of community, on the importance of harmony and consensus, on the programme of practical support for brethren, and on the model of equality within a family, finds its echo in the sermons to the laity.[151] The model of leadership advanced in the sermons to the monks—pastoral, responsive, leading by example as first among equals—is strikingly similar to the Eusebian ideal of clerical authority in a lay community.[152] The arguments of the preachers to the monks—that each individual has ultimate responsibility for his own salvation and must strive and struggle to be worthy of divine grace—extended naturally to the laity as well.[153] Virtue required effort. The Eusebian propensity to stress the role of the individual in self-judging and penitence, while still emphasising the primacy of the group, makes sense if placed in a monastic context. This was the dynamic which marked the path of the coenobite. Some of the same pastoral concerns are evident in the two sets of sermons—overconfidence, excessive security regarding salvation, dissent, individualism, and lack of sufficient effort.

The invasion may thus have been more contested than either our ascetic sources or Markus admit.[154] The monk-bishops had to tread carefully so as not to offend, as the opposition which Caesarius faced testifies.[155] The Eusebius Gallicanus sermons illustrate that the connections between monastery and world did not have to be as antagonistic or coercive in nature as the invasion of Caesarius. Instead, the model of Christian community in this collection tends to ignore divisions rather than pointedly seek to bridge them. The sermons, and the comparison with Caesarius, also provide further evidence of the complexity and variety of the ascetic world in fifth- and sixth-century Gaul.[156] Many different models of ascetic practice led to many different styles of pastoral care, both within the monastery and beyond it. The Eusebius Gallicanus collection itself facilitated this multiplicity, and in its turn became a resource on which future generations of pastors selectively drew to create their own models of congregational care.

What the sermon collection demonstrates most clearly, however, is that for at least some preachers in late antique Gaul, monks and laity were brothers. That is to say, they were Christians who chose to express their faith in different ways and in different contexts, but who were nonetheless to be treated as rough equals. There is little qualitative difference in the pastoral care which each group was offered, or in the problems which the leaders of each expected to face. For the Eusebius Gallicanus preachers, the connection between monastery and world was not a source of anxiety, but rather a natural extension of community.

Conclusion

The Eusebius Gallicanus sermons do not speak in a single voice. They are the work of more than one preacher and they speak to more than one audience. Although the compiler undoubtedly chose for similarity and ironed out some points of divergence, he was not concerned to create a perfectly coherent whole—this was a manual, not a position statement. The collection demonstrates, indeed, that flexibility and adaptability were key features of pastoral care in late antique Gaul, and the popularity of the Eusebius Gallicanus may in part be explained by the fact that it facilitated this approach. It did not impose a particular view but rather enabled preachers to forge their own ways. While we should not, therefore, expect complete consistency from the Eusebius Gallicanus sermons, it does nevertheless hold together as a unit. Sermons within the collection share a series of common concerns and are characterised by common approaches, perhaps reflecting both the interests of their compiler and the shared milieu of their composition.

These points of commonality add up to a distinctive style of pastoral care. The collection is marked, for example, by emphasis on both the importance of community and the extent of individual responsibility. These emerge as the necessary correlates of Christian life. The preachers expended great effort to build up a common identity for their congregations, worked to forge good relations among their members, and accentuated the obligation of each Christian to the group. They tried to ensure that the community was united behind a set of common beliefs and that it was not undermined by conspicuous and unrepentant public sin. They constantly reminded congregation members of the others around them, and of what the Church should be: unified, harmonious, and strong. This attention to community did not, however, take any moral pressure off the individual: quite the opposite. Preachers both emphasised human action and insisted upon some degree of individual self-reliance. Congregants were expected to support their pastor as much as he supported them and to take responsibility for contributing to the group. The individual was instructed to choose virtue in order to merit redemption, since justice demanded that believers should not be dragged unwilling to heaven. The faithful should expect to stand alone before God and his angels on judgment day with only their sins for company, and to understand that they alone could make the necessary expiation while still in this world. Salvation was an individual responsibility, as part of a group effort. This was as much the case for the laity as it was for the monks.

The Eusebius Gallicanus sermons are also marked by a common approach to the problem of how to exercise power. The approach taken by preachers in this collection was almost uniformly indirect. They did not make obvious claims to authority or confrontational statements about who could, or could not, be part of the community. Their tone was most often conciliatory and they played down their own positions of authority. This accommodation did not mean, however, that pastoral power was being relinquished; rather, it was simply being asserted in less obvious ways, notably by urging congregants to police themselves and their own behaviour. Another indirect strategy was to use the goal of consensus to elide difference and sideline dissent. Theology, too, was presented in such a way that dispute or disagreement became almost impossible. Such subtle power plays are more difficult to spot than the tirades of Caesarius of Arles, but the diplomatic tactics of the Eusebian preachers were potentially more effective—difficult for congregants to resist and open to all pastors, even those without the persona of a prophet. This efficacy and accessibility, too, go some way to explaining the collection's popularity and success.

The Eusebian approach is unique, and in the preceding chapters I have tried to establish its distinctive character by highlighting points of divergence from the models of pastoral care offered by Augustine and Caesarius in particular. Both comparisons are important, the former because of Augustine's enormous but contested influence in Gaul, the latter because Caesarius was roughly contemporary with the Eusebian compiler, preached in the same geographical region, and has long dominated our picture of this time and place. The points of divergence which have emerged from these comparisons demonstrate that pastors were making strategic choices about what they said to their congregants. Their needs varied, their own situations varied, and their preaching varied to match. The late antique Church was far from a monolithic entity, to its great advantage.

This was no simple story of difference, however, let alone one of conflict between inimical camps. The styles of these preachers were not incompatible, as their many similarities demonstrate. The differences were matters of nuance, emphasis, and choice. The Church's past was not a burden which directed the course of its heirs, but a storehouse of treasures from which they could take what they would. This past was sufficiently rich that each could find what he needed for a variety of environments and audiences. Moreover, we do not always find differences where we might expect them. The Eusebius Gallicanus sermons are not evidence of conflict, either with other Christians or with non-Christian groups such as pagans or Jews: they are just quietly getting on with the job.

This quiet efficacy is perhaps why the Eusebius Gallicanus sermons have not received the attention they deserve from scholars—conflict always makes better copy. Yet it is not just the content of the

Eusebius Gallicanus which merits examination—even the form of the collection tells us much about the world from which it comes, revealing a Church disunited but not disorganised. Clergy in late antique Gaul could not rely on stable resources of money or power, but they could draw on vast intellectual resources, and the Eusebius Gallicanus repacked the heritage of the Church in convenient, accessible form. It reveals a Church which was not overly concerned with uniformity, but which did want to ensure that preaching was frequent and orthodox. It reveals, too, a Church populated by clergy who needed a preaching manual to get them through the year. It reveals, in short, a Church facing many challenges, but also striving to meet them, and able to do so because of the adaptability which resources such as the Eusebius Gallicanus gave it.

By the time the Christian Church was in a position to centralise religious authority and to impose uniformity, these multiple traditions of pastoral care were well established. Historians have already shown how the Carolingians used the sermons of Augustine, Caesarius, and Gregory the Great in their efforts to reform the Frankish Church.[1] The Carolingians also turned, however, to the sermons of the Eusebius Gallicanus collection, and to many other late antique and early medieval homiletic texts whose influence remains to be traced. In these they found many different models of how to integrate Christianity into the cultures around them. While the reformers may have been frustrated by this diversity, the ability of the Church to adapt proved one of the keys to its success. Medieval Western Europe is known to us as "Christendom" because Christianity suffused its culture, society, politics, identity, and ideologies. This process was not singular, coherent, or always on the terms of the religious elites, but it was a success.

Epilogue

This book has focused on the primary moments in the life of the Eusebius Gallicanus sermons: their composition in the fifth century and their compilation into a collection in the sixth. Their story did not end there, however. The sermons survive in 447 manuscripts produced between the seventh century and the dawn of the age of print. The collection continued to be copied, in whole and in part, while sermons were excerpted from it and incorporated into other homiliaries, into monastic resource books, and into collections of material on specific saints. It was quoted by florilegists, drawn on by Carolingian homilists, and read by theologians. Sections of it were even absorbed into the liturgy.[1] This subsequent history is important for several reasons. It helps students of the Eusebius Gallicanus understand the nature and purpose of the collection, and it gives a sense of the ongoing influence of the pastoral strategies in it. The sermons of the Eusebius Gallicanus had, quite unrecognised, an important place in the developing intellectual tradition of the Church. No account of them would be complete without some recognition of this.

The history of the sermons has relevance also to students of medieval preaching in general. It reminds us that it is not enough to describe the emergence of new preachers and to study freshly composed sermons: to get a full picture of medieval homiletics we need also to trace the ongoing use of older texts. The adaptation and application of these texts can tell us much about cultural and religious continuities, but it can also highlight points of departure and difference. Medieval people lived with a very present past, and the Eusebius Gallicanus sermons were part of it.

This epilogue will not provide a systematic analysis of the manuscript tradition of the Eusebius Gallicanus sermons. That work has already been done by Glorie and Leroy, and my comments rely heavily on their meticulous scholarship.[2] Here I wish merely to draw out some of the implications of their work. Although Leroy and Glorie were both striving to produce an edition, their manuscript work reveals the result as representing but one part of the sermons' history. Many scholars now recognise the limitations of an edition. Even the best ones efface the "essential plurality" of medieval texts as they appear in manuscripts.[3] They freeze one moment in a continuous history of writing and reify that moment as a true and proper statement of what the text is.[4] The misleading view of the text which can result from this treatment is especially clear in the case of the Eusebius Gallicanus. The collection was not stable or hermetically sealed and it was never considered as such by those who used it. Instead, as we have already noted, it was cannibalised, edited, and reworked from almost the moment of its inception, and it may itself have been the product of such processes. While the compiler's intention may well have been to make preaching more stable and predictable by fixing a number of approved texts in a convenient collection, he relinquished control as soon as the collection was made. As Cerquiglini notes, "the work copied by hand, manipulated, always open and as good as unfinished, invited intervention, annotation and commentary."[5] Those who came after edited and reworked, stole and discarded. The Eusebius Gallicanus collection as we have it is but one act in an ongoing plagiaristic sequence.

The Eusebius Gallicanus collection was not, therefore, a final or definitive statement of a particular pastoral ideology. Instead it was a group of texts, united by a common approach and often appearing together, but still separable in practice and constantly evolving.[6] To capture this sense of the Eusebius Gallicanus properly, it is necessary to step away from the comfort of the edition and into the murky and far less stable world of the manuscripts. Each manuscript tells a story of one way in which the sermons were used. Some stories are more decipherable than others, however, and here I must confess that I am no paleographer. I dabble from a sense of the importance of manuscripts, but without expertise. I rely on what the experts have said, and where they cannot conclude or agree I am forced to silence. Nonetheless, some observations can be made with confidence, and they are worth making. There are clues which suggest a manuscript's usage and audience, both intended and actual.

The contents of a manuscript are the first guide. Some contain only sermons from the Eusebius Gallicanus collection, but most manuscripts combined the Eusebian sermons with other texts. These could be sermons by other late antique or early medieval preachers, readings from scripture, biblical commentaries, monastic rules, medical texts, letters, theological treatises, *sententiae,* hymns, and more. The range is in itself extraordinary and bespeaks a variety of usages. The contents of a manuscript can indicate its intended purpose: liturgical homiliary for a church or monastery, devotional text, clerical resource, and so forth.

Physical characteristics are also suggestive. As Taylor notes, "the precise physical form of a particular manuscript or edition is a vital part of any given text's meaning and social function."[7] Many of the manuscripts are very large and would have required a reading stand such as those found in a church or monastic library.[8] At least one, however, is tiny—137 × 78mm—and would have been an easily portable devotional text, ill suited to reading in a public context.[9] Most of the manuscripts are utilitarian rather than ornamental, inscribed on poor parchment, contain few illustrations, and include rubrics and capitals only to help a reader quickly find his or her place.

Aesthetic considerations did not rank highly with the copyists of these works. They were not texts intended to impress or to be displayed. Instead, these codices were designed to be used. Their scribes imagined them being read from and frequently referred to. The condition of these manuscripts gives the impression, and of course it can only ever be an impression, that they were pored over, fingered, damaged by use, and scribbled on by those seeking to keep them up to date, seeking to keep them useful and alive. Some manuscripts containing Eusebius Gallicanus sermons, however, are luxury items, beautifully put together and still immaculate today. Combining all of this information permits an educated guess as to a manuscript's usage.

The manuscripts also make clear that the Eusebius Gallicanus sermons were not all equally popular. Those which had the greatest resonance, or which were considered to be the most useful, were the series on Easter (sermons twelve to twenty-four) and the series "to the monks" (sermons thirty-six to forty-five).[10] The Eusebius Gallicanus sermons which were incorporated into successful homiliaries also gained widespread exposure. Paul the Deacon included sermons thirteen (part of the Easter series), fifty-one (for the burial of a bishop), and forty-seven (for the feast of a church) into his collection, while Alain of Farfa ensured that sermons twelve A and twenty-two (both for Easter), twenty-eight (on the Ascension), fifty-one, forty-seven and forty-nine (for the dedication of a church) would have a lasting influence.[11] Other popular sermons in the collection included Eusebian sermons one (for Christmas), nine and ten (on the creed), twenty-seven (on the Ascension), thirty-four (on the Trinity) and sixty-one (a castigation of disobedience, frequently copied with sermons to monks).[12] Most others were copied far less frequently. The choices which scribes made when excerpting the collection can tell us a great deal about what issues were felt to be relevant at particular times and in particular places.

To illustrate in practice the implications of these general observations, I have analysed a sample of the manuscripts, covering the period between the seventh and the fifteenth centuries. The sample is not necessarily representative, as it consists of those manuscripts which I have been able to examine in person and/or for which there are reasonably detailed published descriptions. The sample is large enough, however, to permit some conclusions about the changing ways in which the Eusebius Gallicanus sermons were used.

The earliest manuscripts of the Eusebius Gallicanus sermons illustrate that in the first two centuries after their compilation they were already being reused and reinterpreted in a variety of contexts and over a broad geographical area. Several were aimed at a monastic audience. F[0], for example, is a luxurious codex written, according to the dedication, in the late seventh century at St-Médard's abbey in Soissons by order of the abbot Nomedius, and intended for the education and instruction of the monks under his care.[13] Four sermons from the Eusebian series to monks (thirty-nine, forty, forty-one, and forty-four) are mixed in with sermons by Caesarius.[14] Alongside these are Pelagius' *Verba seniorum,* the beginning of the Gelasian decretal, and a commentary on the four Gospels sometimes attributed to Theophilus of Antioch, but more likely a seventh-century Merovingian work.[15] Hen argues that the codex can be linked to the monastic reform movements of the seventh century and their pedagogical goals.[16] Na, an eighth-century palimpsest manuscript from Bobbio, contains Eusebian sermons thirty-eight and thirty-nine on its secondary level amidst an eccentric combination of other texts. These include Gennadius' *Liber de viris illustribus,* letters of Augustine and Jerome, *florilegia* from various fathers on the relation between grace and free will, a panegyric, treatises on various grammatical forms and rhetorical arts, and a work on the physical wonders of the world.[17] This manuscript was also most likely intended for monastic education, or as a resource book.

SΣ[0], a scrap of seventh-century papyrus, perhaps originating in Italy, contains a selection from Isidore of Seville's *Synonyma* and two of the Eusebian sermons to monks (numbers thirty-seven and thirty-eight), along with corrections, comments, and a prayer added in the eighth century.[18] SΣ[1], a mid-eighth-century palimpsest probably produced at the monastery of St. Gall, placed five Eusebian sermons to monks (thirty-eight through forty-one, and forty-four) alongside a series of Caesarius' monastic sermons, some works of Isidore and a number of other homiletic works.[19] These were standard collections designed for monastic reference and devotional reading. In condition, they were coarse, practical, and show signs of repeated use.

P⁰ is a little different. This plain manuscript, produced in Fulda in the late eighth or early ninth century, combines an educational collection, centred on the themes of wealth and almsgiving, with a doctrinal and disciplinary *florilegia,* the original version of which may date to the late sixth century.[20] It places Eusebian sermon twelve A, on Easter, alongside selections from John Chrysostom's treatise *De compunctione cordis* and some of his sermons, with responses by Severian of Gabala; homilies by Augustine, Pope Leo, and Fulgentius; Paulinus' Life of Ambrose; an apocryphal letter of Jerome; fragments from letters of Gelasius, Pope John II, and Athanasius; parts of Augustine's *De regulis ad Petrum;* and Ambrose's exposition on Psalm 118.[21] P⁰ reflects a very specific set of clerical interests, though marks on the manuscript indicate that it was itself later used as a source for *florilegia.*[22] It may have been a resource book for a pastor, or a collection of items for education and contemplation.

Finally, two of the early manuscripts show that the Eusebian sermons were rapidly incorporated into liturgical homiliaries. At the beginning of the eighth century, Eusebian sermon twelve A was copied by the priest Agimund into V⁰, a homiliary for the use of the Basilica of Philip and James in Rome. This vast work, which now contains some 300 pieces (representing two-thirds of the original total) includes sermons attributed to Leo, Jerome, Augustine, Chrysostom, Ambrose, Gregory of Nazianzus, Hilary of Poitiers, and Gregory the Great.[23] It moves through the Church calendar, providing sermons for all the major feasts, and indicates the accompanying scriptural readings. It was intended to guide the preachers in this Roman church through the liturgical year.[24] This manuscript is very large, suitable for public reading, and, although it was not a luxury manuscript, damage was carefully repaired on numerous occasions. Later marks on the manuscript indicate where a reader should pause in delivery, while abbreviations are spelt out, alternative vocabulary given, and additions made to the text. V⁰, in other words, was a manuscript in continued use for a long period. Be is a similar example from northern Italy, dating from the late eighth or early ninth century. It bears the title "sermones legendi in festivitatibus ecclesiae" and was written for the cathedral library at Verona under the instruction of Bishop Egino.[25] Like V[0], the "Codex Eginonis Veronensis" was designed to take the preacher through the circuit of the year, enabling the proper celebration of the martyrs and confessors and the feasts of the Church.[26] It even provided an index of its contents for easy reference.[27] From the Eusebius Gallicanus the compiler chose to include one sermon on Easter (twenty-two), one on the Ascension (twenty-eight), and a selection of sermons for particular occasions: the burial of a bishop (fifty-one), the dedication of a church (forty-nine), and the celebration of its anniversary (forty-seven). These were accompanied by sermons credited to Augustine, Jerome, Pope Leo, and Isidore. Both V[0] and Be drew heavily on homiliaries from the sixth and seventh centuries, and were themselves drawn on and plundered by later compilers.[28] They formed part of the wave of interlinked homiletic collections which predated the Carolingians, but swelled to astonishing proportions under their enthusiastic encouragement.[29]

It is in the Carolingian era, indeed, that we see the most extensive use of the Eusebius Gallicanus sermons in homiliaries. The purpose of some of the homiliaries from this period has been debated by historians and it is not clear that all were intended as preaching guides for clergy addressing the laity.[30] Nonetheless, the facilitation of preaching to the laity was undoubtedly one of the goals of the reformers, as was increasing the level of clerical education.[31] It is reasonable to suppose that at least some of the large numbers of homiliaries produced in this period were intended for these ends. Part of the issue, as d'Avray points out for a later period, is that audiences were multiple and envisaged as such. Model sermon collections, he suggests, were a multipurpose genre. They could provide reading material for clergy and monks, sermons to be preached to them, and sermons for lay congregations.[32] Even in the thirteenth century, collections could include sermons directed to different audiences.[33]

Moreover, the very indeterminacy of the audience of some of these collections, d'Avray argues, indicates that the cultural lines between clergy, laity, and monks were not always as sharp as we might imagine.[34]

The Carolingians are well known for plundering, reusing, and transforming their patristic and Merovingian cultural heritage, and the Eusebius Gallicanus was one of the sources they turned to.[35] They produced a series of ninth-century homiliaries based on the Eusebian collection. F^1, for example, probably initially contained the entire collection, and only one sermon of other origin.[36] V^1 is another ninth-century volume heavily reliant on the Eusebius Gallicanus, containing sermons one through thirty-five alongside a few works attributed to Jerome and Nicetas of Remesiana. Both manuscripts were of a size and style suitable for preaching and show signs of revision and highlighting to facilitate use.

More often, however, the Eusebian sermons were only one part of a Carolingian homiliary. Ch, for example, is an early ninth-century liturgical homiliary containing Eusebian sermon forty-seven (on the anniversary of a church), alongside sermons attributed to Augustine, Leo, Maximus, and Caesarius.[37] The manuscript was the work of five different hands and shows extensive later marginalia, corrections, and repairs.[38] K^0 is a very large volume which mixes works attributed to Augustine, John Chrysostom, Bede, Gregory the Great, and Leo with ten of the Eusebius Gallicanus sermons on Easter.[39] T^0 contains 162 homilies, or parts thereof, intercut with the incipits of the biblical readings which they should accompany.[40] Only two of its homilies are from the Eusebius Gallicanus collection. 313 is very similar, interspersing sermons from Jerome, Bede, Gregory the Great, Maximus of Turin, Augustine, and the Eusebius Gallicanus with brief indications of the biblical readings which they would accompany.[41] Rn contains 105 sermons, including Eusebius Gallicanus sixty-four (on prayer), and had page markers to aid users in finding the beginnings of the text they wanted.[42] All of these were standard types of homiliary in that period. They were rough, practical texts with minimal ornamentation and an emphasis on utility.

Some manuscripts from the Carolingian period testify clearly to the ongoing monastic interest in the sermons. Q^0 is a tiny, portable manuscript from the ninth century, probably designed as a devotional text. It contains four of the Eusebian sermons to monks, some homilies of Caesarius and others, a section of one of Cassian's conferences, and part of the *synonyma* of Isidore. 399 is larger but provides a similar collection of texts: nine sermons to monks, ten sermons on Easter and the good thief, one on the Trinity, and two on the creed, all from the Eusebius Gallicanus collection. Alongside these we find more sections from Cassian's conferences and various other sermons and sections of treatises by patristic authors, all of monastic interest.[43] A^1, which dates from the tenth century, combines these same Eusebian sermons with those of Jerome and Augustine, as well as instructions on the legal protection of monastic property. These were practical rather than luxurious texts and exhibit signs of ongoing use in their marginalia, corrections, and repairs. They show that the Eusebian sermons still had resonance in the monastic milieu long after their composition.

It is striking that the end of the Carolingian era, and of their efforts to encourage popular preaching, sees also a sharp decline in homiliaries which use the Eusebius Gallicanus to address a lay audience. Instead, it was the monastic interest in the Eusebian collection which accounted for most copies of the sermons in the eleventh century. Some were still intended as preaching guides, but their contents suggest a cloistered audience, while others are clearly devotional or inspirational in character. P^1, for example, contains forty-two Eusebian sermons on a variety of topics, but combines these with lives of monks, letters, and miracle accounts which suggest an ascetic interest. 312 contains texts of items important to the monastery of Echternach, including hagiographical texts, a mélange of materials touching on the monastic life, the dialogues of Gregory the Great, an abridged chronicle of the abbots of Echternach, a 1063 charter for the monastery, a work of Alcuin, and four of the Eusebius Gallicanus sermons to monks. P^2 is also a resource book of sorts. It comes from Corbie and was perhaps compiled in response to renewed concern about the doctrines of Paschasius Radbertus, who had been a monk there. Alongside Eusebius Gallicanus sermon seventeen (on Easter, but with particular reference to the body and blood of Christ) it contained sections from the writings of Paschasius, patristic extracts in support of his position, and some *sententiae* on relevant themes.[44] P[2] is a beautiful manuscript, carefully ornamented, with a striking first folio illustration of monastic scribes at work and offering the completed text to the monastery's patron, St. Peter. The whole is intended as a defense of Paschasius' orthodoxy and the manuscript no doubt formed part of the weaponry upon which the monks of Corbie could draw.

Ru may be from the eleventh or the twelfth century and was produced in the monastery of St. Emigdius, but was of a rather different character.[45] It is an enormous volume, 62 × 40 cms and 327 folios in length. Such a manuscript would have been very expensive to produce, but it is not especially ornamented. Most of its contents are sermons organised according to the liturgical calendar, with a particular focus on sermons on saints, and including also some hagiography and passions of the martyrs. The sermons are attributed to Augustine, Gregory the Great, Bede, Jerome, Leo, John Chrysostom, Ambrose, and Isidore, while from the Eusebius Gallicanus collection we find sermons twenty-seven (on the Ascension), thirty (on John the Baptist), and forty-seven (on the anniversary of a church). The manuscript is in good condition, but shows signs of continued use, including sections which have been rewritten for clarity and changes made in the dates of festivals for saints. There is no obvious indexing, but paragraphs are marked by means of capitals which extrude to the left, perhaps making it easier to find one's place. This manuscript may have been intended for reading during refectory, at monastic services, or simply as a guide to the liturgical year.

This monastic interest in the Eusebius Gallicanus sermons continued into the twelfth century. A number of monastic resource books similar to those described above also survive from this later period. Q[1] is a large lectionary from Cluny, possibly designed for reading in the refectory.[46] It contains Eusebius Gallicanus sermons twelve to twenty-four (on Easter and the good thief) alongside saints' lives and a number of other homilies, to which Peter the Venerable's *Contra Iudaeos* was later added.[47] O[1] contains the series of ten Eusebian sermons to monks, as well as most of those on Easter, together with a treatise of Ambrose, sermons by Leo, the lives of a series of abbots associated with Cluny, and a hymn. P[4] contains nine of the sermons "to the monks" (identified here as the work of Eusebius of Caesarea), another sermon to monks attributed to Faustus, a sermon of Augustine on penance, a work on the desolation of Jerusalem, a book of the divine office, a tractate on ecclesiastical offices, the meditations of St. Bernard, and a book of Lothar on the vileness of the human condition. A number of other twelfth-century monastic books of a similar kind survive, containing sermons from the Eusebius Gallicanus amidst their variant contents.[48]

However, the twelfth century also saw a revival in the use of the Eusebius Gallicanus in clerical education and the facilitation of preaching. Some manuscripts are clerical resource books, containing items of use to a conscientious pastor. P[6] is an example of this: a collection of materials by various authors chiefly relating to St. Denys, but also including some sermons of John Chrysostom, some treatises of Isidore of Seville, a calendar list of scriptural lessons, a series of poetic or rhythmical works, some *florilegia* fragments, and some anonymous poems to the Virgin as well the series of paschal sermons from the Eusebius Gallicanus. Other manuscripts from this period are liturgical homiliaries which exclude sermons to monks. T[1] contains 133 sermons covering the liturgical year, including Eusebian sermon twelve A, on Easter. Many of the sermons are on the same topic, indicating that preachers could choose between the thoughts of different authors on a single theme. The homiliary Ge, meanwhile, is very reliant on the Eusebius Gallicanus and includes sermons one to thirty-five from it in its total of 110.

Two other manuscripts from this period are interesting, but less clear in audience. B[1] and B[2] constitute a two-volume homiliary put together at Benedictine abbey at Haffligem. This homiliary contains twenty-eight sermons from the Eusebius Gallicanus collection, including those on Christmas, on Epiphany, the good thief, most of the Easter series, and those on the universal martyrs. These are mixed in with sermons attributed to Augustine, John Chrysostom, Gregory, Maximus, and Bede, as well as instructions on scriptural readings and miracle accounts. The homiliary may have been designed to facilitate preaching to the monks, but its contents display no specifically ascetic focus or interest, which leaves open the possibility of a wider application. P[7], which dates from the twelfth or thirteenth century, also excludes the ascetic sermons in its selection of Eusebius Gallicanus texts and chooses twenty-six focused on the major Church feasts and on moralising topics.[49] Even if these homiliaries were designed to be used by monks, this does not exclude the possibility that the sermons were heard by the laity. The twelfth century was the golden age of monastic preaching, both within and beyond monasteries.[50] It is interesting to speculate whether the Eusebius Gallicanus sermons, with their sense of a Christian community which cut across the walls of the cloister, held a particular appeal for preaching monks.

If this was so, however, it did not last. The thirteenth century saw the rise of the mendicant orders and a decline in the use and popularity of the Eusebian sermons. This was not, of course, for lack of interest in preaching or model sermon collections. The thirteenth century was, in many ways, the great age of homiletics.[51] Friars placed enormous emphasis on the importance of spreading the word and developed a vast textual and educational infrastructure to support their efforts.[52] Preaching guides and resource books were produced in greater quantities than ever before.[53] In the production of these guides and manuals, however, the friars do not seem to have turned to the Eusebius Gallicanus. Their preaching was in a new style and it addressed new issues; hence their resources took a different form.[54] The Eusebius Gallicanus was no longer as relevant, and although it did not cease being read, there are fewer manuscripts containing Eusebius Gallicanus sermons from this period, and those that survive were beautiful, ornamental pieces, rather than practical collections. S[2], for example, is a very expensive series of what would originally have been eight volumes, mostly consisting of saints' lives ordered according to feast days. Among these is Eusebius Gallicanus sermon thirty-five, on Maximus of Riez.[55] This sermon was also selected for inclusion in F², another collection of saints' lives and martyrdoms, this time running to two volumes. These were large, carefully decorated, and expensively rebound in the seventeenth century, indicating an ongoing importance as a status text.[56] It is possible that friars still encountered the Eusebius Gallicanus sermons at some point in their education, but their interest in the sermons as sermons appears to have faded.

The final manuscript in my brief survey exemplifies the changed role of the Eusebius Gallicanus sermons. V³ is a beautiful fifteenth-century manuscript, with an exquisite initial illumination, elaborate initials, and high quality parchment. It contains sermons attributed to Augustine, among which is Eusebius Gallicanus sermon one, on Christmas, but this was no preaching manual. It may have been a scholarly text, as suggested by the marginal comments and glosses throughout, and it is filled with whimsical illustrations of men, women, and animals in various garb and in various forms. Individual Eusebius Gallicanus sermons were still of interest, but the collection had lost its force as a resource for either popular preaching or monastic contemplation. It would not be long before it was revived in the first early modern editions, but here it would be a subject for scholarly inquiry, no longer a practical guide to how to teach or how to live.

Eusebius Gallicanus Manuscripts and Their Sigla

This list comprises only those mentioned in the course of this work. For a full list of manuscripts and their locations, see Glorie, *Eusebius "Gallicanus,"* 902–34.

A^1	Bibliothèque municipale d'Angers 144
B^1	Deutsche Staatsbibliothek Theo. lat. fol. 269
B^2	Deutsche Staatsbibliothek Theo. lat. fol. 270
Be	Deutsche Staatsbibliothek 50
Ch	Newberry Library F.I
F^0	Koninklijke Bibliotheek 9850-52
F^1	Koninklijke Bibliotheek 1651-52
F^2	Koninklijke Bibliotheek 7461
Ge	Bibliothèque publique et universitaire de Genève 24
I^0	Bibliothèque municipale d'Albi 38-bis

K^0	Badische Landesbibliothek Augiensis Perg. XV
M^1	Biblioteca dell'Abbazia 109GG
Na	Biblioteca Nazionale Vindobonensis lat. 2
O^1	Bodleian Library Rawlinson A. 46
P^0	Bibliothèque Nationale lat. 1771
P^1	Bibliothèque Nationale lat. 2628
P^2	Bibliothèque Nationale lat. 12299
P^3	Bibliothèque Nationale lat. 2811
P^4	Bibliothèque Nationale lat. 13333
P^5	Bibliothèque Nationale lat. 17415
P^6	Bibliothèque Nationale lat. 2445A
P^7	Bibliothèque Nationale lat. 2169
P^8	Bibliothèque Nationale lat. 2167
P^9	Bibliothèque Nationale lat. 2780
Q^0	Bibliothèque Nationale Nouv. acq. lat. 1436
Q^1	Bibliothèque Nationale Nouv. acq. lat. 1436
Rn	Biblioteca Nazionale Vittorio Emanuele II, V.E. 1190
Ru	Biblioteca Vallicelliana Tom. XXV
S^2	Bibliothèque municipale de Saint-Omer 716
$S\Sigma^0$	Stiftsbibliothek 226
$S\Sigma^1$	Stiftsbibliothek 194
T^0	Bibliothèque municipale de Troyes 154
T^1	Bibliothèque municipale de Troyes 188
V^0	Bibliotheca Apostolica Vaticana, Vaticanus lat. 3835-3836
V^1	Bibliotheca Apostolica Vaticana, Reginensis lat. 131
V^3	Bibliotheca Apostolica Vaticana, Vaticanus lat. 479
6	Staats- und Stadtbibliothek, 2^0.Augsb. 320
66	Cambridge, Trinity Hall 26
312	Bibliothèque Nationale lat. 8996
313	Bibliothèque Nationale lat. 11699
399	Bibliotheca Apostolica Vaticana, Reginensis lat. 140s

Introduction

1. See the epilogue for discussion of the Eusebius Gallicanus manuscript tradition.

2. Carle, "Homélie de pâques," "Sermon de s. Fauste de Riez"; Buchem, *Homélie pseudo-Eusébienne.*

3. Triacca, "Maternità feconda" and "'Cultus' in Eusebio 'Gallicano.'"

4. Kasper, *Theologie und Askese;* Nürnberg, *Askese als sozialer Impuls;* Beaujard, *Culte des saints;* Harries, "Christianity and the City"; Leyser, "This Sainted Isle."

5. Weiss, "Statut du prédicateur."

6. Bruzzone, "Similitudine, metafore e contesto sociale."

7. See the detailed discussion of the debates over the authorship of the sermons in chapter 2.

8. This figure excludes the *Sermones extrauagantes,* sermons which became associated with the Eusebius Gallicanus in the manuscript tradition, although they did not form part of the original collection. Since the focus of this dissertation is on the original production and compilation of the Eu-

sebian sermons, the *Sermones extrauagantes* have not been included in this study. They are edited by Glorie in *CCSL* 101B.

9. These manuscripts are P[7] and F[1].

10. This point is also noted by Simonetti, "Eusebius Gallicanus."

11. Contrast, for example, the extensive exegetical material in the collections of Peter Chrysologus and Caesarius of Arles.

12. These are Eusebius Gallicanus 7, 8, 37–44, 72.

13. See chapter 6 for more details.

14. For a more detailed analysis of language in the Eusebius Gallicanus sermons see Leroy, "Oeuvre oratoire," 1:213–52, and Triacca, "Maternità feconda," 367–70, 379–80. On *sermo humilis* see the discussion in chapter 1.

15. Bruzzone, "Similitudine, metafore e contesto sociale," 127, 135.

16. Almost certainly none were gleaned from the original source, but via other Christian authors. On this see Courcelle, "Nouveaux aspects," 379–409.

17. See more detailed discussion in chapter 4.

18. See chapter 3.

19. Scholars working on the Eusebius Gallicanus have taken such a context as read, without feeling the need to defend it. Triacca stresses the liturgical nature of the sermons, "'Cultus' in Eusebio 'Gallicano,'" 110, and "Maternità feconda," 352. The Eusebius Gallicanus sermons show no signs of being intended for anything other than an urban audience, so I will not be focusing on the situation of the Gallic countryside. See, however, the interesting work on rural communities being done by Klingshirn, *Caesarius of Arles,* 201–43; Bowes, "'Christianization' and the Rural Home," 143–70; Clark, "Pastoral Care"; Stancliffe, "From Town to Country"; Wood, "Early Merovingian Devotion"; Fouracre, "Work of Audoenus of Rouen."

20. Triacca, "'Cultus' in Eusebio 'Gallicano,'" 110, and "Maternità feconda," 352–55; Bruzzone, "Similitudine, metafore e contesto sociale," 125.

21. For the variety of ways in which the sermons were used subsequent to their compilation see the epilogue.

22. Of course, the exact constitutions of these groups fluctuated.

23. Markus, "Roman Empire," 343–44.

24. Orosius, *Seven Books of History Against the Pagans* 5.22, 6.20.

25. Markus, "Roman Empire," 346–49, and *Saeculum,* 39–44.

26. On the attempts made by the bishops of Rome to establish their authority in fifth-century Gaul see Mathisen, *Ecclesiastical Factionalism,*

44–68. Smith, *Europe after Rome,* 281–82 notes the ongoing limitations on their power and influence in this period.

27. For Gaul see, for example, the work of Van Dam, *Leadership and Community;* Klingshirn, *Caesarius of Arles;* Barcellona, "Fausto di Riez"; Beaujard, "Évêque dans la cité"; Heinzelmann, *Bischofherrschaft in Gallien.*

28. Smith, *Europe after Rome,* 223–24.

29. For the records of the Gallic councils see *Concilia Galliae.*

30. Godding, *Prêtres en Gaule,* 278–82.

31. Godding, *Prêtres en Gaule,* 51–71; Aubrun, "Clergé rural," 15–27.

32. On the financial support of the clergy see Jones, *Later Roman Empire,* 2:894–907 and Godding, *Prêtres en Gaule,* 331–58.

33. Brown, *Cult of the Saints;* Van Dam, *Saints and Their Miracles;* Beaujard, *Culte des saints;* Harries, "Christianity and the City."

34. Rapp, *Holy Bishops;* Sterk, *Renouncing the World.* Note that the work of Peter Brown has here also served as a foundational inspiration, starting with "Rise and Function of the Holy Man."

35. Prinz, *Frühes Mönchtum;* Heinzelmann, *Bischofherrschaft in Gallien;* Van Dam, *Leadership and Community;* Rousseau, *Ascetics, Authority and the Church;* Mathisen, *Ecclesiastical Factionalism.*

36. Leyser, *Authority and Asceticism;* Demacopoulos, *Five Models;* Markus, *End of Ancient Christianity.*

37. For example, Klingshirn, *Caesarius of Arles;* Stewart, *Cassian the Monk.*

38. Casiday comments that: "many Church historians over the centuries have been so committed to [the idea of a semi-pelagian controversy] that they cannot bear to leave a Gallic Christian of the fifth century unaffiliated to Pelagius or to Augustine." *Tradition and Theology,* 19 n. 6, and again at 41.

39. See the brief summary in Leyser, "Semi-Pelagianism," 761.

40. Important recent works include Weaver, *Divine Grace;* Smith, *De Gratia;* Leyser, "Semi-Pelagianism"; Markus, "Legacy of Pelagius"; Tibiletti, "Rassegna di studi."

41. Leyser, "Semi-Pelagianism," 763; O'Donnell, "Authority of Augustine," 17.

42. Weaver, *Divine Grace,* 234–49; Smith, *De Gratia,* 70–71, 227; Leyser, "Semi-Pelagianism," 764.

43. See, for example, Weaver's description of the controversy as "a conflict between two different sets of issues, two different social contexts, and two different theological traditions," *Divine Grace,* x.

44. Weaver, *Divine Grace*, x.

45. Weaver, *Divine Grace*, x.

46. Leyser, "Semi-Pelagianism," 764; Weaver, *Divine Grace*, 162; Smith, *De Gratia*, 59; Stewart, *Cassian the Monk*, 24.

47. Weaver, *Divine Grace*, 177; Smith, *De Gratia*, 216; Pontal, *Histoire des conciles mérovingiens*, 90.

48. Weaver, *Divine Grace*, 233; Pontal, *Histoire des conciles mérovingiens*, 91, 99.

49. Leroy states that "le recueil dit d'Eusèbe d'Emèse respire le semi-pélagianisme," "Oeuvre oratoire," 1:304. The association of the sermons with Faustus of Riez has also drawn them into the "semi-pelagian" side. On Faustus and semi-pelagianism see Smith, *De Gratia*; Leyser, "Semi-Pelagianism," 764; Weigel, *Faustus of Riez*, 88–109; Tibiletti, "Salvezza umana." The question of Faustus' authorship of the sermons is discussed in chapter 2. The monastery of Lérins, with which some of the Eusebian sermons were undoubtedly connected, has also been seen as a centre of opposition to Augustine. On this see Kasper, *Theologie und Askese*, 224–48; Leyser, "This Sainted Isle," 192–93; Weaver, *Divine Grace*, 38, 157; Markus, "Legacy of Pelagius," 222; Pontal, *Histoire des conciles mérovingiens*, 90; Weigel, *Faustus of Riez*, 101. The connection of the sermons to the monastery at Lérins is discussed in chapter six.

50. Casiday: "It is far from obvious what constitutes anti-Augustinianism in Late Antiquity or even, with the exception of Julian of Eclanum and perhaps a few others, who these anti-Augustinians were supposed to be. For that matter, apart from the ringing claims of Prosper himself, we have no real evidence for 'Augustinianism' for another seven centuries and consequently we have no real reason to suppose that there was a monolithic, theological juggernaut ('Augustinian theology') that attracted systematic opposition during this period." *Tradition and Theology*, 7.

51. Kleinberg, "*De agone christiano*," 16–33.

52. Hen, *Royal Patronage*, 28–33.

53. On the Gallic councils see Pontal, *Histoire des conciles mérovingiens*.

54. Smith, *Europe after Rome*, 223.

55. On the relations and divisions between clergy and laity in this period see Faivre, "Clerc/Laïc," 195–220.

56. On the medieval concept of the Church as a corporation which cannot die see Kantorowicz, *King's Two Bodies*, 291–94.

57. See Allen and Mayer for a very useful survey of the literature and the problems with it, "Through a Bishop's Eyes," 345–97.

58. Beck, *Pastoral Care.*

59. Maxwell, *Christianization and Communication;* Demacopoulos, *Five Models.* Demacopoulos defines "spiritual direction" as "the modus operandi by which religious authorities (in both lay and monastic communities) sought to advance the spiritual condition of those under their care." He adds: "Throughout the text, I will use the terms *spiritual direction* and *pastoral care* almost interchangeably. The term *pastoral care* conveys a certain set of modern preconceptions about clerical ministry, but it was also a term employed by late ancient Christians, especially Pope Gregory I, to describe the responsibilities of spiritual leadership." *Five Models,* 1 nn. 2–3. I am very grateful to George Demacopoulos for kindly allowing me to see sections of this work prior to its publication. The new prominence of pastoral care is reflected in the fact that the recent *Cambridge History of Christianity* volume on late antiquity includes a chapter on it: Greer, "Pastoral Care and Discipline."

Chapter 1. Preaching in Late Antique Gaul

1. Although the terms *sermo* and *homilia* have technically different meanings, they were used interchangeably during the period discussed here and they are treated as synonyms in this book, as are "sermonnary" and "homiliary." See Grégoire, *Homéliaires du Moyen Âge,* 6; Kienzle, "Introduction," in Kienzle, ed., *The Sermon,* 161; Hall, "Early Medieval Sermon," 205; Longère, *Prédication médiévale,* 27.

2. "Velis depictis adumbrantur plateae, eclesiae curtinis albentibus adurnantur, baptistirium conponitur, balsama difunduntur, micant flagrantes odorem cerei, totumque templum baptistirii divino respergetur ab odore, talemque ibi gratiam adstantibus Deus tribuit, ut aestimarent se paradisi odoribus collocari." Gregory of Tours, *LH* 2.31, ed. Krusch and Levison, 77, trans. Thorpe, 144.

3. "populus ingens sexu ex utroque, quem capacissima basilica non caperet quamlibet cincta diffusis cryptoporticibus . . . de loci sane turbarumque compressu deque numerosis luminibus inlatis nimis anheli." Sidonius Apollinaris, *Epistula* 5.17.3, ed. and trans. Anderson, 228–29.

4. This account excludes sermons to monks, for which see chapter 6.

5. On the internal spaces and architectural features of late antique Gallic churches see for example the descriptions in Sidonius Apollinaris, *Epistula* 2.10.4; Gregory of Tours, *LH* 2.14, 2.16; *GC* 34, 88; *GM* 27, 64;

VJ 2, 9; *VM* 1.31. See also Van Dam, *Leadership and Community,* 245. For a description of the "characteristic" late antique basilica and smaller churches see Stalley, *Early Medieval Architecture,* 23–24, 29–34. On the architecture of churches in Gaul see Griffe, *Gaule chrétienne,* 3:12–42 and the *Topographie chrétienne* series.

6. Sidonius praised the gilded ceiling, coloured marble, stones, and glass in the church built by Patiens in Lyon, *Epistula* 2.10.4. According to Gregory of Tours, the church built by Namatius in Clermont-Ferrand boasted mosaic work made of many varieties of marble and he describes Namatius' wife directing the decorations and coloured frescoes to be painted in the extramural shrine of St. Stephen, *LH* 2.16–17. Gregory was outraged when Eberulf's manservants sneaked into the church of St. Martin at Tours and gaped at the wall paintings, *LH* 7.22. See also *Vita Caesarii* 1.32; Gregory of Tours, *LH* 10.31; *VP* 12.2; *VJ* 20, 44; *GC* 34; *GM* 61, 64, 71, 93 and 102. There are descriptions of curtains and draperies against the walls in *VJ* 20; *VM* 1.13, 2.23.

7. On windows see Gregory of Tours, *LH* 2.14, 2.16; for lamps and candles, see *GC* 2, 20, 68, 69; *GM* 5, 14, 33, 78. In *GM* 104 Gregory told of a man attending vigils at the church of St. Felix who was wearied by the smoke in the church. The fragrance from incense and scattered herbs is described in *LH* 2.16; *GC* 94; *GM* 34, 70; *VP* 6.7, 8.6; *VM* 2.38.

8. The abbess of the nunnery at Poitiers was accused by her rebellious nuns of cutting up a silk altar cloth to make a dress for her niece and using gold leaf from its edge to make a necklace, Gregory of Tours, *LH* 10.15. See also references to silken altar cloths and precious liturgical vessels (both of which were a constant temptation to thieves) in *LH* 6.10, 7.22; *GC* 62; *GM* 45, 65, 71, 85, 91, 94; *VP* 8.11. Gregory told of Rauching's wife travelling to church for the feast day of Saints Crispin and Crispian, bedecked with gold and jewels, accompanied by a troop of servants, *LH* 9.9. Caesarius railed against those who went to church covered with precious stones, gold, and expensive clothing, but who were internally stained with vice. He did not suggest, however, that the faithful should come to church in old and stained garments—clothing should be bright and becoming. Caesarius of Arles, *Sermo* 224.2. See also 14.1. For clergy dressed in white, see Gregory of Tours, *GC* 20. On the question of appropriate dress in general, see Effros, "Appearance and Ideology," 7–24.

9. *Vita Caesarii* 1.19; Gregory of Tours, *LH* 8.3; *GC* 94; *GM* 34, 74, 75; *VP* 8.2.

10. For the presence of both men and women in church see Caesarius of Arles, *Sermones* 44.2–3, 50.3, 78.1; for different classes, see Caesarius of Arles, *Sermones* 30, 117.6; Gregory of Tours, *VM* 1.31; and discussion in Clark, "Pastoral Care," 271. Gregory told the story of a monk who had come to the festival of St. Julian at Briode but was unable to enter either the church or the tomb due to the crowds of people. An angelic guide later instructed him to visit the tomb after hours, when it was empty. *VJ* 28. Those who were locked into churches after hours in Gregory's stories often found the space and silence frightening; see for example *VM* 2.33; *GM* 33.

11. Compare for example the account of Salvius, who went to heaven but was sent back to earth: "Deinde per portam luce ista clariorem introductus sum in illud habitaculum, in quo omne pavimentum erat quasi aurum argentumque renitens, lux ineffabilis, amplitudo inenarrabilis; quam ita multitudo promiscui sexus obtexerat, ut longitudo ac latitudo catervae prorsus pervidere non possit . . . Stans igitur in loco in quo iussus sum, operuit me odor nimiae suavitatis, ita ut, ab hac suavitate refectus, nullum adhuc cybum potumque desiderarem." Gregory of Tours, *LH* 7.1, ed. Krusch and Levison, 325. Gregory provided numerous descriptions of saints and angels engaged in an ideal liturgy with light, incense, and chanted psalms. See for example *GC* 29, 72; *GM* 33. Van Dam comments: "When people entered a church, it was possible for them to experience, even if only for brief moments, the celestial atmosphere in which saints lived all the time. In churches the lights, sounds, and scents could evoke the impression, if not the very image, of Paradise." *Leadership and Community,* 239.

12. For stories of miracles during the liturgy see Gregory of Tours, *VJ* 47; *VM* 2.14, 2.25, 2.30; and Augustine of Hippo, *Sermo* 323.4.

13. Caesarius of Arles, *Sermones* 13.3, 50.3, 55, 72.1–3, 76.2, 77.7, 78.1, 80.1; Gregory of Tours, *GM* 57; Augustine of Hippo, *Sermones* Dolbeau 2.5, 27. See also Klingshirn, *Caesarius of Arles,* 154.

14. *Vita Caesarii* 1.27; Caesarius of Arles, *Sermones* 72.1, 73, 74.1–3, 76.1–3, 77.1–2, 78.1, 208.3; Augustine of Hippo, *Sermo* Dolbeau 2. For canons against leaving church during the service, see Council of Agde, a. 506, c. 47; Council of Orléans, a. 511, c. 26; Council of Orléans, a. 538, c. 32.

15. Augustine's *Sermo* Dolbeau 2 gives a good sense of the mobility of both congregation and preacher and also of the level of interaction between them.

16. Caesarius of Arles, *Sermo* 55; Gregory of Tours, *GM* 35, 89; *VJ* 15, 18; Valerian of Cimiez, *Homilia* 19. Sidonius described playing games, chatting, and exchanging poetry during breaks between services for the fes-

tival of St. Justus in Lyon. *Epistula* 5.17.3–10. See also Brown, "Enjoying the Saints," 1–24, and *Cult of the Saints,* 26–27; Van Dam, *Leadership and Community,* 232–33.

17. For only a few of the many examples, see Gregory of Tours, *LH* 4.43, 7.22, 7.38, 8.31.

18. This may have been the case in other parts of Europe as well—it is not clear whether the more extensive evidence for preaching in Gaul is an accident of source-survival or a signal of exceptionalism. Most scholars have been wary of generalising. For a summary of the evidence in Spain, Italy, and England, see Amos, "Origin and Nature," 90–138. Allen, "Identity of Sixth-Century Preachers," 245–53, argues that preaching continued to be common in the East through the early Byzantine period. See also Cunningham, "Preaching and the Community," 29–47 and the articles in Cunningham and Allen, eds., *Preacher and Audience.*

19. See Council of Agde, a. 506, c. 13; St-Jean-de-Losne, a. 673–75, c.18; pseudo-Germanus: "Homiliae autem sanctorum quae leguntur pro sola praedicatione ponuntur, ut quicquid Propheta, Apostolus vel Evengelium mandavit, hoc doctor vel pastor Ecclesiae apertiori sermone populo praedicet, ita arte temperans ut nec rusticitas sapientes offendat, nec honesta loquacitas obscura rusticis fiat." Quoted in Duchesne, *Christian Worship,* 197. See also Grégoire, "Homily"; Mara, "Mass"; Amos, "Origin and Nature," 16, 19, 22–23; Mayeski, "Reading the Word," 71–74; Thibaut, *Ancienne liturgie gallicane,* 40–41. McLaughlin maintains that it is "fanciful" to assume that there was a weekly Sunday sermon, but he relies for this judgement upon nineteenth-century secondary literature and does not address either the case of Gaul or the period before 700. McLaughlin, "The Word Eclipsed?" 78, 102–3.

20. Caesarius of Arles, *Sermones* 1.10, 4.3. Discussion in Klingshirn, *Caesarius of Arles,* 146–47. Augustine may have preached up to four times a week during certain periods of the year; Harmless, *Augustine and the Catechumenate,* 161, and Augustine of Hippo, *Sermo* Dolbeau 2.4.

21. Note the "visitation" sermons by Augustine of Hippo: *Sermones* 82, 301A; *Sermones* Dolbeau 7, 21, 25, and 27. Caesarius lamented that he was not able to visit some rural congregations as often as he would like: *Sermones* 6, 151. Some priests were diligent; Gregory of Tours told of Severus who traveled between two villages every Sunday to give mass, *GC* 49.

22. Women, monks, and lay people also preached, but of this activity there is very little record. See Kienzle, "Preaching as a Touchstone," 33–44; "Introduction," in Kienzle, ed., *The Sermon,* 166–67.

23. It is very difficult to reconstruct the late antique Gallic liturgy from the surviving evidence, but it seems clear that these were the main elements in most services. For an evocative account of the liturgy based on the later pseudo-Germanus source see Duchesne, *Christian Worship*, 189–226. The problems of this source are discussed by Mensbrugghe, "Pseudo-Germanus Reconsidered," 172–84 and Cabié, "Lettres attribuées à saint Germain de Paris," 13–57. Yitzhak Hen emphasises the diversity of liturgical practices in Gaul. *Royal Patronage*, 28, 32–33, and "Unity in Diversity," 19–30.

24. On the elaboration for special festivals see Duchesne, *Christian Worship*, 229–93. On the shorter daily offices see Beck, *Pastoral Care*, 110–19; Van Dam, *Leadership and Community*, 283.

25. Beck, *Pastoral Care*, 136; Dix, *Shape of the Liturgy*, 13; Chelini, "Pratique dominicale des laics," 166.

26. The bishops gathered in Agde insisted that any lay person "qui Natale Domini, Pascha, Pentecosten non communicauerint, catholici non credantur, nec inter catholicos habeantur." Council of Agde, a. 506, c. 18, ed. Munier, 202. Church councils also tried to enforce frequent attendance at church—see, for example, Council of Orleans a. 538, c. 31; and St-Jean-de-Losne, a. 673–75, c. 8. Gregory of Tours' *Miracula* collections are full of punishments for those who work or play on Sundays instead of attending church. See, for example, *GM* 15; *VP* 7.5, 15.3; *VJ* 11, and discussion of these issues in Van Dam, *Leadership and Community*, 66.

27. For example, the woman who went to church every day to attend the mass that she had ordered for her deceased husband. Gregory of Tours, *GC* 64. The authors of the *Vita Caesarii* wrote that the bishop of Arles instituted Terce, Sext, and None so that anyone who wanted to be present at the daily offices could easily do so (1.15).

28. Ramsey MacMullen doubts whether any city had a church or churches large enough to accommodate more than a minority of the total resident population, although Amos notes that the number of churches in Gaul was increasing exponentially at this time. MacMullen, "The Preacher's Audience," 510; Amos, "Origin and Nature," 23. For an assessment of the size and number of churches in Gaul and estimates of the populations of the towns see Griffe, *Gaule chrétienne*, 3:5–42.

29. Van Dam, *Leadership and Community*, 281–82; Baldovin, *Urban Character*, 251, 254; Beaujard, *Culte des saints*, 158, 493; Dix, *Shape of the Liturgy*, 1–2.

30. Buc, *Dangers of Ritual*, 255.

31. Augustine of Hippo, *Sermo* Dolbeau 2; *Vita Caesarii* 1.27; Bell, *Ritual Theory,* 8, 215.

32. Buc, *Dangers of Ritual,* 252; Bell, *Ritual Theory,* 189.

33. Buc, *Dangers of Ritual,* 256; Bell, *Ritual Theory,* 210.

34. Constantius of Lyon, *Vita Germani* 7; Gregory of Tours, *LH* 10.1.

35. I am here extending to speech Catherine Bell's notion of ritualisation as an exercise in drawing contrasts with other ways of acting. See, in particular, *Ritual Theory,* 7–8, 74, 90–91.

36. Bell notes these as common strategies of ritualisation. *Ritual Theory,* 92.

37. Kienzle, "Preaching as a Touchstone," 22, and "Conclusion," in Kienzle, ed., *The Sermon,* 978; Hen, "Martin of Braga," 42; Rebillard, *In hora mortis,* 3; Amos, "Early Medieval Sermons," 1–14.

38. McKitterick, *Carolingians and the Written Word,* 8–22, and "Latin and Romance," 130–45; Wright, *Late Latin,* ix–xi, 1; Lloyd, "On the Names of Languages," 9–18; Van Uytfanghe, "Consciousness of a Linguistic Dichotomy," 114–29; Smith, *Europe after Rome,* 25; Banniard, "Latin et communication orale," 61.

39. Preachers therefore did not face the problems which d'Avray refers to in the translation of Latin preaching aids into vernacular spoken words, *Preaching of the Friars,* 20–21.

40. Hilary of Arles was known to change his style and language depending on the composition of his audience, *Vita Hilarii* 14. [The numeration used is that of the *PL* 50 edition.] Sidonius Apollinaris delivered a sermon filled with allusions to classical history and literature to the people of Bourges on the occasion of their episcopal election. *Epistula* 7.9.

41. Augustine of Hippo, *De doctrina christiana* 4.24–25. For discussion of Augustine's arguments and their implications for the Christian tradition, see Auerbach, *Literary Language,* 27–66; Kaster, *Guardians of Language,* 84–88. For the application in Augustine's own preaching, see Banniard, "Variations langagières," 73–93.

42. Banniard, *Viva voce,* 35–39.

43. Banniard, *Viva voce,* 67–79. The clearest example of this principle is Gregory the Great's *Regula pastoralis,* with its detailed breakdown of strategies depending on audience type.

44. Caesarius of Arles made a number of such programmatic statements. See *Sermones* 1.12–13, 1.20, 86.1, 87.5, and discussions in Klingshirn, *Caesarius of Arles,* 148–49; Clerici, "Sermo humilis," 339–64; Rapisarda, "Stile umile," 115–59. See also the similar statements of Peter

Chrysologus, *Sermones* 43, 106.2. On the use of such methods in the Eusebius Gallicanus collection, see Bruzzone, "Similitudine, metafore e contesto sociale," 127–29.

45. On the use of quotidian analogies in late antique preaching, see Salvatore, "Uso delle similitudini," 177–225 and Bruzzone, "Similitudine, metafore e contesto sociale," 126–29. This does not necessarily mean, however, that *sermo humilis* was straightforwardly directed to uneducated audiences, as Salvatore tends to assume.

46. *Vita Hilarii* 15; Augustine of Hippo, *Sermo* Dolbeau 198.

47. Caesarius usually spoke for less than half an hour, and deliberately kept things brief to ensure attendance and attention. See *Sermones* 22.1, 23.2, 76.3, 91.8. Palardy, *St. Peter Chrysologus,* 30, estimates the length of Peter Chrysologus' sermons as fifteen minutes, and there are signs that he sometimes broke larger discussions into smaller parts, for example, *Sermones* 51.5 and 63.5. The sermons of the Eusebius Gallicanus collection are a comparable length.

48. On this see Amos, "Early Medieval Sermons." Not all scholars agree with this assessment. McLaughlin, for example, questions whether "individual members of an oral community would have possessed the mental tools to appreciate the products of a literate society." He doubts "whether an ordinary fifth-century Christian would have been able to follow the train of thought and argument" of the preaching of the bishop of Hippo. "The Word Eclipsed?" 100, and 100 n. 111. For such scepticism, however, McLaughlin has no positive evidence and cites only the example of Charlemagne's daughters struggling with Augustine's sermons almost four hundred years later. Given Augustine's repeatedly stated intention to be comprehensible, the burden of proof must lie with those who doubt that he was. Even should such proof surface, moreover, it would scarcely apply to later preachers who simplified, reworked, and adapted Augustine's sermons to suit their own audiences.

49. Caesarius of Arles, *Sermones* 2, 4.2–3, 130.4, 145.1, 217.3.

50. Caesarius of Arles, *Sermo* 1. See also Peter Chrysologus, *Sermo* 173.1–2.

51. Caesarius of Arles, *Sermones* 1.15, 2; *Vita Caesarii* 1.18, 1.54–55; Morin, "Homilies of St. Caesarius," 481–86.

52. Caesarius of Arles, *Sermones* 4.4, 5.1–5, 6.1–3, 6.8, 8.1–2, 13.3, 74.4; Ferreiro, "'Frequenter legere,'" 5–15.

53. Caesarius of Arles, *Sermones* 73.1–4, 74.1–3, 145.1, 208.3; *Vita Caesarii* 1.27.

54. Gennadius of Marseille, *Liber de viris illustribus* 21, 40, 53, 57, 67, 69, 73, 77,79, 90, 93 [the numeration used is that of the *PL* 58 edition]; Sidonius Apollinaris, *Epistula* 9.3.5; Gregory of Tours, *LH* 10.1, *VP* 17.2.

55. Arator quoted by Beck, *Pastoral Care,* 259; Sulpicius Severus, *Vita Martini* 15; Hilary of Arles, *Sermo sancti Honorati* 26, 29; Constantius of Lyon, *Vita Germani* 14; Audoenus of Rouen, *Vita Eligii* 14; *Vita Hilarii* 14–15; *Vita Caesarii* 17–18, 54–55.

56. Gennadius mentions sermons and collections by Salvian and Musaeus of Marseille, *Liber de viris illustribus* 79; the author of the Life of Hilary of Arles claims many more homilies for him than the single surviving example, *Vita Hilarii* 14; the Life of Eligius of Noyon contains a sermon by him which is not otherwise transmitted [*Vita Eligii* 15], though this may be a later insertion. See Klingshirn, *Caesarius of Arles,* 275. Eucherius of Lyon, Maximus of Riez, and Lupus of Troyes may also have composed sermons which do not survive. Amos, "Origin and Nature," 21. On the large numbers of unedited early medieval sermons, see Amos, "Preaching and the Sermon," 47–49.

57. On the importance of sermons for the Carolingian reforms, see Amos, "Preaching and the Sermon," 47–48; McKitterick, *Frankish Church,* 81–113.

58. Amos, "Origin and Nature," 139–372, clearly demonstrates their indebtedness.

59. McKitterick, *Carolingians and the Written Word,* 213; Smith, *Europe after Rome,* 40–41.

60. On the education of clergy in late antique Gaul see Godding, *Prêtres en Gaule,* 54–71; Riché, *Education and Culture,* 122–28.

61. Amos, "Origin and Nature," 18; Weiss, "Statut du prédicateur," 25–26; McLaughlin, "The Word Eclipsed?" 101. On the long-standing association of preaching with heresy and disobedience, see Kienzle, "Preaching as a Touchstone"; Longère, *Prédication médiévale,* 78–82; Muessig, "Sermon, Preacher and Society," 83–84.

62. Gennadius of Marseille, *Liber de viris illustribus* 67 and 79; *Eusebius Gallicanus* 67–71. See Weiss, "Statut du prédicateur," 25–37, 45–47. The practice of having priests preach was not unknown elsewhere—see Weiss, "Statut du prédicateur," 24–25. The famous examples are John Chrysostom and Augustine of Hippo, who both preached "on behalf of" their bishops.

63. Celestine I, *Epistula* 21.1.2.

64. *Vita Caesarii* 1.53; Caesarius of Arles, *Sermo* 1.15.

65. Council of Vaison, a. 529, c. 2: "Hoc etiam pro aedificatione omnium ecclesiarum et pro utelitate totius populi nobis placuit, ut non solum
in ciuitatibus, sed etiam in omnibus parrociis uerbum faciendi daremus
presbyteris potestatem, ita ut, si presbyter aliqua infirmitate prohibente per
se ipsum non potuerit praedicare, sanctorum patrum homiliae a diaconibus
recitentur; si enim digni sunt diaconi, quod Christus in euangelio locutus
est, legere, quare indigni iudicentur sanctorum patrum expositiones publice
recitare?" Ed. de Clercq, 78–79.

66. On this use of sermon collections see Grégoire, *Homéliaires liturgiques médiévaux,* 21; Amos, "Origin and Nature," 30–33; Hall, "Early Medieval Sermon," 213; McKitterick, *Frankish Church,* 92; Longère, *Prédication médiévale,* 31, 35; Weiss, "Statut du prédicateur," 31, 45–47.

67. Susan Ashbrook Harvey has argued that the Church used liturgy
to try to control and to incorporate charismatic authority in much the same
way. "The Stylite's Liturgy," 523–39.

68. On the methodological problems which this causes see Kienzle,
"Introduction," in Kienzle, ed., *Sermon,* 170–73; and Kienzle, "Medieval
Sermons," 89–90. Note interesting parallels with the challenges and opportunities presented by the use of *formulae* as sources. See the thoughtful
discussion in Rio, "Charters, law codes and formulae."

69. For example the sermon *De castigatione rusticorum* by Martin of
Braga is a letter instructing an acquaintance on what to tell his congregation, so it is unclear in what form, if any, it was ever delivered. See Ferreiro,
"Missionary Labours," 11–26. Caesarius of Arles, *Sermones* 1 and 2 were
almost certainly also letters.

70. McLaughlin, "The Word Eclipsed?," 93, 106–7. McLaughlin is
building on a longstanding "dark-age" narrative of preaching beautifully
epitomised in the chapter headings to Dargan's *A History of Preaching:*
"The Culmination of Ancient Preaching in the Fourth Century"; "The Decline of Preaching in the Fifth and Sixth Centuries"; "The Low Estate of
Preaching in the Seventh and Eighth Centuries"; "Voices in the Night, or
Preaching during the Ninth, Tenth and Eleventh Centuries"; "Heralds of
the Dawn in the Eleventh and Twelfth Centuries." Dargan's text was first
published in 1905, but the outlook and imagery persists in more recent
scholarship on preaching. Hughes Oliphant Old describes Leo I as "a most
brilliant ray in the sunset of classical civilization" and Gregory the Great as
"the evening star of the patristic age." *Reading and Preaching,* 2:410, 425.
Old also agrees with McLaughlin's view on the "decline" of improvisation
and spontaneity in preaching—*Reading and Preaching,* 3:143, 154.

71. On the explosion in numbers of homiliaries see Hall, "Early Medieval Sermon," 221; Grégoire, "Homiliary" and "Homéliaires mérovingiens," 901–17.

72. McKitterick, "Some Carolingian Law-Books," 13–27; Mathisen, "The 'Second Council of Arles,'" 511–54; Vessey, "Origins of the *Collectio Sirmondiana*," 178–99; Rochais, "Contribution à l'histoire des florilèges," 246–91; Morin, "'Breviarium fidei,'" 35–53; Grégoire, *Homéliaires du Moyen Âge*, 2–6; Stansbury, "Early Medieval Biblical Commentaries," 49–82; O'Donnell, "Authority of Augustine," 18–19; Hen, *Royal Patronage*, 11–12, and "Merovingian Commentary," 167–87. I am indebted to Yitzhak Hen for allowing me to read this article prior to its publication.

73. Bloch, "Symbols, Song, Dance," 68. Bloch points out that this high level of "formalisation" could have the effect of detaching the speaker from the words spoken—he became a representative rather than an individual (74–75). The implications of Bloch's arguments are discussed in Kienzle, "Medieval Sermons," 93.

74. On the influence of Caesarius' formulaic sermon endings, see Amos, "Origin and Nature," 37.

75. Caesarius' sermons contain many phrases and formulas repeated from one sermon to another. The same is true of the sermons in the Eusebius Gallicanus collection.

76. Hamman, "Transmission des sermons," 327. See also the comments of Rebillard, who argues that sermons directly touched a greater number of people than any other genre of Christian literature. *In hora mortis*, 3.

77. Heffernan, *Sacred Biography*, 6. Heffernan uses the phrase in reference to hagiography, but it applies equally well to homiletics.

78. For more on this process see the epilogue.

79. McLaughlin, "The Word Eclipsed?" 78.

80. This is the case, for example, in the following studies: Amos, "Origin and Nature"; Beck, *Pastoral Care;* Hen, *Culture and Religion;* McLaughlin, "The Word Eclipsed?"; Longère, *Prédication médiévale;* Markus, *End of Ancient Christianity,* and "From Caesarius to Boniface"; Brown, *Rise of Western Christendom,* 150; Old, *Reading and Preaching,* 3:74–81. There are also a large number of studies specifically of Caesarius. See in particular Klingshirn, *Caesarius of Arles;* Milleman, "Caesarius von Arles," 12–27; Bardy, "Prédication de saint Césaire"; Clerici, "Sermo humilis"; Morin, "Homilies of St. Caesarius"; Rapisarda, "Stile umile"; Arnold, *Caesarius von Arelate;* Daly, "Caesarius of Arles," 1–28; Ferreiro, "Early Medieval Missionary Tactics," 225–38.

81. In particular MacMullen, "The Preacher's Audience," and Mc-Laughlin, "The Word Eclipsed?"

82. As Beverly Mayne Kienzle notes, "any communicative discourse is persuasive to some extent, but the sermon is highly persuasive." Kienzle, "Introduction," in Kienzle, ed., *Sermon,* 155.

83. On the lay audience for the collection, see the discussion in chapter 2. For sermons to monks, see the discussion in chapter 6.

84. For a definition of pastoral care and discussion of the literature on it, see the introduction.

85. Kienzle, "Medieval Sermons," 92, 95–96.

86. Rebillard, "Interaction between the Preacher and the Audience," 86–96. See also the expansion of this point in Rebillard, *In hora mortis.*

87. De Bruyn, "Ambivalence within a 'Totalizing Discourse,'" 405–21. See also Kleinberg, *"De agone christiano,"* 16–33.

88. Rebillard, "Interaction between the Preacher and the Audience," 96. Rebillard was building on the work of Raoul Manselli, who claimed that Christianity was forced into "un infatigable dialogue avec les masses," and Aron Gurevich, who explored the "ongoing hidden dialogue between official doctrine and folkloric consciousness." Manselli, *Religion populaire,* 24, and Gurevich, *Medieval Popular Culture,* 5.

89. Maxwell, *Christianization and Communication,* 1–4, 120, 170–71.

90. On the power of the ancient rhetor to do this see De Bruyn, "Ambivalence within a 'Totalizing Discourse,'" 407.

91. Bloch, "Symbols, Song, Dance," 64.

92. Bell, *Ritual Theory,* 120–21.

93. Bloch, "Symbols, Song, Dance," 79.

94. Bell, *Ritual Theory,* 121.

95. Bell, following Foucault, notes that the existence of freedom is necessary to the exercise of power, as distinct from the force of necessity. *Ritual Theory,* 201.

Chapter 2. The Eusebius Gallicanus Sermon Collection

1. See the epilogue for a detailed discussion of the manuscript history of the sermons.

2. Dolbeau, *"Serminator uerborum,"* 71–86.

3. See Glorie, *Eusebius "Gallicanus,"* xliv.

4. See for example the list of inscriptions in Glorie, *Eusebius "Gallicanus,"* 10.

5. Buytaert, *Héritage littéraire d'Eusèbe d'Émèse,* 159–61; Leroy, "Oeuvre oratoire," 1:283–84; Buchem, *Homélie pseudo-Eusébienne,* 54.

6. Morin, "Collection gallicane," 107; Griffe, "Sermons de Fauste de Riez," 32; Leroy and Glorie, "'Eusèbe d'Alexandrie,'" 33–70; MacCoull, "Who Was Eusebius of Alexandria?" 9–18.

7. See for example the attributions in manuscripts 6 (to Columbanus), 66 (to Isidore), P⁹ (to Faustus), P⁵ (to Caesarius), V³ (to Augustine), I⁰ (to Faustinus), K⁰ (to Leo) and M¹ (to Maximus). All manuscript *sigla* are those of Glorie. Lettered manuscripts are those used for his edition, numbers are used for the remainder. See the appendix for full manuscript titles.

8. See for example the differing designations in Griffe, "Sermons de Fauste de Riez"; Leeming, "False Decretals," 122–40; Leroy, "Oeuvre oratoire"; Morin, "Collection gallicane"; Souter, "Observations on the Pseudo-Eusebian Collection," 47–57.

9. Leroy, "Oeuvre oratoire," 1:57.

10. On the editions of the collection see Leroy, "Oeuvre oratoire," 1:10–56; Morin, "Collection gallicane," 92–93 and Glorie, *Eusebius "Gallicanus,"* xliii–xliv.

11. For example, sermons 9 and 10 were edited by Caspari in *Kirchenhistorische Anecdota* 1, under the name of Faustus of Riez; 11 appeared in *PL* 50 as a sermon of Eucherius of Lyon; 13 in *PL* 57 as a sermon of Maximus of Turin; and large parts of the paschal series appeared in *PL* 67 as the work of Caesarius of Arles.

12. Leroy prepared an edition of the collection for his doctoral thesis, submitted in 1954, but sadly died before completing the preparations for publication. The *CCSL* edition produced by Glorie is based on Leroy's work.

13. See the analysis in Glorie, *Eusebius "Gallicanus,"* 1045–83.

14. See the analysis in Glorie, *Eusebius "Gallicanus,"* 1091–96.

15. See Leroy, "Oeuvre oratoire," 1:212–13 for a summary of his arguments.

16. Leroy, "Oeuvre oratoire," 1:2, 282–410.

17. Leroy, "Oeuvre oratoire," 1:1–2, 389.

18. Engelbrecht, *Studien über die Schriften;* Griffe, "Sermons de Fauste de Riez"; Leeming, "False Decretals"; Souter, "Observations on the Pseudo-Eusebian Collection"; Buchem, *Homélie pseudo-Eusébienne;* Carle, "Homélie de pâques" and "Sermon de s. Fauste de Riez"; Nürnberg, *Askese als sozialer Impuls.* Griffe published a reaffirmation of his position after the publication of Glorie's edition: "Nouveau plaidoyer," 187–92.

19. Morin, "Collection gallicane," 107; Stancliffe, "Thirteen Sermons," 118–24.

20. Stancliffe, "Thirteen Sermons," 119.

21. Candidates include Honoratus and Hilary of Arles, Maximus of Riez, Patiens of Lyon, Eucherius of Lyon, and the latter's sons Salonius of Geneva and Veranus of Vence.

22. Bergmann, *Studien zu einer kritischen Sichtung*, 7–8; Morin, "Critique des sermons," 49–61.

23. Glorie, *Eusebius "Gallicanus,"* x–xii.

24. The most frequently mentioned candidates are sermons 12, 17, 28, 51, 72, and the *ad monachos* series.

25. Harries and Weiss suspect Eucherius of Lyon. Harries, *Sidonius Apollinaris*, 44; Weiss, "Statut du prédicateur," 43. Mathisen argues for Eucherius' successor, Patiens, *Ecclesiastical Factionalism*, 233. See also Bailey, "Building Urban Christian Communities," 5.

26. Samuel Cavallin argues that the sermon was originally written by Hilary of Arles, and this is supported by the preacher's intimate reference to the city's topography and by Pietri's argument that the sermon was responding to a specific situation in Arles at the time of Hilary's episcopate. Cavallin, "Saint Genès le notaire," 150–75; Pietri, "Culte des saints," 357; Beaujard, *Culte des saints*, 79–80. Also arguing for a bishop of Arles are Harries, *Sidonius Apollinaris*, 51, and Weiss, "Statut du prédicateur," 43. The extensive use of the third person in the sermon, however, may suggest some subsequent distancing.

27. Rivet, *Histoire littéraire de la France*, 2:606.

28. Kasper, *Theologie und Askese*, 377–78.

29. Glorie, *Eusebius "Gallicanus,"* ix.

30. Glorie, *Eusebius "Gallicanus,"* viii–xvii, xxi, 949.

31. Glorie, *Eusebius "Gallicanus,"* xii. The stylistic disunity of the collection is also emphasised by Bruzzone, "Similitudine, metafore e contesto sociale," 125.

32. Stancliffe, "Thirteen Sermons," 119; Leeming, "False Decretals," 134–35; Weiss, "Statut du prédicateur," 43–44.

33. Morin, "Collection gallicane," 102, 113–14; Leroy, "Oeuvre oratoire," 1:293–96; Griffe, "Sermons de Fauste de Riez," 32.

34. In addition to comments in the following chapters, see Stancliffe, "Thirteen Sermons," 133–38.

35. See Morin, "Collection gallicane."

36. Bergmann, *Studien zu einer kritischen Sichtung*, 1, 3–4, 72–78.

37. Kasper, *Theologie und Askese*, 377.

38. Weiss, "Statut du prédicateur," 43–44; Weigel, *Faustus of Riez,* 161–63.

39. Morin, "Collection gallicane," 92; Souter, "Observations on the Pseudo-Eusebian Collection," 47; Stancliffe, "Thirteen Sermons," 118; Weiss, "Statut du prédicateur," 43–44.

40. Morin, "Collection gallicane," 94, 107; Stancliffe, "Thirteen Sermons," 118–19; Glorie, *Eusebius "Gallicanus,"* viii, ix, xiii, xix.

41. The archives of the church at Hippo operated in a similar fashion and contributed to the incorporation of inauthentic sermons into the corpus of Augustine's work at an early stage. See Hamman, "Transmission des sermons," 312–13.

42. On the practice of circulating works at the time, see Mathisen, "Letters of Ruricius of Limoges," 101–15, and "Epistolography," 95–109; Vessey, "*Epistula Rusticii ad Eucherium,*" 278–97.

43. Eucherius of Lyon had set up a monastery on the neighbouring island, but joined the group at Lérins by 420. Hilary of Arles, Maximus of Riez, and Faustus, his successor as bishop, were all graduates of the monastery. Patiens is also known to have been connected to Faustus and other Lérinian alumni. On the ties within the Lérinian circle, see Mathisen, *Ecclesiastical Factionalism* and Harries, *Sidonius Apollinaris,* 40–43.

44. On episcopal libraries in late antiquity see Vessey, "*Epistula Rusticii ad Eucherium.*"

45. Women copied texts in monastic *scriptoria,* but if these texts were compiled from an episcopal archive, the collector was probably a cleric. On female scribes, see McKitterick, "Nuns' Scriptoria," 1–35.

46. *Eusebius Gallicanus* 67–71. On these see Weiss, "Statut du prédicateur," 44–45.

47. Bruzzone also sees the Eusebius Gallicanus primarily as a preaching "handbook" or anthology. "Similitudine, metafore e contesto sociale," 126.

48. *Vita Caesarii* 1.55; Morin, "Homilies of St. Caesarius," 481–86; Klingshirn, *Caesarius of Arles,* 10–11; Amos, "Origin and Nature," 31–37.

49. Caesarius of Arles, *Sermones* 1.15, 2.

50. Dolbeau, "*Serminator uerborum,*" 82–84.

Chapter 3. Building Community

1. "[Christianity] was not in its origins a 'community' religion, whose boundaries coincided with the boundaries of the local community and

whose practices conformed to local traditions, attitudes, and expectations. It was rather an 'organized' religion, whose self-defined hierarchy, strict criteria of inclusion and exclusion, and highly regulated code of conduct and belief had all been devised by outside religious specialists and were in many ways ill-suited to the demands of local communities." Klingshirn, *Caesarius of Arles*, 1–2.

2. Important works on Christian communities in Gaul include Van Dam, *Leadership and Community* and *Saints and their Miracles;* Beaujard, *Culte des saints,* "Cités, évêques et martyrs," and "Évêque dans la cité"; Klingshirn, *Caesarius of Arles;* Markus, "From Caesarius to Boniface"; Brown, *Rise of Western Christendom,* 145–65; Heinzelmann, *Bischofherrschaft in Gallien;* Hen, *Culture and Religion;* Prinz, *Frühes Mönchtum;* and various articles in Rebillard and Sotinel, eds., *Évêque dans la cité.*

3. See discussion in chapter 6 and Bailey, "Monks and Lay Communities."

4. 1 Corinthians 12.12–27.

5. In the sixth century Gregory the Great would make this the cornerstone of his view of ministry. The clergy were like the eyes, he argued, who guided the feet, and he wrote of the responsibility of a pastor to "condescend" to the level of his congregants—to bend down from his position of superiority to reach into their world. *Moralia in Iob* 19.15.45; *Regula pastoralis* 2.7; Markus, *Gregory the Great,* 27. On the ancient background of the metaphor, and Paul's use of it, see Mitchell, *Paul and the Rhetoric of Reconciliation,* 157–61.

6. Mitchell, *Paul and the Rhetoric of Reconciliation,* 300; Burke, "Paul's Role as Father."

7. On Stoic ideas of community, see Schofield, *Stoic Idea of the City,* 72; Colish, *Stoic Tradition,* 1:37–38. Colish discusses the influence of Stoicism on both Cassian and Faustus of Riez, *Stoic Tradition,* 2:114–15, 128–29. The fantasy that Seneca corresponded with Paul reflects the close connections between their ideas.

8. On the ideal of Christian consensus, see Oehler, "Consensus omnium," 103–29; Gaudemet, "Unanimité et majorité"; Hannig, *Consensus fidelium;* Stocking, *Bishops, Councils and Consensus.*

9. It appears this way, for example, in the work of Vincent of Lérins, *Commonitoria* 2–4, and was one of the weapons used against the Donatists. Gaddis, *There Is No Crime,* 7, 21. Stocking emphasises its coercive potential. *Bishops, Councils and Consensus,* 12, 24.

10. On this process, see Lim, "Christian Triumph and Controversy."

11. On the community-building strategies in these sermons, see also Bailey, "Building Urban Christian Communities."

12. A sermon by Hilary of Arles on Genesius (not the one in our collection) gives us some of this context, discussing a miraculous rescue which happened in the course of a procession between the saints' holy sites on his feast day. Hilary of Arles, *Sermo seu narratio de miraculo s. Genesii martyris Arelatensis*. The same event is described in Gregory of Tours, *GM* 68. On the celebrations in general, see Brown, "Enjoying the Saints."

13. The works of Gregory of Tours are filled, for example, with miracles taking place in the course of saints' day celebrations. *GM* 35, 57, 85, 89, 90; *GC* 5, 20, 28, 94, 97. Note also the sermons by Augustine of Hippo in which he comments on a miracle which took place in church while he was preaching about St. Stephen. *Sermo* 323.

14. Bell, *Ritual Theory*, 210.

15. The collection also contains sermons on saints common to the Church as a whole, but these display none of the community-building strategies discussed here. See Bailey, "Building Urban Christian Communities," 15–16.

16. On the authorship of these and the other sermons on local saints, see chapter 2. The intense parochialism of these sermons is another argument against Faustus of Riez as their author.

17. Gregory of Tours records that their bodies were to be found in the crypt of the basilica of St John in Lyon, along with that of Irenaeus. *GM* 49. For a summary of the evidence see Amore, "Epipodio e Alessandro."

18. "Et ideo, indigenarum martyrum cultus, et honor specialium patronorum: sicut peculiare dat gaudium, ita proprium requirit affectum." *Eusebius Gallicanus* 55.1, ed. Glorie, 639.

19. "ut, sicut eorum per unius parentis gremium iure nascendi cognati sumus, ita nobis erga eos pietatis et gratiae priuilegium uindicemus, atque ad eos fidei deuotione prius accedamus, ut: quorum esse ciues gratulamur in terris, cum his *municipatum* habere mereamur *in caelis*." *Eusebius Gallicanus* 55.2, ed. Glorie, 639. Philippians 3.20.

20. "Nonne nobis ad cor nostrum clamat, cognati uiua uox sanguinis?" *Eusebius Gallicanus* 55.6, ed. Glorie, 640.

21. "*Quae cum ita sint*, carissimi, ad tenendam fidem, ad excolendam religionem: non nobis aliqua de longinquo sunt exspectanda documenta; paternis instruimur magisteriis, ac domesticis admonemur exemplis."

Eusebius Gallicanus 55.6, ed. Glorie, 640. The phrase is Ciceronian, but the author may have taken it from Augustine, where it is frequently used. See Glorie, 640. Compare the similar sentiment in Maximus of Turin, *Sermo* 12.2, discussed in Chaffin, "Civic Values in Maximus of Turin."

22. "Duplicia itaque Ephypodii et Alexandri tropaea ecclesiae nostrae fides . . . concelebrat, non aduenticiis festa reliquiis, sed intemeratis patrii sinus festa monumentis." *Eusebius Gallicanus* 55.3, ed. Glorie, 639.

23. "quod uniuerso mundo possit sufficere, intra gremium ciuitatis huius peculiariter conclusum tenemus; et geminas palmas triumphi aemulas apostolicae urbi attolimus, atque, habentes et nos Petrum Paulumque nostrum, cum sublimi illa sede binos suffragatores certamus." *Eusebius Gallicanus* 55.4, ed. Glorie, 639–40.

24. On the significance of the use of such language, see Beaujard, *Culte des saints*, 333.

25. Blandina and her cohorts were far more prominent figures than were Epipodius and Alexander, and by the fifth century they enjoyed an established cult in Lyon. Reynaud, "Premiers édifices," 279–87.

26. "te coronauit innocentia morientium, me gloria triumphantium; tui in praemium regni sine conscientia peruenere martyrii, mei autem cruciatibus afflicti, suppliciis explorati, saeuis ignibus sacrificii more decocti." *Eusebius Gallicanus* 11.3, ed. Glorie, 132; Matthew 2.6. On the personification of and address to cities in the rhetorical tradition see Kennedy, *Art of Rhetoric*, 561–65, 582–85; Rees, *Layers of Loyalty*, 176–77; Cameron, *Claudian*, 105–77, 352–55, 365–66.

27. "Exsultant urbium populi, etsi unius saltem martyris reliquiis muniantur; ecce nos populos martyrum possidemus. Gaudeat terra nostra nutricia caelestium militum et tantarum parens fecunda uirtutum." *Eusebius Gallicanus* 11.2, ed. Glorie, 131.

28. *Eusebius Gallicanus* 11.6.

29. Gadille, ed., *Diocèse de Lyon*, 11–18.

30. Gadille, ed., *Diocèse de Lyon*, 5, 11, 19; Harries, *Sidonius Apollinaris*, 37–38, 46; Reynaud, "Premiers édifices," 282; Harries, "Christianity and the City," 88. Coville emphasises, however, that Christianity was very firmly established in Lyon by the fifth century. *Recherches sur l'histoire de Lyon*, 437.

31. Benoît, "Arles," 16–18; Février, "Arles aux IVe et Ve siècles," 149–51; Loseby, "Arles in Late Antiquity," 46.

32. Février, "Arles aux IVe et Ve siècles," 149; Loseby, "Arles in Late Antiquity," 46; Klingshirn, *Caesarius of Arles*, 51–57, 65–69.

33. On Caesarius' career in Arles see Klingshirn, *Caesarius of Arles*; Arnold, *Caesarius von Arelate*.

34. For the diffusion of the cult of Genesius see Prete, "Genesio di Arles." Gregory of Tours records the veneration of the relics of Genesius in Embrun and Clermont, as well as describing his cult in Arles. See *GM* 46, 66, 67 and 68. The sermon survives only in a ninth-century manuscript of the collection, F[1], but already existed to be adapted into a *passio* in the sixth century. Cavallin, "Saint Genès le notaire," 170–73. On the *passio*, see also Cavalieri, "S. Genesio di Arelate," 203–29.

35. Benoît, "Arles," 19; Février, "Arles aux IVe et Ve siècles," 135; Pietri, "Culte des saints," 357–58.

36. Pietri, "Culte des saints," 357–58.

37. Hubert, "Topographie religieuse," 17; *Topographie chrétienne* 3: 83–84.

38. *Eusebius Gallicanus* 56.6.

39. The passage as a whole reads: "Iustius ergo isti celebrantur natales: quibus sancti ex corruptibili luce in nouam illam futuri saeculi ueniunt claritatem, et filii hominum *in adoptionem* diuinae paternitatis ascendunt, et consortes paulo ante mortalium subito *ciues* incipiunt esse *angelorum.*" *Eusebius Gallicanus* 56.2, ed. Glorie, 651. Ephesians 1.5, 2.19.

40. "Sub ipsa itaque felicissimae ciuitatis moenia, fidelium humeris funus inclyti uictoris infertur . . . Fideles itaque populi, peculiarius exsultantes de perpetui propugnatoris auxilio." *Eusebius Gallicanus* 56.6–7, ed. Glorie, 653.

41. Weiss, "Statut du prédicateur," 42; Leroy, "Oeuvre oratoire," 1:303.

42. Février, "Riez," 39; *Topographie chrétienne*, 2:39.

43. Février, "Riez," 40; *Topographie chrétienne*, 2:38.

44. "quae territorii ac finium suorum incolam uelut proprium amplectebatur indigenam." *Eusebius Gallicanus* 35.8, ed. Glorie, 407.

45. Maximus was born in Châteaux-Redon, just north of Riez. Garrigues, "Massimo di Riez." The "flight" of the saint in the face of threatened episcopal election is a standard hagiographic *topos*. For other examples, see *Vita Caesarii* 1.14 and *Vita Ambrosii* 8.

46. "Quocumque latitas, incassum te patriae per fugam denegas." *Eusebius Gallicanus* 35.9, ed. Glorie, 408.

47. *Eusebius Gallicanus* 35.9.

48. *Eusebius Gallicanus* 35.5.

49. See Heinzelmann, "'Affair' of Hilary of Arles," 239–51, and Weiss, "Statut du prédicateur," 30. Such tensions continued into the sixth century, as Gregory, a native of Clermont, found when he became bishop of Tours. Loseby, "Gregory's Cities," 242, and Van Dam, *Leadership and Community*, 213. The dispute also illustrates the shrinking conception of "foreignness" in fifth century Gaul—see Beaujard, "Pèlerinages vus par Grégoire de Tours," 263–70.

50. Faustus was probably born in Britain. Viard, "Fauste de Riez."

51. See Heinzelmann, "Pater populi," 47–56; Stevenson, "Ideal Benefactor," 421–36; Burke, "Paul's Role as Father"; Mitchell, *Paul and the Rhetoric of Reconciliation*, 300; Hellerman, *Ancient Church as Family*; Penn, *Kissing Christians*, 30–31.

52. Hellerman, *Ancient Church as Family*, 93, 99; Burke, "Paul's Role as Father," 96.

53. Heinzelmann, "Pater populi," 47; Burke, "Paul's Role as Father," 113.

54. Hellerman, *Ancient Church as Family*, 12, 220; Burke, "Paul's Role as Father," 108.

55. "Omnes enim nos *fratres sumus*, ex uno auctore progeniti, et ex eadem massa generati ex primo homine, ex Christo et ecclesia duplici uinculo adstricti, naturae et gratiae iure copulati, in unam fidem uocati, uno pretio restituti. *Fratres*, inquam, *sumus* . . . et, si meruerimus, etiam in angelorum fraternitatem unius patris hereditate sociandi . . . *Fratres* uterini *sumus* per unius fontis lauacrum, consanguinei sumus per unum salutare commercium." *Eusebius Gallicanus* 54.1–2, ed. Glorie, 629–30. The preacher specified that the scriptural passage did not solely refer to monastic or blood brotherhood: "Non hic specialiter de nexu fratrum aut de copula germanorum, sed generaliter de nobis omnibus loquitur." *Eusebius Gallicanus* 54.1, ed. Glorie, 629.

56. "continuo imbecillam suscipiunt fortiores et quasi sedulam ac mutuam ad inuicem curam etiam peregrinatio docet." *Eusebius Gallicanus* 50.3, ed. Glorie, 584.

57. *Eusebius Gallicanus* 50.3.

58. Augustine, *Enarrationes in Psalmos* 41.4; Pliny, *Naturalis historia* 8.114.

59. Augustine, *Enarrationes in Psalmos* 41.4–5.

60. "Ac sic inuicem laboribus suis animalia bruta famulantur, et reddunt sibi mutuam seruitutem: quae nesciunt caritatem. Quid nos facere debemus: quibus auctor rationis contulit intellectum, quibus redemptor

praebuit dilectionis *exemplum?*" *Eusebius Gallicanus* 50.3–4, ed. Glorie, 585. John 13.15.

61. "*In humilitate alter alterum superiorem existimantes, non quae sua sunt singuli considerantes, sed quae aliorum.*" *Eusebius Gallicanus* 50.4, ed. Glorie, 585. Philippians 2.3–4.

62. "id est: mutuis necessitatibus in alterutrum consulentes." *Eusebius Gallicanus* 50.4, ed. Glorie, 585.

63. "ne, sicut arundines quae *omni uento circumferuntur* et inuicem se leui implusione collidunt: ita nos animorum mobilitate in proximorum feramur iniurias et sit in nobis infirmitas ad adiuuandum et facilitas ad laedendum. Sed magis, utilitates mutuas cogitantes: *alter alterius* commodis studeamus et inuicem labores et *onera* nostra *portemus.*" *Eusebius Gallicanus* 50.2, ed. Glorie, 583–84. Ephesians 4.14, Galatians 6.2.

64. On the use of sibling terminology in Christianity, see Hellerman, *Ancient Church as Family,* 12, 220.

65. *Eusebius Gallicanus* 53.5–8. Luke 18.10–14. See also *Eusebius Gallicanus* 64.10.

66. See, for example, *Eusebius Gallicanus* 2.2, 4.6, 60.7.

67. The passage as a whole reads: "Sed forsitan dicas: 'Quid me ita constringis, quasi solus acceperim? quid me, in publico munere, priuata lege obligas? In munere utique, quod omnibus deus in commune largitus est, unumquemque specialiter non constringet ad debitum generale beneficium!' Non ita est; nec ideo unus minus debet: si et alius idem debeat." *Eusebius Gallicanus* 53.13, ed. Glorie, 622.

68. "Sed forte aliquis sibi dicat: 'Debeo curare de corpore meo; debeo sollicitus esse de uictu meo.' Numquid homo, dilectissimi, *ad imaginem dei* factus, illam primam curam debet putare, quam sibi uidet communem esse cum pecude?" *Eusebius Gallicanus* 48.3, ed. Glorie, 567.

69. Nathan, "Rogation Ceremonies," 275–303.

70. Sidonius Apollinaris, *Epistula* 7.1, and Avitus of Vienne, *Homilia* 5.

71. "Exoraturi enim sumus ut dominus infirmitatibus, plagis, tribulationibus interdicat: malum pestilentiae, hostilitatis, grandinis, siccitatis, repellat; caeli temperiem pro salute corporum, pro terrarum fecunditate, componat; elementorum pacem cum temporum tranquillitate concedat; peccata dimittat, flagella submoueat." *Eusebius Gallicanus* 25.1, ed. Glorie, 295.

72. "'Quid nobis profuit ante laborasse et uires cordis nostri in gemitus et lacrimas profudisse?' . . . 'Quid nobis profuit orasse et tota spiritus contritione laborasse?'" *Eusebius Gallicanus* 25.2, ed. Glorie, 295.

73. "Inter haec autem ille se ab oblatione communi reddat alienum, qui se his periculis non sentit obnoxium." *Eusebius Gallicanus* 25.2, ed. Glorie, 295.

74. Gregory the Great's *Regula pastoralis* is the prime example of such an approach. See Banniard, *Viva voce*, 41–44, 76.

75. See, for example, Augustine of Hippo, *Sermones* 47.6, 80.8, 88.19, 223.2; Caesarius of Arles, *Sermones* 25.1–2, 30.1, 42, 43, 44.2, 50.3, 52.4–5, 78.4, 118.3, 156.5, 228.6.

76. *Eusebius Gallicanus* 30.6.

77. *Eusebius Gallicanus* 51.6.

78. "Vobis enim, iste *athleta Christi*, in illo agone sudauit . . . sibi illic serens, uobis colligebat; sibi quaerens, uobis nescius acquirebat: sibi paraturus *pecuniam*, uobis soluturus *usuram*." *Eusebius Gallicanus* 35.4, ed. Glorie, 403.

79. "Vir ille praecipuus illic doctus, ut hic doceret; illic ditatus, ut hic feneraret; illic illuminatus, ut hic refulgeret; illic purificatus, ut hic sanctificaret; et, ut hic exercere posset confectionem *curationum*, illuc quaesiuit aromata et pigmenta *uirtutum*." *Eusebius Gallicanus* 35.5, ed. Glorie, 404. 1 Corinthians 12.9–10.

80. "Ditate, dixi: quia quot<idem> fructus uestri, illius thesauri sunt; et, cum iuxta apostolum: *Parentes filiis thesaurizant*, nunc patrem filii locupletent. Et cum illius uita, uestra sit gloria: mutuo commerci<o> uestra salus, illius sit corona; ut, qui[a] a domino donatus est desideriis uestris, commendetur domino meritis uestris." *Eusebius Gallicanus* 65.3, ed. Glorie, 742. 2 Corinthians 12.14.

81. "subeunte<s> tanti honoris sarcinam: subleuate per oboedientiam, quem meruistis sublimare per gratiam." *Eusebius Gallicanus* 65.3, ed. Glorie, 742.

82. "Erudientis sedulitas, obtemperantis utilitas est; studium exhortantis, lucris militat audientis, quinimmo et lucrum exhortantis operatur." *Eusebius Gallicanus* 61.1, ed. Glorie, 697.

83. "Agnosce operis tui meritum etiam per meae exsultationis affectum; intellege quantum tu gratulaberis de munere acquisitae salutis, si ego tantum gratulor de mercede sermonis." *Eusebius Gallicanus* 61.2, ed. Glorie, 697.

84. "unam fuisse in tot uocibus uocem, unamque in tot pectoribus uoluntatem; et, quod, apud sacra primordia nascentis ecclesiae, apostolica uerba concelebrant: *Erat illis,* inquit, *cor et anima una* . . . hoc, insinuante Christo, sub una uidemus impletum tantorum conspiratione populorum.

Gratulamur ergo domino: in innumeras multitudines, clamoribus atque animis discrepantes, per unius uiri magnificam eminentemque personam, unius consessus transisse concordiam." *Eusebius Gallicanus* 65.1–2, ed. Glorie, 741. Acts 4.32.

85. *Eusebius Gallicanus* 61.1.

86. "nemo ergo aestimet quod sacerdoti praestet, si oboediat sacerdoti." *Eusebius Gallicanus* 61.1, ed. Glorie, 697.

87. For instances when paternal imagery is used to describe other pastors, see *Eusebius Gallicanus* 35, 72.

88. "Ideo enim illum huic terrae nostrae, huic regioni, dominus dedit: ut omnem uitae nostrae actum, ad illius informemus exemplum; et animarum nostrarum facies, ad eum respicientes tamquam ad speculum, componamus; et, quasi boni filii, similitudinem patris excolamus in nobis." *Eusebius Gallicanus* 51.10, ed. Glorie, 601.

89. *Eusebius Gallicanus* 51.10.

90. *Eusebius Gallicanus* 51.10. Note that this image of the holy man as a painter's model was also used by Basil of Caesarea, *Epistula* 2.3.

91. "Secundum haec ergo: animarum nostrarum uultibus, illius uiri unusquisque uirtutis tamquam pretiosos superducamus colores. Rapiat sibi de eo alter gratam speciem compunctionis, alter pigmentum candidissimum nitidae castitatis, pallorem ille abstinentiae, ruborem iste uerecundiae." *Eusebius Gallicanus* 51.10, ed. Glorie, 602.

92. *Eusebius Gallicanus* 51.10.

93. "Rapiat unusquisque quod possumus de bonis intestati parentis: hic de hereditate eius assumat holosericam, gestorum uarietate pretiosissimam; hic mansuetudinis ac simplicitatis occupet talentum; ille decus pectoris beneuolentiae ac sapientiae monile sibi uindicet; hic margaritum compunctionis et thesaurum castitatis inuadat . . . Ita ergo agamus, bona illius consectantes: ut, qui in aeternam gloriam suscitandus est sub fine saeculorum, redditus ecclesiae suae per rediuiua in filiis merita iam resurgat." *Eusebius Gallicanus* 35.14, ed. Glorie, 412.

94. "per quae et ad uiam salutis possint uenire qui cupiunt, et excusationem non possint inuenire qui neglegunt." *Eusebius Gallicanus* 35.5, ed. Glorie, 404.

95. "omnes in nobis habere possumus *claues regni caelorum*." *Eusebius Gallicanus* 33.4, ed. Glorie, 379. Matthew 16.19.

96. "caritas prona sit ad misericordiam, non insultans peccantibus sed condolens—facilis enim est lapsus ad uitia; et fragilitas conditionis humanae." *Eusebius Gallicanus* 21.5, ed. Glorie, 251.

97. "Nescio autem, carissimi, cur nobis uitiorum ac superbiae *itinera aspera* et confragosa magis placeant, cum magis humilium *uiae* molles, *planae atque directae* sint. Vbi est enim humilitas, ibi quies, ibi tranquillitas, ibi omnis serenitas . . . At uero e contrario uiae superborum plenae sunt offendiculis, plenae praeruptissimis praecipitiis; quia: ubi est superbia, ibi est indignitas, ibi animositas, ibi labor, ibi tribulatio." *Eusebius Gallicanus* 4.5, ed. Glorie, 49–50. Isaiah 40.4, Luke 3.5. Compare Valerian of Cimiez, *Homiliae* 2 and 3, which emphasise the narrowness and difficulty of the path to heaven.

98. *Eusebius Gallicanus* 4.5.

99. See, for example, Caesarius of Arles, *Sermones* 1.4–5, 1.16, 1.19, 4.4, 5.5, 8.5, 13.5, 19.5, 78.5, 231.2, and discussion of this model of authority in Klingshirn, *Caesarius of Arles,* 158.

100. Caesarius of Arles, *Sermo* 1.19.

101. "Si enim bono et sollicito corde consideramus grave periculum et infinitum pondus imminere cervicibus omnium sacerdotum . . ." Caesarius of Arles, *Sermo* 1.3, ed. Morin, 2, trans. Mueller, 31:4. See also *Sermones* 4.2, 5.5, 183.1.

102. "animarum illorum sanguis de nostris manibus requiratur," Caesarius of Arles, *Sermo* 4.2, ed. Morin, 23, trans. Mueller, 31:30. See also *Sermones* 1.15, 5.1, 43.9, 44.8, 46.8.

103. Caesarius of Arles, *Sermo* 1.19.

104. Caesarius of Arles, *Sermo* 5.1.

105. "Volentibus audire verbum dei offerendum est, fastidientibus ingerendum," Caesarius of Arles, *Sermo* 4.2, ed. Morin, 23, trans. Mueller, 31:29–30.

106. Caesarius of Arles, *Sermo* 4.2. Caesarius is drawing on a line of argument developed by Augustine—see in particular Augustine of Hippo, *Sermo* 46.14.

107. The passage reads in full: "Beatus tamen Iohannes plena et perfecta libertate maluit iniusta sustinere, quam iusta non dicere." Caesarius of Arles, *Sermo* 217.3, ed. Morin, 863, trans. Mueller, 66:123. Caesarius used this to comment on confrontational and non-confrontational styles of preaching, noting that he preferred the former, like the Baptist. His attraction to this model of "prophetic" leadership is clear in other sermons, where he reiterates that preachers should "Cry, cease not, lift up thy voice like a trumpet and show my people their sins." (Isaiah 58.1) *Sermones* 1.3, 4.2, 5.1, 57.1, 80.2, 115.4, 183.1, 230.3, and discussion in Klingshirn, *Caesarius of Arles,* 147.

108. *Eusebius Gallicanus* 30.6.

109. "Itaque, etiam quando pastor absentat: praesens sit futuri iudicii timor, praesens sit mordacissima aeternarum necessitatum sollicitudo; atque, etiamsi deest qui perurgere possit ad implenda quotidianae redemptionis officia, perurgeat se homo ipse qui solus *stabit ante tribunal* dei *cum actibus suis*." *Eusebius Gallicanus* 63.6, ed. Glorie, 718. Romans 14.10, Colossians 3.9.

110. *Eusebius Gallicanus* 63.6.

111. *Eusebius Gallicanus* 63.8.

112. See, for example, Caesarius of Arles, *Sermones* 42–47 and 50–55. For scholarly discussions of these sermons see Hen, *Culture and Religion*; Flint, *Rise of Magic;* Harmening, *Superstitio*; Klingshirn, *Caesarius of Arles*; Manselli, "Resistenze dei culti antichi," 1:57–108; Markus, "From Caesarius to Boniface"; Milleman, "Caesarius von Arles"; Bailey, "These Are Not Men."

113. Caesarius of Arles, *Sermones* 42.2, 43.5, 47.6, 225.4–5. He was here building on Paul's comments in 1 Corinthians 5.

114. Caesarius of Arles, *Sermo* 53.2.

115. Caesarius of Arles, *Sermo* 225.4.

116. *Eusebius Gallicanus* 59.

117. Adultery is mentioned in *Eusebius Gallicanus* 6.6 and 19.6.

118. *Eusebius Gallicanus* 19.3.

119. Caesarius of Arles, *Sermones* 42.2–5, 43.3–5, 44.4–6.

120. Caesarius of Arles, *Sermones* 13.4–5, 44.2, 46.1, 46.8, 47.4–5, 50.1, 52.5–6, 53.1, 54.1, 54.6, 55.2.

121. See, for example, *Vita Eugendii* 141–44; Gregory of Tours, *LH* 4.16, 5.14; Council of Auxerre, a. 561/605, c. 3 and c. 4. See also the discussion in Flint, *Rise of Magic*, 74–76.

122. *Vita Caesarii* 1.21, 1.27, 1.29–31, and 1.36.

123. *Vita Caesarii* 1.21, 1.29–31, and 1.36.

124. Caesarius of Arles, *Sermones* 42.6, 43.9.

Chapter 4. Explaining the Faith

1. Van Dam, *Becoming Christian,* 3–4.

2. See detailed discussions in chapters 1 and 2. Note, also, that the Eusebius Gallicanus sermons were most likely addressed to audiences located in or near urban centres, and not to the "peasants" to whom Van Dam refers.

3. See, for example, Auerbach, *Literary Language,* esp. 25–66; Brown, *Power and Persuasion;* Cameron, *Christianity and the Rhetoric of Empire;* Kaster, *Guardians of Language,* esp. 70–95; Marrou, *Histoire de l'éducation,* 416–34; Riché, *Education and Culture;* Rousseau, *Early Christian Centuries,* 124–52.

4. For examples of these constructions see Matthew 11.25, Luke 10.21, Acts 4.13, Romans 1.18–20; 1 Corinthians 1.18–28 and 3.18. See also the discussion in Auerbach, *Literary Language,* 43–53.

5. Kelly, *Early Christian Doctrines,* 37.

6. One thinks especially of Gnosticism and Manichaeism, but the more immediate examples for fifth-century Gaul would have been Donatism, Pelagianism and perhaps Priscillianism. Moreover, this was not an issue confined to heretical sects. Ascetics also came under suspicion because of their calls for purity and seeming exclusivity. On the late antique debates over asceticism, see Hunter, "Rereading the Jovinianist Controversy," 454–70; Markus, *End of Ancient Christianity,* 38–40.

7. Cameron, *Christianity and the Rhetoric of Empire,* 8.

8. The New Testament epistles are filled with anxiety about "false teaching" and misinterpretation. See, for example, 1 Corinthians 1.10–17; 2 Corinthians 11.3–6; Galatians 1.6–9; Colossians 2.8 and 2.16–23; 1 Timothy 1.3–7, 4.1–16, and 6.3–5; 2 Peter 2.1–9; 1 John 2.18–29.

9. Brown, *Rise of Western Christendom,* 450.

10. Bloch, "Symbols, Song, Dance," 71.

11. Bloch, "Symbols, Song, Dance," 63–64, 66, 68.

12. On the power of this impoverishment see Bloch, "Symbols, Song, Dance," 60–63.

13. Bloch identifies this as a limit on formalisation. "Symbols, Song, Dance," 65.

14. See the discussion of Edelman's arguments and their relation to Roman history in Morstein-Marx, *Mass Oratory,* 241.

15. Such preaching, as Morstein-Marx noted of Roman public oratory, "quietly foreclosed the development of a more active, assertive form of deliberative participation." *Mass Oratory,* 33.

16. See discussion in chapter 3.

17. I owe this concept to Professor John Bishop in the philosophy department at the University of Auckland.

18. C. S. Lewis develops this idea in a modern context in "On Obstinacy in Belief."

19. See, for example, Augustine of Hippo, *Sermones* 43, 126.1–3, *Sermo* Dolbeau 25.15–16.

20. Cameron, *Christianity and the Rhetoric of Empire,* 155ff. The phrase is also used by Brown, *Power and Persuasion,* 74.

21. Cameron, *Christianity and the Rhetoric of Empire,* 159.

22. Kierkegaard, *Concluding Unscientific Postscript,* 177–82.

23. Augustine of Hippo, *Sermo* 117.5, 16–17. He is here evoking 1 Corinthians 3.2.

24. Peter Chrysologus, *Sermo* 61.

25. "Quomodo sane deus Pater genuerit Filium, nolo discutias. Credendus est ergo deus esse Pater unici Filii sui domini nostri, non discutiendus: neque enim fas est servo de natalibus domini disputare . . . Pater ipsum esse dicit Filium suum, et ipsum audire iubet: quis est qui neget esse verum, quod Veritas dicit?" Caesarius of Arles, *Sermo* 9, ed. Morin, 48.

26. "Vides quas sibi tenebras infidelitas facit: non vis scire quod deus noluit ignorari, et vis scire quod deus non iussit inquiri . . . Utrum genitus, an ingenitus sit, requiris. Nihil ex hoc eloquia sacra cecinerunt: nefas est inrumpere divina silentia. Quod deus in scripturis suis indicandum esse non credidit, interrogare vel scire superflua curiositate te noluit." Caesarius of Arles, *Sermo* 213.1–2, ed. Morin, 848.

27. The creed presented in sermon nine is as follows: *Credo in deum patrem omnipotentem et in filium eius Iesum Christum qui conceptus est de spiritu sancto, natus ex Maria uirgine, mortuus est et resurrexit, ascendit ad caelos, sedet ad dexteram dei patris omnipotentis, inde uenturus est iudicare uiuos et mortuos. Credo in sanctum spiritum, credo sanctam ecclesiam catholicam, peccatorum remissionem.* The creed presented in sermon ten is: *Credo in deum. Credo et in filium eius unicum, dominum nostrum Iesum Christum qui conceptus est de spiritu sancto, natus ex Maria uirgine, crucifixus est et sepultus, tertia die resurrexit, ascendit ad caelos, sedet ad dexteram dei patris omnipotentis, inde uenturus iudicare uiuos et mortuos. Credo in spiritum sanctum, sanctam ecclesiam catholicam, sanctorum communionem, abremissa peccatorum, credo carnis resurrectionem, (uitam aeternam).* See Glorie, *Eusebius "Gallicanus,"* 898–99. The form of these creeds is derived from the Old Roman Creed and is related to those laid out by Caesarius of Arles and by Cyprian of Toulon. See Kelly, *Early Christian Creeds,* 178–81; Morin, "Symbole de saint Césaire d'Arles," 178–89.

28. Kelly, *Early Christian Creeds,* 49–52; Beck, *Pastoral Care,* 173–77.

29. Augustine of Hippo, *Sermo* 214.12. The passage reads: "Quod ideo Symbolum dicitur, quia ibi nostrae societatis fides placita continetur, et ejus confessione tamquam signo dato christianus fidelis agnoscitur." *PL* 38:1072.

30. Caesarius of Arles, *Sermo* 10.1.

31. The passage as a whole reads: "Satis agite, carissimi, nouella adoptio diuinitatis: ut hos, quam paucos, tam pretiosos sub illuminato corpore sermones, imis animae uisceribus imprimatis; ut hunc spei uestrae aeternum thesaurum, in omni loco, in omni tempore fides credat, spes augeat, memoria retineat, uita custodiat." *Eusebius Gallicanus* 10.14, ed. Glorie, 126.

32. "quod facile possit implere nuda paupertas, despecta mediocritas, indocta simplicitas." *Eusebius Gallicanus* 10.2, ed. Glorie, 114.

33. "uerba breuia et certa, expedita sententiis sed diffusa mysteriis . . . angusta sermonibus sed diuersa sensibus." *Eusebius Gallicanus* 9.1, ed. Glorie, 97.

34. "de utroque testamento totius corporis uirtus in paucas est diffusa sententias, ut facilius animae thesaurus non in arca sed in memoria portaretur." *Eusebius Gallicanus* 9.1, ed. Glorie, 97–98. Here, and elsewhere, the author(s) of these sermons may have been drawing on Cassian. He too describes the creed as a brief compendium of Christian wisdom, which any Christian, no matter how "simplex et imperita," can grasp with the mind and hold easily in memory. *De incarnatione* 6.3. See also Rufinus of Aquileia, *Expositio symboli* 2, and Augustine of Hippo, *Sermo* 213.1: "Symbolum est breviter complexa regula fidei, ut mentem instruat, nec oneret memoriam; paucis verbis dicitur, unde multum acquiratur." *PL* 38:1060.

35. "Ita et ecclesiarum magistri, studiosissimi salutis nostrae negotiatores, in scripturis sanctis de magnis maxima separauerunt mentium pagina inscribenda, ut cuilibet cordi, quamlibet angusto, quamlibet rustico, sine ullius difficultatis impedimento facile possit insinuari ueritatis agnitio, ut ad parandum et tenendum caelestis sapientiae uitale carmen et salubritas inuitaret et breuitas." *Eusebius Gallicanus* 9.1, ed. Glorie, 98. For the "ecclesiarum patres," see *Eusebius Gallicanus* 9.1, ed. Glorie, 97.

36. "quando tibi aliqua dei gesta referuntu . . . non cogites nec intra te dicas: *Quomodo* aut quo ordine *hoc fieri potuit?;* diuina opera *non discutienda* sunt *sed credenda*. Non te confundat nec trepidum faciat rerum nouitas, sed sufficiat tibi omnipotentis auctoritas." *Eusebius Gallicanus* 9.3, ed. Glorie, 101. Luke 1.34.

37. "non decauseris si non subiaceat sensui tuo ordinationum caelestium magnitudo: *excedit* diuini opificii dignitas, *humanae mentis angustias*." *Eusebius Gallicanus* 9.3, ed. Glorie, 101. The phrase "angustias humanae mentis excedit" is also found in Faustus of Riez, *Epistula* 5, ed. Engelbrecht, 194–95.

38. "diuinas dispensationes quantum difficilius inuestigare te uideris, tantum reuerentius admireris." *Eusebius Gallicanus* 9.3, ed. Glorie, 102.

39. *Eusebius Gallicanus* 10.1, evoking Luke 6.49. The preacher goes on to note: "Hanc ergo nobis fidem uelut magnam lampadem Christus adueniens errantibus uiam monstraturus exhibuit, per quam possit *deus ignotus* requiri, quaesitus credi, creditus inueniri." Ed. Glorie, 113. See also Caesarius of Arles, *Sermo* 9: "Qui divina mysteria intellegendo se magis capere aestimat quam credendo, sic facit, quomodo si aliquis relicta via petat devium, vel sine fundamento construat aedificium, vel per obiectum parietem requirat ingressum." Ed. Morin, 46–47.

40. On the image of the Virgin Mary in the Eusebius Gallicanus sermons see also Triacca, "Maternità feconda."

41. The passage as a whole reads: "Sed: '*Quomodo*' inquis '*potuit* uirgo esse, post filium?' . . . Non ergo contra fidem tuam uenias, nec dicas: *Quomodo hoc fieri potuit?*" *Eusebius Gallicanus* 76.2 and 76.7, ed. Glorie, 809 and 812. The preacher is evoking Mary's own astonishment, expressed in Luke 1.34.

42. The passage as a whole reads: "Quando audis deum ex homine natum esse et maiestatem sub fragilitate latuisse, uirginem prole ditatum nec tamen uirginitatem fuisse solutam, non se obiciat sensibus tuis nouitas operis sed uirtus operantis; nec dicas: 'Illud impossibile est, illud fieri non potest.'" *Eusebius Gallicanus* 10.4, ed. Glorie, 115. See also *Eusebius Gallicanus* 9.3.

43. "Virgo concepit, miramini: virgo peperit, plus miramini: post partum, virgo permansit." Augustine of Hippo, *Sermo* 196.1, *PL* 38:1019, trans. Hill, 3.6:61.

44. The passage as a whole reads: "Concepit virgo, virgo peperit, non te conceptus turbet, partus te non confundat auditus, quando virginitas quidquid est humani pudoris excusat." Peter Chrysologus, *Sermo* 148, *PL* 52:597, trans. Ganss, 17:249.

45. See in particular the canons of the councils of Nicaea (325), Constantinople (381) and Ephesus (431).

46. Price, "Marian piety," 31–38.

47. Cameron, "Cult of the Virgin," 1–21.

48. "Obstupescit natura rerum . . . creator ex creatura sua nascitur, et fructus uteri sui mater innupta miratur, ac femina auctoris sui auctor efficitur!" *Eusebius Gallicanus* 2.3, ed. Glorie, 24.

49. "In operibus dei sollicito quamlibet homini, magis admiratio se potest offerre quam ratio." *Eusebius Gallicanus* 76.7, ed. Glorie, 812.

50. "si de factis eius dubitas, imbecillitatem omnipotentis accusas." *Eusebius Gallicanus* 10.4, ed. Glorie, 115. See also *Eusebius Gallicanus* 9.6: "Quid mirum, si non est uiolata partu, quae magis est sanctificata conceptu? aut quid incredibile, si Christus *ex uirgine,* id est integritas de integritate processit?—*Natus ex Maria uirgine:* non enim nasci decebat ex corruptione uirtus." Ed. Glorie, 104.

51. "qui te credere in *omnipotentem* prima confessione testatus es." *Eusebius Gallicanus* 76.7, ed. Glorie, 812.

52. *Eusebius Gallicanus* 2.3.

53. *Eusebius Gallicanus* 27.2–5. Elsewhere in the collection, the miracle of the virgin birth is used in turn to support the idea that it was possible for Jesus to enter through the closed doors. *Eusebius Gallicanus* 2.3, 23.2, 22.4: "Quid mirum, si dominus ad discipulos glorificatum corpus, claustris stupentibus, intromisit: qui, illaeso materni pudoris signaculo, ianuam mundi huius intrauit; cuius ortum natura nesciuit?" Ed. Glorie, 259.

54. "Quid hic rationem quaerimus? quid intellectum fatigamus humanum? . . . quid nouitatem stupemus, ubi cernimus maiestatem? Miramur dominum nostrum absque ullius uiri semine intra uirginea uiscera hominem consummasse, quem scimus caeli terraeque immensitatem *ex nihilo* condidisse." *Eusebius Gallicanus* 2.3, ed. Glorie, 25. 2. Maccabees 7.28. See also *Eusebius Gallicanus* 9.3.

55. "Mirabiliter natus. Quid mirabilius virginis partu? Concipit, et virgo est; parit, et virgo est." Augustine of Hippo, *Sermo* 189.2, *PL* 38:1005, trans. Hill, 3.6:34.

56. "Quis comprehendat novitatem novam, inusitatam, unicam in mundo, incredibilem credibilem factam, et toto mundo incredibiliter creditam: ut virgo conciperet, virgo pareret, virgo pariens permaneret? Quod humana ratio non invenit, fides capit: et ubi humana ratio deficit, fides proficit." Augustine of Hippo, *Sermo* 190.2, *PL* 38:1008, trans. Hill, 3.6:39. Note also 192.1: "Miramur virginis partum, et novum ipsum nascendi modum incredulis persuadere conamur, quod in utero non seminato germen prolis exortum est, et a complexu carnis viscera immunia filium hominis protulerunt, cujus patrem hominem non tulerunt: quod virginitatis integritas et in conceptu clausa, et in partu incorrupta permansit. Mira est ista potentia, sed plus est miranda misericordia, quod ille qui sic nasci potuit, nasci voluit." *PL* 39:1012.

57. Augustine of Hippo, *Sermo* 191.2: "Porro si fides Deum natum credit in carne, Deo non dubitat utrumque possibile; ut et corpus majoris aetatis non reserato aditu domus, intus positis praesentaret, et sponsus in-

fans de thalamo suo, hoc est utero virginali, illaesa matris virginitate procederet." *PL* 38:1010.

58. "Et quando dicimus, natus est de virgine, magna res, miraris. Deus est, noli mirari: transeat admiratio, accedat laudatio." Augustine of Hippo, *Sermo* 189.4, *MA* 1:211, trans. Hill, 3.6:36.

59. Peter Chrysologus, *Sermones* 117, 145, 146.

60. Peter Chrysologus, *Sermones* 148, 141.

61. Simonetti, *Biblical Interpretation,* 34–85.

62. Young, *Biblical Exegesis,* 299; Simonetti, *Biblical Interpretation,* 1; McGoldrick, "Liturgy: the Context of Patristic Exegesis," 31; Markus, *Signs and Meanings,* 4–9, 39. Sermons were not the only way in which the laity were exposed to scripture. In church they were surrounded by Biblical imagery and language—in the illustrations on the walls and in the readings, psalms and prayers. Sermons are, however, the only place in which scholars can see the process of interpretation for the ordinary faithful.

63. For summaries of the various early Christian disputes over the meanings of scripture, see Kelly, *Early Christian Doctrines,* 29–79. See also Clark, *Origenist Controversy* and Simonetti, *Biblical Interpretation.*

64. Augustine, *Confessiones* 6.4; Brown, *Augustine of Hippo,* 39.

65. Auerbach, *Literary Language,* 51. See also Oberhelman, *Rhetoric and Homiletics,* 117.

66. See the classic statements of Augustine, *De doctrina christiana* 2.6–9, 2.15, 3.12–13.

67. *Eusebius Gallicanus* 14.1, 15.2, 16.1.

68. *Eusebius Gallicanus* 17.2–8.

69. "Si enim bene respicimus, quodammodo in aquis ipsis similitudo baptismatis et regenerationis exponitur: dum enim aliud ex alio intra se efficitur, dum inferior creatura in speciem meliorem secreta conuersione transfunditur, mysterium secundae natiuitatis peragitur. Mutantur subito aquae, homines postmodum mutaturae." *Eusebius Gallicanus* 5.2, ed. Glorie, 58. Note that there are very similar passages in a sermon attributed by Engelbrecht to Faustus of Riez, and in one found in the collections of Caesarius. Compare: "inplentur hydriae, mutantur subito aquae homines postmodum mutaturae et, dum in melius mutantur, uelut baptismatis uim loquuntur. quodam modo in illis similitudo regenerationis exprimitur et, dum aliud ex alio efficiuntur, dum in speciem gratiorem inferior creatura transfertur, mysterium secundae natiuitatis aperitur." Faustus of Riez (?), *Sermo* 7, ed. Engelbrecht, 250. On the problems with the attribution of this and other sermons to Faustus, see chapter 6, note 108. Compare also:

"implentur hydriae, mutantur subito aquae, homines postmodum mutaturae: et dum in melius reformantur, velud baptismatis vim locuntur, quodam modo in illis similitudo regenerationis exprimitur: et dum aliut ex alio
efficiuntur, dum in speciem gratiorem inferior creatura transfertur, mysterium secundae nativitatis aperitur." Caesarius of Arles, *Sermo* 168.3, ed.
Morin, 689. My translation of the Eusebian passage is based in part on the
translation of this Caesarian passage by Mueller, 47:410.

70. *Eusebius Gallicanus* 47.1. On these linkages, see Mayeski, "Reading
the Word," 64; McGoldrick, "Liturgy: The Context of Patristic Exegesis,"
27–37.

71. For identical exegesis, see Caesarius of Arles, *Sermones* 97.1, 161.1,
167.1, 168.3; Augustine of Hippo, *Sermones* 4.9, 363.2; Maximus of Turin,
Sermones 65.1, 67.3.

72. See, for example, Caesarius of Arles, *Sermones* 82, 118, 119, 120.

73. Peter Chrysologus, *Sermones* 11, 36, 170.

74. Of Caesarius' 238 sermons, 105 focused explicitly on the interpretation of scripture. Peter Chrysologus' sermons were also primarily exegetical. As Kelly notes, Augustine "employed allegory with the greatest freedom,
delighting particularly in the mystical significance of names and numbers."
Early Christian Doctrines, 75.

75. Peter Chrysologus, *Sermones* 36, 120; Augustine of Hippo, *Sermones* 32.1, 32.6, 51.5, 54.1–2, *Sermo* Dolbeau 22.22; Caesarius of Arles,
Sermones 84.5, 85.1, 89.1, 94.3, 96.4, 100.1, 105.1–2, 113.1, 124.1,
146.1.

76. For just a few examples of problematic scriptural passages which
Caesarius and Augustine attempt to explain, but which the Eusebian preachers and compiler ignore, see Augustine of Hippo, *Sermones* 6.1–2, 12.1–2,
50, 51.7, 54.1, 63B; Caesarius of Arles, *Sermones* 88.2 or .4, 89.1, 91.1–3,
108.3, 109, 114.1, 125.2 and 127.1.

77. See, for example, Caesarius of Arles, *Sermones* 6, 7, 8, 75.3; Augustine of Hippo, *De doctrina christiana,* prologue 9. See also the discussions in
Ferreiro, "'Frequenter legere,'" 5–15; Van Uytfanghe, "Bible et l'instruction
des laïcs," 67–123.

78. Uhalde, *Expectations of Justice.* See also discussion of this material
in Bailey, "No Use Crying."

79. The literature on this topic is extensive. For samplings of recent
philosophical and theological views, see Pía Lara, ed., *Rethinking Evil;*
Howard-Synder, ed., *Evidential Argument from Evil;* Weisberger, "Argument

from Evil." For a more historical perspective, see Kremer and Latzer, eds., *Problem of Evil*.

80. "In isto enim saeculo felicitas malorum fouea est peccatorum. Solent autem hinc maueri homines, et plerumque religiosi, et qui non audent reprehendere dominum, tamen mirari apud semetipsos, quare sint mali plerumque felices; et maxime hii mouentur, qui, cum se melius uiuere nouerint, miseriis et ca<la>mitatibus aguntur. Ipsi enim uident malos in omnibus, licet terrenis et temporalibus, tamen bonis omni felicitate pollere; et suspirant in miseriis suis, et uix a reprehensione dei sua corda refrenant." Augustine of Hippo, *Sermo* 25A.1, ed. Germain Morin, "Deux nouveaux sermons retrouvés de St Augustin." *Revue bénédictine* 36 (1924): 187, trans. Hill, 3.2:88. For other examples of such anxieties reflected in sermons see Augustine of Hippo, *Sermo* Dolbeau 29.1–2; Caesarius of Arles, *Sermones* 114.1, 125.1 and 3, 127.1.

81. The more complete passage reads: "Sed inter haec fortasse, carissimi, quando boni et sancti *tanta* hic mala *patiuntur,* aliquis intra se cogitet et dicat: 'Certum est rerum dominum non respicere quae nostra sunt, neglegere humana, non curare terrena' . . . Sed inter haec aliquis secum cogitet et dicat: 'Deus potentiae, deus habitans in arce iustitiae: aut peccata si non damnat ignorat, aut fauet peccatis si damnare dissimulat.'. . . 'Cur,' inquit, 'non statim peccantem reum punit?'" *Eusebius Gallicanus* 55.8, 12–13, ed. Glorie, 641–43. Galatians 3.4.

82. Augustine of Hippo, *Sermones* 25.4–6; 32.15, 19, and 28; 38.1–3.

83. Augustine of Hippo, *Sermo* 26.15. He is drawing here on the ideas expressed by Paul in Romans 9.20–21.

84. Augustine of Hippo, *Sermones* 21.8, *Sermo* Dolbeau 21.4.

85. "non dubitet pietas, etsi non comprehendit infirmitas." Augustine of Hippo, *Sermo* Dolbeau 29.10, ed. Dolbeau. "Sermon inédit de saint Augustin sur la providence divine." *Revue des études augustiniennes* 41 (1995): 287, trans. Hill, 3.11:60. See also Augustine of Hippo, *Sermo* 27.4: "Exspectas a me fortasse ut dicam tibi, quare *cui vult miseretur, et quem vult obdurat?* Exspectas a me, homo?" *PL* 38:179. Romans 9.14–15.

86. Augustine of Hippo, *Sermo* 27.6.

87. As Theodore De Bruyn puts it: "Like their pagan neighbours, Christians expected material benefits from religious observances, and grumbled when their God seemed oblivious to the prosperity of their enemies." "Ambivalence within a 'Totalizing Discourse,'" 410.

88. See, for example, *Eusebius Gallicanus* 25, which implies that peace, good weather and flourishing crops will be the reward of proper prayer.

89. Kleinberg, "*De agone christiano,*" 16–33; Weaver, *Divine Grace,* 152–53.

90. "Sed, etsi aliquis deputatus fuerit perditioni praeiudicata sorte nascendi, ecce descenditur in fontem tamquam in sepulcrum." *Eusebius Gallicanus* 15.4, ed. Glorie, 178. For the position of Eusebius Gallicanus preachers see also 18.5, 32.4. Casiday discusses such views in late antique Gaul, *Tradition and Theology,* 43.

91. Augustine admits the power of doubts over the justice of predestination: "Sed movet me, inquis, quod ille perit, ille baptizatur: movet me, movet tanquam hominem. Si verum vis audire, et me movet quia homo sum." Augustine of Hippo, *Sermo* 26.15, *PL* 38:178. Compare Faustus of Riez, *De gratia* 2.12. This seems to have been the mainstream position on grace and free will in fifth-century Gaul—see Smith, *De Gratia,* 59; Leyser, "Semi-Pelagianism," 761–65. Augustine had his Gallic defenders too, in particular Prosper of Aquitaine, Avitus of Vienne, Fulgentius of Ruspe, and Julianus Pomerius. See Weaver, *Divine Grace,* 117–54 and 180–98; Tibiletti, "Teologia della grazia," 489–506.

92. The more complete passage reads: "Quia humana conditio, quae per trangressionis culpam obnoxia tenebatur inimico, non imperio erat eruenda sed *pretio,* necesse erat ut pietati iustitia misceretur . . . Propterea homo, si inoboedientiae lapsu et liberae mentis assensu a diabolo seductus fuerat, non coactus: a totius rationis et aequitatis auctore inuitandus erat, non attrahendus; iniquissimum siquidem uideretur, ut, qui ceciderat uoluntarius, erigeretur inuitus. Vides quia dignatissimi medici studium, infirmi sui requirit assensum. Per liberum arbitrium est excepta captiuitas, per liberum rursus arbitrium erat restituenda libertas: dominus enim, qui ianuam reserat, etiam sollicitudinem pulsantis exspectat." *Eusebius Gallicanus* 19.7, ed. Glorie, 229. 1 Corinthians 6.20.

93. The more complete passage reads: "si homo de potestate diaboli per dei potentiam et, ut sic dictum sit, per uiolentiam tolleretur, potuerat diabolus, qui hominem proprio uitio debitum possidebat, aliquid rationis afferre ac deo dicere: 'Iuste rerum arbiter: tuus quidem est homo per creaturam, sed meus coepit esse per culpam; tuus per naturam, meus per inoboedientiam, quia maluit audire seductionem meam quam legem . . . tuus est opere, meus uoluntate, quia potuit praeceptum tuum seruare sed noluit.'" *Eusebius Gallicanus* 19.7, ed. Glorie, 230.

94. "Sed forte hic aliquis in corde suo dicat: 'Quid est hoc, quod *semetipsam* diuinitas *humiliauit?* . . . Prima iustitiae causa est . . . Peccauerat enim

primus homo suo uitio et inoboedientiae lapsu et propriae uoluntatis impulsu, seductus a diabolo, non coactus . . . et ideo per misericordiam poterat quasi reus redimi, non debebat per potentiam quasi innocens liberari." *Eusebius Gallicanus* 18.4–5, ed. Glorie, 216–17. The preacher expands on the necessity of God acting "justly" through the rest of this sermon.

95. "Potuerat quidem dominus noster, carissimi, hostem humani generis sola maiestate prosternere sine incarnationis humilitate, sine certamine passionis; sed homo, qui proprio transgressionis crimine tenebatur obnoxius, qui per culpam suam incurrerat seruitutem, non uiolentia liberandus fuit sed misericordia." *Eusebius Gallicanus* 22.3, ed. Glorie, 258.

96. "Aequius et salubrius fuit, ut: qui per superbiam a diabolo persuasus fuerat ad mortem, a deo per humilitatem sollicitaretur ad uitam; iusto ergo ordine: qui per calliditatem maleuoli serpentis non impulsus sed seductus fuerat ad perditionem, rursum per sapientiam beneuoli redemptoris non compelleretur sed duceretur ad salutem." *Eusebius Gallicanus* 22.3, ed. Glorie, 258–59.

97. For Caesarius of Arles as an Augustinian, see Lejay, "Rôle théologique de Césaire d'Arles," 135–82; Rivière, "Rédemption chez saint Césaire d'Arles," 3–20; Pontal, *Histoire des conciles mérovingiens*, 91–92; and the discussion in Daly, "Caesarius of Arles," 6–7. Christophe, *Cassien et Césaire*, 74, shares my less doctrinaire view of Caesarius.

98. "Multos, fratres carissimi, tangit ista suspicio; multos parvae scientiae homines in scrupulum mittit huiuscemodi cogitatio; dicunt enim: Quare dominus Iesus Christus, virtus et sapientia Patris, salutem hominis non potestate divina et solo est operatus imperio, sed humilitate corporea et humana conluctatione." Caesarius of Arles, *Sermo* 11.1, ed. Morin, 54, trans. Mueller, 31:62.

99. "Mihi se homo propria voluntate coniunxit; a te eadem voluntate, non invitus, distraxit," Caesarius of Arles, *Sermo* 11.2, ed. Morin, 55, trans. Mueller, 31:63.

100. Caesarius of Arles, *Sermo* 11.3.

101. See, for example, Caesarius of Arles, *Sermo* 220.3 and the discussion in Klingshirn, *Caesarius of Arles*, 143.

102. Pastors throughout Christian history have recognised the problem with preaching predestination, and despite being condemned, semipelagianism became the effective pastoral theology of the Catholic Church through the Middle Ages, as the Calvinists took great delight in pointing out. See also Weaver, *Divine Grace*, ix.

103. Caesarius of Arles, *Sermones* 70.1: "Quotiens, fratres carissimi, aliquae adversitates adveniunt, quotiens aut hostilitas aut siccitas aut mortalitas iusto dei iudicio nobis fuerit inrogata, non eius iniustitae, sed nostris hoc peccatis imputare debemus," ed. Morin, 295; and *Sermones* 71.1: "Quanta sint istius temporis mala, carissimi, quantaeque miserae, quibus assidua afflictione conterimur, neminem inter vos credo esse tam fatuum, qui non possit advertere peccatorum nostrum meritis hoc moveri: et ideo paene omnia aut accidunt aut aguntur, nosque in hoc saeculo adfligunt." Ed. Morin, 300. The same argument is also prevalent in the sermons of Peter Chrysologus, and can be found in the collection of Valerian of Cimiez. See, for example, Peter Chrysologus, *Sermones* 47, 101, 111, 112; Valerian of Cimiez, *Homilia* 1.3–5.

104. Christophe discusses similar approaches in the monastic context, *Cassien et Césaire.*

Chapter 5.   Dealing with Sin

1. Caesarius of Arles made this point about the pastoral response to men who kept concubines: "This great crime is not so punished by priests because it is committed by so many. If only one or two or four or five presumed to do this evil, they could and should not only be suspended from communion, but even separated from the conversation and banquets of Christian people . . . However, as was already said, the number of those who commit the sin prevents the priests of the Lord from segregating them." Caesarius of Arles, *Sermo* 43.5, trans. Mueller, 31:217. See comment by Uhalde, *Expectations of Justice,* 128–29.

2. "facilis enim est lapsus ad uitia; et fragilitas conditionis humanae." *Eusebius Gallicanus* 21.5, Glorie, 251.

3. De Jong emphasises the "extremely diverse" character of penitential practice in the West. "What Was Public," 866.

4. Eusebius Gallicanus 64.13. On the functioning of this kind of indirect power, see Bell, *Ritual Theory,* 201. For an elaboration of some of the points raised in this chapter, see Bailey, "Our Own Most Severe Judges."

5. Vogel, *Discipline pénitentielle,* 49–51. On Augustine as a defender of "Christian mediocrity," see Markus, *End of Ancient Christianity,* 45–62.

6. Uhalde, *Expectations of Justice,* 105–34.

7. Fitzgerald, *Conversion through Penance,* 2.

8. On this change, see Brown, "Pelagius and His Supporters," 107–14; Rebillard, *In hora mortis,* 129ff. Rebillard argues that there was a shift over this period from a "baptismal spirituality" to a "penitential spirituality" (232).

9. See, for example, the discussions in Brown, "Decline of the Empire of God," 51–85; Rebillard, *In hora mortis;* Weaver, *Divine Grace.* On Augustine's view of baptism, see Cramer, *Baptism and Change,* 87–129. For other Christian thinkers grappling with similar ideas, see Fitzgerald, *Conversion through Penance,* 41–42, 59–60.

10. Similar movements can be found outside North Africa around this time, see Fitzgerald, *Conversion through Penance,* 11.

11. Fitzgerald, *Conversion through Penance,* 14.

12. Symbolised, for example, in the Donatist practice of whitewashing Catholic Churches before use. Gaddis, *There Is No Crime,* 120–21.

13. Brown, *Augustine of Hippo,* 212–25.

14. For examples of this view in Augustine's preaching, see *Sermones* 25.4, 47.6, 80.8, 88.18–22, 223.1–2, 311.10, *Sermo* Dolbeau 6, 29.8.

15. "Quid festinatis . . . Videtis zizania inter frumentum, videtis malos christianos inter bonos; eradicare vultis malos: quiescite, non est tempus messis . . ." Augustine of Hippo, *Sermo* 73.1–3, *PL* 38:470, trans. Hill, 3.3:291–3. On this strain in Augustine's thought and its relation to the Donatist challenge, see Straw, "Augustine as Pastoral Theologian," 129–51.

16. "fieri potest ut qui hodie sunt zizania, cras sint frumentum." Augustine of Hippo, *Sermo* 73.1–3, *PL* 38:471, trans. Hill, 3.3:291–3.

17. Brown, "Pelagius and his Supporters," 104–5; Rebillard, *In hora mortis,* 145; Markus, "Legacy of Pelagius," 215.

18. TeSelle, "Pelagius, Pelagianism," in Fitzgerald, ed., *Augustine through the Ages,* 635; Brown, "Decline of the Empire of God," 51.

19. Brown, "Pelagius and his Supporters," 107ff; Rebillard, *In hora mortis,* 151–57.

20. Augustine of Hippo, *Sermones* 9.17–19, 58.10, 181.

21. Augustine of Hippo, *Sermones* 9.17, 56.12, 179A.6.

22. "Qui baptizantur et exeunt, sine debito ascendunt, sine debito pergunt. Qui autem baptizantur et tenentur in hac vita, de fragilitate mortali contrahunt aliquid, unde et si non naufragatur, tamen oportet ut sentinetur. Quia si non sentinatur, paulatim ingreditur unde tota navis mergatur." Augustine of Hippo, *Sermo* 56.11, *PL* 38:382, trans. Hill, 3.3:101.

23. Brown, *Rise of Western Christendom,* 256; Rebillard, *In hora mortis,* 162.

24. "donec ad illam pacem veniamus, ubi nullum hostem habebimus, diu et fideliter strenueque pugnemus, ut a domino deo coronari mereamur." Augustine of Hippo, *Sermo* 77A.3, *MA* 1:578, trans. Hill, 3.3:329.

25. The complete passage reads: "Non contemnantur vel minora. Per angustas rimulas navis insudat aqua, impletur sentina, et si contemnatur sentina, mergitur navis. Sed non cessatur a nautis ambulant manus: ambulant, ut quotidie sentinae exhauriantur. Sic et tuae manus ambulent, ut quotidie sentines." Augustine of Hippo, *Sermo* 58.10, *PL* 38:398, trans. Hill, 3.3:123.

26. Peter Chrysologus, *Sermones* 30, 91. See also discussion in Rebillard, *In hora mortis,* 171–76.

27. Avitus of Vienne, *Homilia* 5.

28. Caesarius of Arles, *Sermo* 158.2.

29. "Cum enim nullum diem possimus sine peccato transigere, quae ratio est, ut, dum paulatim minuta peccata congerimus, de parvissimis guttis infinitos gurgites faciamus?" Caesarius of Arles, *Sermo* 61.1, ed. Morin, 267, trans. Mueller, 31:300.

30. Caesarius of Arles, *Sermones* 63.1, 144.4, 209.2–3.

31. "In baptismo regeneramur ad uitam, post baptismum confirmamur ad pugnam; in baptismo abluimur, post baptismum roboramur. Ac sic continuo transituris sufficiunt regenerationis beneficia, uicturis autem necessaria sunt confirmationis auxilia. Regeneratio per se saluat mox in pace beati saeculi recipiendos, confirmatio armat et instruit ad agones mundi huius et proelia reseruandos." *Eusebius Gallicanus* 29.2, ed. Glorie, 338. For a similar idea, see Caesarius of Arles, *Sermo* 209.1.

32. For examples of this imagery used in relation to both baptism and expiation, see *Eusebius Gallicanus* 6.4–6, 15.2, 17.3, 20.4, 26.5, 27.8, 45.1, 51.6, 53.8 and 53.11, 54.8, 58.6, 64.4. On the connection between baptism and penance in the earlier period, see Fitzgerald, *Conversion through Penance,* 59; Rebillard, *In hora mortis,* 225.

33. The complete quotation reads: "Et [istos quoque uir ille apostolicus,] appositis paenitentiae medicamentis, uelut *quatriduanum foetentem,* increpationum fremitu suscitabat; et, emendatione suscepta, de mendiis mortis faucibus erutos, temporiua resurrectione, uitae restituebat." *Eusebius Gallicanus* 51.8, ed. Glorie, 600. John 11.38–9.

34. Faustus of Riez, *Epistula* 5, ed. Engelbrecht, 183–95. For discussion of this letter see Nodes, *"De subitanea paenitentia,"* 30–40; Weigel, *Faustus of Riez,* 88–90.

35. Weigel writes, for example, that Faustus answered Paulinus "in a chilly tone of the utmost severity," and contrasts the response of Avitus, *Faustus of Riez,* 89–90. See also Vogel, *Discipline pénitentielle,* 49–51. Gallic bishops were rebuked by Pope Innocent in 405 and by Pope Celestine in 428 because they refused to grant penance to the dying on the grounds that redemption of their sins had not yet been, and could not be, properly earned. Innocent I, *Epistula* 6.2; Celestine I, *Epistula* 4.2.

36. Rebillard points out that Faustus was talking only about those who had serious sins, and their chance of salvation, not about whether comfort should be offered to the dying. *In hora mortis,* 222–23. Barcellona also sees Faustus as motivated by compassion and solicitiousness in his pastoral care. "Fausto di Riez," 779.

37. Uhalde, *Expectations of Justice,* 123; Demacopoulos, *Five Models,* 110–25.

38. See discussion in De Jong, "Transformations of Penance."

39. "Si leuia sunt fortasse delicta, uerbi gratia si homo uel in sermone uel in aliqua reprehensibili uoluntate, si oculo peccauit aut corde: uerborum et cogitationum maculae, quotidiana oratione curandae et priuata compunctione tergendae sunt. Si uero quisque, conscientiam suam intus interrogans, facinus aliquod capitale commisit, aut si fidem suam falso testimonio expugnauit ac prodidit, ac sacrum ueritatis nomen periurii temeritate uiolauit, si <ni>ueam baptismi tunicam et speciosam uirginitatis holosericam caeno commaculati pudoris infecit, si in semetipso nouum hominem nece hominis occidit, si per *augeres et diuinos atque incantatores* captiuum se diabolo tradidit: haec atque huiusmodi commissa expiari penitus communi et mediocri uel secreta satisfactione non possunt; sed graues causae grauiores et acriores et publicas curas requirunt." *Eusebius Gallicanus* 45.3, ed. Glorie, 536–37. Glorie identifies a series of Church councils as the possible source of the quotation, though it is a common phrase (537). Compare Caesarius of Arles, *Sermones* 197.2, 189.2. This distinction is a standard one which can also be found in Augustine's sermons, and elsewhere in the preaching corpus of Caesarius of Arles. See, for example, Augustine of Hippo, *Sermones* 56.12, 351.2–7, 352.7–8, 392.3; Caesarius of Arles, *Sermones* 44.6, 179.2–7.

40. De Jong, "What Was Public," 863–902, and "Transformations of Penance," 196–207; Meens, "Frequency and Nature," 47–54; Uhalde, *Expectations of Justice,* 105–34. For examples of historians who construct a penitential schema around the distinction between public and private,

see Beck, *Pastoral Care,* 188–99; Vogel, *Discipline pénitentielle,* 88–101; Poschmann, *Penance and the Anointing of the Sick;* and discussions in Meens, "Frequency and Nature," 36–37, and De Jong, "What Was Public," 866–71.

41. "qui cum plurimorum destructione se perdidit, simili modo cum plurimorum aedificatione se redimat." *Eusebius Gallicanus* 45.3, ed. Glorie, 537. The same passage occurs in Caesarius of Arles, *Sermones* 197.2 and 189.2 and is closely echoed in 179.7. A similar argument is offered in *Eusebius Gallicanus* 8.5, probably directed to monks: "Sicut ergo, quando aliquis peccat sub conscientia ac destructione plurimorum, de pluribus incurrit reatum . . . ita autem, e contrario, quando quisque de ecclesiae filiis aliquod bonum profitetur in publicum, crescit deuotio meritorum turba mirantium; ac de tantis acquiruntur bonorum operum fructus, quantorum uelut balsami suauitate condiuntur affectus bonorum turba paenitentium, qui secundus ordo est neophytorum. Sicut ibi fide est acquisita, hic opere et lacrimis: crimina diluuntur." Ed. Glorie, 88.

42. "Non pudeat paenitere, quos peccare non puduit." *Eusebius Gallicanus* 58.6, ed. Glorie, 668. Caesarius echoed these sentiments. "Erubescimus modo parvo tempore paenitentiam agere, et non timemus sine ullo termino aeterna supplicia sustinere. O infelix homo, de ipso vulnere non erubescis, et de ligatura vulneris erubescis!" Caesarius of Arles, *Sermo* 64.1, ed. Morin, 275.

43. *Eusebius Gallicanus* 45.4. Note the parallel passages in Caesarius of Arles, *Sermones* 197.3, 189.3.

44. De Jong, "Transformations of Penance," 190.

45. De Jong observes that penitents were often recruited into the clergy—they had already "left the world" and required no lengthy purification. "Transformations of Penance," 203–5.

46. "Paenitentia quidem praecipuum, sed extremum remedium est. Peruenistis ad illud. Tenete illud quasi primum, custodite quasi solum. Sicut in Christo renatis iam aliud baptismum non potest subuenire nisi sola paenitentiae medicina, ita post paenitentiam nulla res subuenit." *Eusebius Gallicanus* 58.1, ed. Glorie, 667.

47. *Eusebius Gallicanus* 58.2–3.

48. *Eusebius Gallicanus* 58.4.

49. "ita soli operam date emendationi: quasi quotidie de hoc saeculo transituri." *Eusebius Gallicanus* 58.4, ed. Glorie, 668.

50. Caesarius of Arles, *Sermo* 56.3.

51. Fitzgerald, *Conversion through Penance,* 193ff.

52. *Eusebius Gallicanus* 64.1, 53.11.

53. *Eusebius Gallicanus* 74.8, 26.4–5.

54. *Eusebius Gallicanus* 74.2–4.

55. *Eusebius Gallicanus* 60.8. Note the parallel passage in Caesarius of Arles, *Sermo* 58.3.

56. *Eusebius Gallicanus* 45.5. Daniel 4.24, Luke 19.1–10.

57. *Eusebius Gallicanus* 8.4. The first part of the sermon, moreover, was dedicated to fasting. The author of sermon forty-six, drawing on Faustus of Riez's treatise *De gratia,* described almsgiving as part of the commerce between man and God. *Eusebius Gallicanus* 46.6. The author of sermon twenty-one included almsgiving and compassion to the poor in a long list of how Christians could preserve their faith. *Eusebius Gallicanus* 21.5.

58. The Eusebian sermons may have been describing the Rogations, or some predecessor of them. On the Rogations, see chapter 3.

59. *Eusebius Gallicanus* 25.2–4.

60. Caesarius of Arles, *Sermo* 207.3.

61. Avitus of Vienne, *Homilia* 5, and Caesarius of Arles, *Sermo* 144.3.

62. "At vero, cum contra hostem communem multitudinis pugnat assensus, trahit etiam timidum militem virtus aliena." Avitus of Vienne, *Sermo* 5, ed. Chevalier, 297.

63. Maximus of Turin, *Sermo* 81.2–4.

64. "Tota igitur in tribulatione Niniuitarum ciuitas ieiunauit . . . Vnde et nos, fratres, temporum angustias sustinentes omnes pariter ieiunare debemus, et misericordiam dei cunctorum abstinentia deplorare." Maximus of Turin, *Sermo* 81.4, ed. Mutzenbecher, 334. See also *Sermo* 50 on the importance of fasting in unison as a community during Lent.

65. Ambrose of Milan, *Sermo* 25.3. See also *Sermo* 26.3. On Ambrose and almsgiving, see Vasey, *Social Ideas.*

66. "Ergo elemosina quodammodo animarum aliud est lauacrum, ut si qui forte post baptismum humana fragilitate deliquerit, supersit ei, ut iterum elemosina emundetur." Maximus of Turin, *Sermo* 22A.4, ed. Mutzenbecher, 89. Lizzi sees Maximus' emphasis on the expiatory-penitential character of the act of charity as a "significant novelty" in North Italian spirituality. Lizzi, *Vescovi e strutture ecclesiastiche,* 187–88. On Maximus see also Fitzgerald, *Conversion through Penance,* 242–48; Rebillard, *In hora mortis,* 163–64; Padovese, *Originalita cristiana,* 193–211; Merkt, *Maximus I. von Turin,* 113–41.

67. "Nullum enim tam graue delictum est, quod non purgetur abstinentia elemosinis extinguatur." Maximus of Turin, *Sermo* 61.1, ed. Mutzenbecher, 244. Fitzgerald argues that Maximus gave almsgiving the place and role one would normally expect for formal penance. *Conversion through Penance,* 128.

68. "Quamuis ergo pollutus quamuis multis criminibus circumseptus, si elemosinas feceris, innocens esse coepisti." Maximus of Turin, *Sermo* 22.1, ed. Mutzenbecher, 83.

69. Peter Chrysologus, *Sermo* 8. See also *Sermones* 42, 43, and 41: "Abstinentia est hominis prima medicina, sed ad plenam curam, misericordiae requirit expensas." *PL* 52:316. On Peter Chrysologus and almsgiving, see Fitzgerald, *Conversion through Penance,* 297–300; Rebillard, *In hora mortis,* 178–79, 185.

70. Caesarius of Arles, *Sermo* 199.2, 6. Clement of Alexandria presented a similar ranking, in which almsgiving was more important than fasting or prayer. Fitzgerald, *Conversion through Penance,* 194. For a general discussion, see Ramsey, "Almsgiving in the Latin Church," 226–59. The idea was also present in Eastern homiletics. John Chrysostom had made it central to his exhortations to repentance and maintained that "regardless of how many other sins you have, your almsgiving counterbalances all of them." John Chrysostom, *Homily* 3.6, trans. Christo, 31. "Repentance without almsgiving is a corpse," he said in another sermon, "and is without wings. Repentance cannot fly high without the wing of almsgiving." John Chrysostom, *Homily* 7.21, trans. Christo, 103. On the rise of the idea to prominence during the persecutions, see Countryman, *Rich Christian,* 189, 196, and Fitzgerald, *Conversion through Penance,* 194.

71. For Eusebius Gallicanus sermons which allude to the expiatory power of almsgiving, see 45.6 and 46.6. In both instances the discussion is general and almsgiving receives no especial emphasis as a penitential act.

72. *Eusebius Gallicanus* 58.6.

73. For example, Augustine of Hippo, *Sermo* 388.1. Frahier, Lizzi, and Ramsey all note the restricted power of almsgiving in Augustine's works. Frahier, "Interprétation du récit du jugement dernier," 70–84; Lizzi, *Vescovi e strutture ecclesiastiche,* 188; Ramsey, "Almsgiving in the Latin Church," 243.

74. "Et quodammodo in orationibus vestris a cottidianus levibus minoribusque peccatis cottide purgamini, si ex animo dixeritis, si veraciter dixeritis, si fideliter dixeritis: *Dimitte nobis debita nostra, sicut et nos dimitti-*

mus debitoribus nostris." Augustine of Hippo, *Sermo* 179A.6, *MA* 1:679, trans. Hill, 3.5:311. Matthew 6.12.

75. "Remissio peccatorum una est, quae semel datur . . . in sancto Baptismate; alia, quae quamdiu vivimus hic, datur in Dominica oratione. Propter quod dicimus, *Dimitte nobis debita nostra.*" Augustine of Hippo, *Sermo* 58.6, *PL* 38:396, trans. Hill, 3.3:121. See also *Sermones* 17.5, 56.13, 181.7, 261.10, 354A, 352.7, *Sermo* Dolbeau 17.8.

76. Straw, "Augustine as Pastoral Theologian," 147. Straw claims that "on a practical level Augustine checks the infinitely regressive cycle of grace and human action at prayer and repentance. Prayer is the point where passivity and activity are reconciled for the Christian in his daily life . . . Prayer remains within man's power."

77. *Eusebius Gallicanus* 29.2.

78. "Sed opus est ut ita elaboremus: ne, quod ille abluit, nos iterum polluamus; ne rescindamus uulnera quae ille sanauit; ne, quod semel in nobis diluit unda baptismi, rursum excoquere necesse habeat ignis inferni." *Eusebius Gallicanus* 20.4, ed. Glorie, 242.

79. "'Quod tu in te seuerus agnoscis, ego propitius ignoscam . . . quod tu recordaris in publicum, ego obliuiscar in aeternum. Et quia per paenitentiam tuam praeuenisti sententiam meam: recondam gladium meum.'" *Eusebius Gallicanus* 26.5, ed. Glorie, 306.

80. "Accusanti se, iustitia nata est de peccatis . . . Hic ergo culpas offensasque nostras quotidiana emendatione et contritione damnemus; ipsi in nobis seuerissimi iudices simus, et plena satisfactione futuri examinis sententiam praecurramus. Hic deleat quotidianus gemitus et quotidianus fletus, quidquid concrematurus erat ignis aeternus." *Eusebius Gallicanus* 64.11 and 64.13, ed. Glorie, 734–35.

81. The complete quotation reads: "Qui placiturus est deo: ipse sibi displicet; ipse sibi quodammodo, sub priuatae cognitionis sententia, et testis et accusator et iudex est." *Eusebius Gallicanus* 26.5, ed. Glorie, 305.

82. *Eusebius Gallicanus* 4.6: "Ac sic, fratres, de omnibus neglegentiis nostris *compungamur in cubilibus,* id est, in cordibus *nostris;* ipsi nos condemnemus, ipsi nos accusemus quotidie iudici nostro, et, *dum in hac carne sumus,* contra ipsam carnem quotidie dimicemus." Ed. Glorie, 52. Psalm 4.5, Romans 7.5. *Eusebius Gallicanus* 60.8: "Commendemus nos iudici nostro, et, *dum in hac carne* positi *sumus,* contra ipsam carnem quotidie dimicemus; membra ieiuniis castigemus, corda orationibis concidamus." Ed. Glorie, 689. Romans 7.5, 2 Corinthians 5.6. Compare Caesarius of Arles,

Sermo 58.3: "ipsi nos condemnemus, ipsi nos accusemus cotidie iudici nostro; et dum in hac carne sumus, contra ipsam carnem auxiliante domino cotidie dimicemus." Ed. Morin, 256.

83. *Eusebius Gallicanus* 64.10.

84. *Eusebius Gallicanus* 14.7.

85. "Si laesura aliqua uel querela in prima corporis cute sentitur: curatio medicamenti blandioris apponitur. Si uero in ossibus uulnus absconditum, aut in uiscerum profunda demersum est: austeriorem ac uiolentiorem poscit uis occulta medicinam, ut ulceris magnitudo aut sectione aut exustione super[cur]etur, et dolor dolore pellatur. Similis ratio in aegritudine *interioris hominis* adhibenda est." *Eusebius Gallicanus* 45.2–3, ed. Glorie, 535–36. Note the parallel passages in Caesarius of Arles, *Sermones* 189.2, 197.2. On the use of medical imagery in regard to penance, see Uhalde, *Expectations of Justice,* 109–10; Brown, "Vers la naissance du purgatoire," 1250.

86. See, for example, Augustine of Hippo, *Sermones* 2.3, 15A.8, 16B.1, 20.1, 87.13, 97A.1, 113A.13, 126.4, 174.6, 175.2, 176.4.

87. "Peccatum tuum judicem te habeat, non patronum." Augustine of Hippo, *Sermo* 20.2, *PL* 38:139, trans. Hill, 3.2:16. For other instances where Augustine employed judicial imagery see *Sermones* 9.2, 13.1, and 49.5, although these cases do not relate to penance and expiation.

88. Uhalde, *Expectations of Justice,* 123. Note also Leyser, *Authority and Asceticism,* 48, on Cassian's formulations.

89. Demacopoulos, *Five Models,* 100–5.

90. Augustine of Hippo, *Sermo* Dolbeau 2.

91. Rebillard, *In hora mortis,* 218. Uhalde notes the ascetic origins of such principles, *Expectations of Justice,* 107. For further discussion of this point see chapter 6.

92. "Judam traditorem non tam scelus quod commisit, quam indulgentiae desperatio fecit penitus interire." Augustine of Hippo, *Sermo* 352.8, *PL* 39:1558, trans. Hill, 3.10:147.

93. Augustine of Hippo, *Sermo* 352.9.

94. Augustine of Hippo, *Sermo* Dolbeau 14.6.

95. "Tempus est misericordiae, ut corrigamur: nondum venit tempus judicii . . . Nondum finita est via, nondum clausus est dies, nondum exspiratum est; non desperetur, quod est pejus: quoniam propter ipsa peccata humana et tolerabilia . . . constituit Deus in Ecclesia tempore misericordiae praerogandae quotidianam medicinam, ut dicamus, *Dimitte nobis debita nostra, sicut et nos dimittimus debitoribus nostris.*" Augustine of Hippo, *Sermo*

17.5, *PL* 38:127, trans. Hill, 3.1:369. I have departed slightly from Hill's translation. Matthew 6.12. See also *Sermones* 176.5, 351.12.

96. Augustine of Hippo, *Sermones* 87.4–9, 335M.5. He is evoking Matthew 20.1–16.

97. "Dicimus unde nobis cottidie dimittantur; sed non ideo debemus in flagitiis, in sceleribus, in criminibus quasi securi requiescere." Augustine of Hippo, *Sermo* 229E.2, *MA* 1:469. See also *Sermones* 20.3, 352.9.

98. "Ecce qualem propono, qui dixerit in animo suo: Jam Deus veniam promisit omnibus avertentibus se a peccatis, in quacumque hora conversi fuerint, omnes iniquitates eorum obliviscetur: ergo faciam quidquid volo; quando voluero convertam me, delebiturque quod fecero. Quid dicemus? quia non quando se converterit, curat Deus poenitentem? dimittit Deus omnia peccata praeterita? Si negamus, indulgentiae divinae contradicimus: verbis denique propheticis obviamus, divinis eloquiis repugnamus. Non est hoc fidelis dispensatoris." Augustine of Hippo, *Sermo* 20.3, *PL* 38:140, trans. Hill, 3.2:18.

99. "Quare non hodie? quare non modo? Cras, inquit; indulgentiam mihi Deus promisit. Cras tu tibi promittis?" Augustine of Hippo, *Sermo* 20.4, *PL* 38:141. I have departed slightly from the translation by Hill, for which see 3.2:19.

100. "Nonne multi sani dormierunt et obduruerunt." Augustine of Hippo, *Sermo* 17.7, *PL* 38:128, trans. Hill, 3.1:370.

101. "crastino die te victurum nemo tibi promisit." Augustine of Hippo, *Sermo* 40.5, *PL* 38:245, trans. Hill, 3.2:222–3. See also Augustine of Hippo, *Sermones* 9.2, 17.6, 352.9.

102. Augustine of Hippo, *Sermo* 20.3.

103. "ne nos aut in sinistra perniciosa remissio aut in dextera ruinosa supplantet elatio; ne incipiat aut prauitas de neglegentiis aut uanitas pulluare de meritis; quia illic de infirmitate peccatum, hic de uirtute fit uitium." *Eusebius Gallicanus* 33.5, ed. Glorie, 380. See also *Eusebius Gallicanus* 14.7.

104. "Et ideo, carissimi, conuertamus nos ad meliora dum in nostra sunt potestate remedia," *Eusebius Gallicanus* 6.8, ed. Glorie, 73. Compare the parallel passages in Caesarius of Arles, *Sermones* 167.8, 206.3.

105. "Multo enim inuidiosior et damnabilior erit causa criminum sub assistentium comparatione uirtutum! Quid erit terroris, quid miseriae, quid maeroris: quando sub illo admirabili apostolorum martyrumque concilio, sub illo angelorum sidereo ac praefulgente consessu, cum foetore ueterum delictorum diuersis tetra maculis anima producetur; quando latissimam iniquitatum suarum confusibilis uitae totius historiam ante oculos suos

uidebit exponi, ut illam inauditam, clamantium uox malorum, conscientia obmutescente et deficiente, condemnet? Haec omnia, quae illuc sanari non poterunt, hic redimi possunt!" *Eusebius Gallicanus* 27.8, ed. Glorie, 319–20.

106. "Ac sic: mortificatione praesenti, futurae mortis sententia praeuenitur," *Eusebius Gallicanus* 45.1, ed. Glorie, 535. Compare the parallel passages in Caesarius of Arles, *Sermones* 189.1 and 197.1.

107. *Eusebius Gallicanus* 45.7, 61.9, 64.12.

108. "non ibi emendatio poterit, non ualebit oratio." *Eusebius Gallicanus* 74.7, ed. Glorie, 795.

109. "Nos ergo, < . . . as> adhuc etsi incerta breuitate conceditur curare maculas, lauare culpas, subuenire praeteritis, consulere futuris, et facere infecta de factis," *Eusebius Gallicanus* 74.8, ed. Glorie, 795.

110. *Eusebius Gallicanus* 6.6.

111. "ardens inferni puteus aperietur; descensus erit, reditus non erit." *Eusebius Gallicanus* 6.6, ed. Glorie, 70. Compare Caesarius of Arles, *Sermo* 167.5. This translation is based in part on that of Mueller, 47:406.

112. *Eusebius Gallicanus* 6.6 and 6.7. Compare Caesarius of Arles, *Sermo* 167.7.

113. Brown, "Decline of the Empire of God," 61.

114. Maximus of Turin, *Sermo* 74.1.

115. Pope Celestine also used the example of the thief to defend the practice of deathbed penance. *Epistula* 4.3.

116. The passage reads: "si latro in ipso momento mortis paradisum invasit, et vitam vobis, in articulo temporis quam quaeritis, quis negabit?" Peter Chrysologus, *Sermo* 60, *PL* 52:365, trans. Fitzgerald, *Conversion through Penance,* 311. See also *Sermones* 42, 61, 125, 167, and discussion in Rebillard, *In hora mortis,* 181–84, 226.

117. Avitus of Vienne, *Epistula* 4. Avitus was responding to the letter by Faustus of Riez mentioned above. Note that this is a letter, not a sermon.

118. "ut consolatio ac spes fieret totius populi." *Eusebius Gallicanus* 24.2, ed. Glorie, 281.

119. The passage as a whole reads: "Quare indubitanter credendum est, quod latroni illi ad commendationem fidei suae etiam causa spei nostrae et utilitatis accesserit; immensa enim dei nostri bonitas, libenter tribuit quae etiam generaliter profutura praenoscit." *Eusebius Gallicanus* 24.2, ed. Glorie, 281.

120. "Sed non sine causa tantum meruit." *Eusebius Gallicanus* 24.2, ed. Glorie, 281. The phrase is repeated in 24.3.

121. *Eusebius Gallicanus* 24.3.

122. "ita gratiam adiungit ad merita." *Eusebius Gallicanus* 24.4–5, ed. Glorie, 284.

123. "uideo sub momento, uideo sub exiguo spatio latroni crimina sua fuisse donata, et mihi resoluta." *Eusebius Gallicanus* 24.8, ed. Glorie, 288.

124. "Ipse se inducit et de morte sua ludit, qui hoc cogitat: 'Potest mihi extremi temporis indulgentia subuenire.'" *Eusebius Gallicanus* 24. 8, ed. Glorie, 289.

125. "Quotidie expauescenda transitus nostri et commigrationis incerta—quae et modo uel insperata uel subita sunt—et in aeternum remediis caritura sunt." *Eusebius Gallicanus* 24.8, ed. Glorie, 288.

126. "*Odibile est apud deum,* quando homo, sub fiducia paenitentiae in senectute reseruatae, liberius peccat . . . ars non admittitur ad salutem." *Eusebius Gallicanus* 24.8, ed. Glorie, 289. Ecclesiasticus 10.7.

127. "ille nec salutis tempora sciens distulit, nec remedia status sui in momenta ultima infelici fraude disposuit, nec redemptionis suae spem in desperationis nouissimum reseruauit." *Eusebius Gallicanus* 24.9, ed. Glorie, 289.

128. "illi de Dei misericordia non desperantes, converterunt se ad poenitendum; et pepercit Deus." Augustine of Hippo, *Sermo* 361.20, *PL* 39:1610, trans. Hill, 3.10:238. See also Augustine of Hippo, *Sermones* 72A.1, 346A.3, 351.12, and *Sermo* Dolbeau 5.2.

129. For Augustine's avoidance of the Ninevites in treatises on grace, see Weaver, *Divine Grace,* 179. Augustine gives them careful exegesis in *De civitate dei* 21.24.

130. Maximus of Turin, *Sermones* 81, 82.

131. Merkt, *Maximus I. von Turin,* 39, 59–65, and Padovese, *Originalita cristiana,* 209.

132. Peter Chrysologus, *Sermones* 8, 37.

133. *Eusebius Gallicanus* 26.1.

134. "Vbi sunt: qui negant remedia paenitentiae; qui eam uel accipiendam, uel communionem post labores emeritos munerandam esse, non credunt?" *Eusebius Gallicanus* 26.1, ed. Glorie, 303.

135. "Inter haec fidelis quisque non dubitet: hostias precum, holocausta uotorum, sacrificia lacrimarum ad diuinum familiariter ascendere posse conspectum; ecce ad aurem domini, gemitus etiam brutorum animalium peruenerunt." *Eusebius Gallicanus* 26.3, ed. Glorie, 304.

136. "Ergo niniuitae, per paenitentiam atque abstinentiam, irae desuper imminentis suspenderunt ruinam; et paruuli ac pecora, pariter abstinentes, egressam a domino plagam atque sententiam iam cadentem, ut sic dixerim, retorserunt." *Eusebius Gallicanus* 26.4, ed. Glorie, 305.

137. *Eusebius Gallicanus* 26.5.

138. Straw, "Augustine as Pastoral Theologian," 131, 146.

139. Straw, "Augustine as Pastoral Theologian," 147–48.

140. On Caesarius' attitudes to penance, see also Uhalde, *Expectations of Justice,* 127–31.

141. Compare, in particular, Caesarius' *Sermones* 189 and 197 with *Eusebius Gallicanus* 45; Caesarius' *Sermo* 58 with *Eusebius Gallicanus* 4 and 60; and Caesarius' *Sermones* 167 and 206 with *Eusebius Gallicanus* 6.

142. Caesarius of Arles, *Sermones* 18.2–6, 20.2–4, 41.4, 60.3, 61.1–4, 63.3, 64.1–3, 209.1.

143. "Ad emundanda enim crimina vox paenitentis sola non sufficit: quia in satisfactione ingentium peccatorum non verba tantum, sed opera quaeruntur. Datur quidem etiam in extremis paenitentia, quia non potest denegari: sed auctores tamen nos esse non possumus, quod qui sic petierit mereatur absolvi. Quomodo enim agit paenitentiam lassus, in extremis vitae finibus constitutus? Quomodo potest paenitentiam agere, qui nulla iam pro se potest opera satisfactionis offerre? Et ideo paenitentia, quae ab infirmo petitur, infirma est; paenitentia, quae ab aegroto tantum petitur, aegrotat; paenitentia, quae a moriente tantum petitur, timeo ne et ipsa moriatur." Caesarius of Arles, *Sermo* 62, ed. Morin, 271–2: trans. Mueller, 31:304.

144. "Agens vero paenitentiam ad ultimum et reconciliatus, si securus hinc exeat, ego non sum securus. Paenitentiam dare possum, securitatem dare non possum." Caesarius of Arles, *Sermo* 63.3, ed. Morin, 273–74, trans. Mueller, 31:306.

145. The passage as a whole reads: "Deus tamen, qui omnium conscientias novit, et unumquemque secundum suum meritum iudicabit, ipse scit qua fide aut qua intentione animi paenitentiam petiit." Caesarius of Arles, *Sermo* 60.3, ed. Morin, 265, trans. Mueller, 31:297.

Chapter 6. Sermons to Monks

1. If nonordination is viewed solely as the definitional element of laity, then many monks were technically lay people. It is clear, however, that they were effectively viewed as a distinct group in late antiquity, especially

when cloistered, as the monks addressed in these sermons were. On some of the issues raised by these terms, see Congar, *Lay People,* 4–5; Effros, "Appearance and Ideology"; Lakeland, *Liberation of the Laity,* 12–13; Astell, "Introduction," 9–10; Neill, "Introduction," 16–18; Demacopoulos, *Five Models,* 1–2.

2. See the epilogue for discussion of the manuscript history of these sermons.

3. See, for example, the treatments in Kasper, *Theologie und Askese;* Nouailhat, *Saints et patrons;* Nürnberg, *Askese als sozialer Impuls.*

4. Demacopoulos, *Five Models,* 2.

5. Markus, *End of Ancient Christianity,* title of chapter 14.

6. A point also made by Hausherr, although he draws conclusions different from my own. "Spiritualité monacale," 315–32, and "Vocation chrétienne," 405–85.

7. This is the conclusion of Glorie, *Eusebius "Gallicanus,"* 946; De Vogüé, "Sur une série des emprunts," 119–23, and Kasper, *Theologie und Askese,* 11.

8. See the manuscript incipits in Glorie, *Eusebius "Gallicanus,"* 419.

9. Glorie, *Eusebius "Gallicanus,"* 946; Kasper, *Theologie und Askese,* 11.

10. See the possible allusions to Sallust in section 1, to Cicero, Ovid, Lucretius in section 4, and to Ovid or Virgil in section 6. For an analysis of non-Christian literary allusions by Lérinian monks, see Courcelle, "Nouveaux aspects."

11. *Eusebius Gallicanus* 7.1.

12. For example, Kasper, *Theologie und Askese,* 10–11; Labrousse, *Saint Honorat,* 37–41; Nürnberg, *Askese als sozialer Impuls,* 224; De Vogüé, "Débuts de la vie monastique," 10; Nouailhat, *Saints et patrons,* 16.

13. *Eusebius Gallicanus* 40.3.

14. *Eusebius Gallicanus* 72.12.

15. On Augustine's ascetic withdrawal, see Brown, *Augustine of Hippo,* 115–27; Casiday, *Tradition and Theology,* 47–61. Caesarius had been for a short time a member of the community at Lérins, but in *Sermo* 236.2 he describes himself as a failed drop-out who resisted the efforts of this "uniquely special nurse of all good men." Trans. Mueller, 66:210.

16. Sermons were preached at least every Sunday and fast day at Lérins, and may have been daily occurrences. See Weigel, *Faustus of Riez,* 56; Carrias, "Vie monastique et règle," 207. On preaching by monks in general, see

Amos, "'Monks and Pastoral Care,'" and interesting comments on later developments by Kienzle, "Twelfth-Century Monastic Sermon," in Kienzle, ed., *Sermon*, 271–323.

17. For the basic narrative of Lérins' foundation see Antier, *Lérins*, 77–102; Cooper-Marsdin, *History of the Islands of the Lerins*, 128–36, and Moris, *Abbaye de Lérins*, 16–29, as well as most of the works cited in the following footnote.

18. For examples or accounts of these interpretations, see De Vogüé, "Débuts de la vie monastique," 5; Nouailhat, *Saints et patrons*, 31–33; Prinz, *Frühes Mönchtum*, 47–58; Pricoco, *Isola dei Santi*, 63–64, 70–72, 92–93; Markus, *End of Ancient Christianity*, 199–200, and "Legacy of Pelagius," 221–22; Weaver, *Divine Grace*, 157–58.

19. Nouailhat, *Saints et patrons*, 170.

20. Pricoco, *Isola dei Santi*, 131; Nürnberg, *Askese als sozialer Impuls*, 302.

21. See the summary in Nouailhat, *Saints et patrons*, 182.

22. On the monk-bishop, see Rousseau, "Spiritual Authority of the 'Monk-Bishop.'" Nürnberg also makes use of this term, *Askese als sozialer Impuls*, 299ff. Both are influenced by Prinz's classic account of the "institutionalisation" of charisma in clerical office during this period. Prinz, *Frühes Mönchtum*, 449. Mathisen argues that Lérins was only one of several "monastic cliques" striving to coopt the Gallic episcopate in the fifth century, *Ecclesiastical Factionalism*, xii.

23. An example of the idealist perspective would be Nürnberg, *Askese als sozialer Impuls*. Examples of the cynical would be Leyser, "This Sainted Isle"; Mathisen, *Ecclesiastical Factionalism*; Heinzelmann, *Bischofsherrschaft in Gallien*. Instances of the neutral perspective include Nouailhat, *Saints et patrons*; Prinz, *Frühes Mönchtum*; Pricoco, *Isola dei Santi*.

24. This argument is also put forward in Bailey, "Monks and Lay Communities."

25. Augustine testifies to the power of the *Vita* of Antony, *Confessiones* 8.15 and 8.29.

26. On this process, see Rousseau, *Ascetics, Authority and the Church*, 177–235.

27. On the structures and restrictions of life at Lérins, the most likely original context, see Kasper, *Theologie und Askese*, 21–113; Nouailhat, *Saints et patrons*, 198–222; Klingshirn, *Caesarius of Arles*, 24–29; Carrias, "Vie monastique et règle," 203–7. Scholars have disagreed on whether or not Lérins had a written rule at this time. See discussion in De Vogüé, ed., *Règles*

des saints Père, 21–39; Dunn, *Emergence of Monasticism,* 85–90; Pricoco, *Isola dei santi,* 77–111; Diem, *Keusch und rein,* 126–31.

28. "Numquid serui uestri sumus? . . . Desero atque discedo; hoc ego ferre non patior; ingenuus homo sum! . . . Liber sum!, nihil tibi debeo!" *Eusebius Gallicanus* 38.2, ed. Glorie, 436–37. It is interesting to compare these complaints with those attributed by Gregory of Tours to Clotild, the rebellious nun of Poitiers. "I am going to my royal relations," she is supposed to have said, "to tell them about the insults which we have to suffer, for we are humiliated here as if we were the offspring of low-born serving women, instead of being the daughters of kings!" *LH* 9.39, trans. Thorpe, 526. Such comments provide an intriguing counterbalance to the "servant/slave" motif in hagiographical texts.

29. See Pricoco, *Isola dei santi,* 93–127, and Leyser, "'This Sainted Isle,'" 200, on the vulnerability of Lérins. The *Regula Macharii* and the *Tertia patrum regula* provide further evidence that Gallic monks threatened to leave the communal context and set up on their own. See in particular *Regula Macharii* 27 and *Tertia patrum regula* 10, De Vogüé, ed. *Règles des saints Père.*

30. "obliuisci subito fraternae societatis et consolationis." *Eusebius Gallicanus* 38.4, ed. Glorie, 441.

31. *Eusebius Gallicanus* 38.4.

32. *Eusebius Gallicanus* 38.2.

33. "Isti tales nesciunt quid uouerunt: obliti sunt propter quid hic uenerunt." *Eusebius Gallicanus* 38.2, ed. Glorie, 437.

34. "Quid, inquam, prodest, quod discedis: qui, quocumque loci uadis, te tecum portas? . . . Nemo se fallat: non fugit aduersarium de loco ad locum, de uitio ad uirtutem, de passione ad emendationem: nam si eum taliter fugias, sequitur te." *Eusebius Gallicanus* 38.2, ed. Glorie, 438.

35. "nomen atque habitum professionis suae custodire uideatur, anima uero eius neglegentiis tabescat ac defluat." *Eusebius Gallicanus* 38.4, ed. Glorie, 441.

36. *Eusebius Gallicanus* 39.2, 42.9, 44.1. 1 Corinthians 1.26.

37. "intellectu praeditus, ratione munitus, ita interdum sensu alienus efficeris: ut praeferas dei beneficiis uoluntates uel intentiones tuas, et sequaris proprias cogitationes." *Eusebius Gallicanus* 38.4, ed. Glorie, 442.

38. "*Itinera insipientium recta in conspectu eorum,* et iterum: *Sunt uiae quae uidentur rectae esse hominibus, nouissima autem aerum ueniunt in profundum inferni* . . . sic enim legimus: *Omnis qui audit uerba mea haec et non facit ea, similabitur uiro stulto qui aedificauit domum suam supra arenam.*"

Eusebius Gallicanus 38.3, ed. Glorie, 439–40. Proverbs 12.15, 14.12, 16.25, Matthew 7.26.

39. The passage as a whole reads: "Meliores uero quosque ac seniores, per elationis ac iactantiae malum profectu ipso ac meritis propriis expugnare conatur: ut, dum tempora, dum merita ingerit, per immundissimam uanitatem, humilitatem cordis excidat." *Eusebius Gallicanus* 42.7, ed. Glorie, 501. On the increased risk of pride faced by senior monks, see also *Eusebius Gallicanus* 38.5.

40. *Eusebius Gallicanus* 39.2.

41. "Benedicta illa <a> deo anima, cuius humilitas alterius confundit superbiam, cuius patientia proximi exstinguit iracundiam, cuius oboedientia pigritiam alterius tacite increpat, cuius feruor inertiam alieni teporis exsuscitat!" *Eusebius Gallicanus* 42.5, ed. Glorie, 499.

42. "felix est illa anima, quae, dum bene in congregatione uersatur, multorum gaudium est, et plurimi ex ea uel aedificantur uel illuminantur: bona enim eius, dum multi<s> communicantur, adduntur." *Eusebius Gallicanus* 42.1, ed. Glorie, 497.

43. "Si uero e contrario, per inoboedientiam uel superbiam suam, alios—quod facilius euenire solet—ad maculam compulit: quantos destruxit, de tantis periculum damnationis incurrit." *Eusebius Gallicanus* 42.2, ed. Glorie, 497–98. The preacher adds: "Quamobrem, sicut ille ualde admirandus atque laudandus est: cuius cursus, multorum profectus est; ita ille merito lugendus est: cuius uita, multorum ruina est." Ed. Glorie, 498. Luke 2.34.

44. "Ideoque, carissimi: quae ad aedificationem pertinent, ea, in medio positi, agere studeamus, ne uitia nostra aliorum uirtutibus noceant." *Eusebius Gallicanus* 42.3, ed. Glorie, 498. See also 44.6.

45. "cordis cogitationibus uariis et improbis atque inhonestis agitamur aut uenenatis linguae gladiis uulneramur, pro minimis et paruissimis rebus scandalizantes . . . interdum professionem nostram regulae transgressione uiolamus," *Eusebius Gallicanus* 40.6, ed. Glorie, 480.

46. *Eusebius Gallicanus* 43.3.

47. *Eusebius Gallicanus* 44.3.

48. The full quote reads: "Ille enim, quia non potest aliquem absolute de loco salutis excludere: immittit primum occasiones et causas; immittit inoboedientiae passionem quam semper socia infelicitas comitatur, quae, cum captiuam illaqueauerit mentem, statim intoleranda atque impossibilia facit etiam illa quae parua ac leuia sunt." *Eusebius Gallicanus* 38.2, ed. Glorie, 439.

49. *Eusebius Gallicanus* 42.7.

50. *Eusebius Gallicanus* 38.2.

51. "ut ad suscipienda praecepta nec auctoritate nec ratione flectatur, sed, quod pessimum est, sibi soli credat, et pro omni ratione intentiones suas sequatur, et hoc solum rectum putet quod obdurato corde conceperit." *Eusebius Gallicanus* 38.3, ed. Glorie, 439.

52. "quanto humiliores et oboedientiores fuerimus, tanto super nos leuius ac dulcius *iugum* domini sentiemus; quantum oboedientiores fuerimus praepositis ac patribus nostris, tantum oboediet et deus orationibus nostris." *Eusebius Gallicanus* 38.5, ed. Glorie, 443.

53. "ille enim bene proficit, ille bene consummat: qui quotidie sic agit, quasi semper incipiat." *Eusebius Gallicanus* 38.5, ed. Glorie, 445. See also 38.6: "Verbi gratia: superbiae acquiescere coepi, regulam uiolaui, seniorem laesi, iuniorem destruxi. Si non statim me paenituit tamquam grauiter fuisse praeuentum, ita de die in diem libentissime me rapiet ipsa uiolentia consuetudinis et impetus passionis: ut iam nec delinquere me intellegam, nec peccare me sentiam. Obscurat enim atque obruit intellectum delicti, assiduitas delinquendi." Ed. Glorie, 446. Compare this to Cassian's account of Abbot Pinufius, who repeatedly left his monastery to join another as a novice. *Institutiones* 4.30.2–6 and *Conlationes* 20.1–2.

54. "Quanto ergo plus proficiemus, tanto plus humiliemur, quia, quanto plus humiliati fuerimus, tanto plus proficiemus." *Eusebius Gallicanus* 38.5, ed. Glorie, 445.

55. "*Ego non ueni facere uoluntatem meam, sed uoluntatem illius qui misit me patris.*" *Eusebius Gallicanus* 38.5, ed. Glorie, 444. John 6.38.

56. For this interpretation, see also Nouailhat, *Saints et patrons*, 312.

57. "quaecumque ei uel ordinanda uel gerenda era<n>t, illius tractatu atque iudicio uelut aequissimi examinis libra, pensauit." *Eusebius Gallicanus* 72.5, ed. Glorie, 776.

58. *Eusebius Gallicanus* 72.10. Compare Cassian, *Institutiones* 2.3.3.

59. On the patriarchal terminology and models employed in this sermon, see Kasper, *Theologie und Askese*, 21–28; Nouailhat, *Saints et patrons*, 104. I disagree, however, with their view that this model of leadership meant complete power over the community—Honoratus' position is depicted in this sermon primarily in a service mode.

60. *Eusebius Gallicanus* 72.5 and 72.9.

61. The complete passage reads: "Inter haec, animarum peruigil custos insistebat semper susceptum gregem assiduis exhortationibus erudire et quodammodo in melius commutare. Ac, sicut quaedam bestiae catulos suos

sine ulla specie parere dicuntur, quos rursum lambendo reformare ac sedulo linguae minsterio, asseruntur, ad speciem reuocare faciemque eis reddere et reliquas naturae partes ore perficere: ita et ille magnificus pastor, linguae medicabili blandimento, species mentium componebat, et in multis amissam iam paene Christi imaginem reformabat: alios *ex feris homines*, alios ex hominibus quodammodo angelos *efficiebat.*" *Eusebius Gallicanus* 72.9, ed. Glorie, 778. This view of how infant animals are formed can be found in Pliny, *Naturalis historia* 8.126, and Ovid, *Metamorphoses* 15.379–81. The italicised words in the quotation point to parallels with Hilary of Arles' sermon on Honoratus, *Sermo sancti Honorati* 17.

62. See also Nürnberg, *Askese als sozialer Impuls*, 225.

63. See discussions of these issues in Hunter, "Resistance to the Virginal Ideal," 45–64; Markus, *End of Ancient Christianity*, 38–40.

64. Pelagius, *Epistula ad Demetriadem* 9.2. Brown, "Pelagius and his Supporters," and *Augustine of Hippo*, 342; Bonner, "Augustine and Modern Research," 13.

65. Leyser, *Authority and Asceticism*, 7–13; Demacopoulos, *Five Models*, 105.

66. The complete passage reads: "Unde hortamur Charitatem vestram, maxime quia vos videmus frequentius convenisse, qui propositum altius habetis, id est, in ipso corpore Christi ex ejus munere, non meritis vestris, excellentiorem locum tenetis, habentes conscientiam quae a Deo donata est." Augustine of Hippo, *Sermo* 354.3, *PL* 39:1564, trans. Hill, 3.10:157.

67. "Verumtamen primum id noveritis, charissimi, in corpore Christi excellentiora membra esse non sola. Est enim conjugalis vita laudabilis, et habet in corpore Christi locum suum." Augustine of Hippo, *Sermo* 354.4, *PL* 39:1564: trans. Hill, 3.10:158.

68. Augustine of Hippo, *Sermo* 354.4. See also 354.9.

69. Augustine of Hippo, *Sermo* 354.8.

70. "Minorem locum habebit mater in regno coelorum, quoniam maritata est, quam filia, quoniam virgo est. Majorem enim locum filia virgo, minorem locum mater maritata, ambae tamen ibi: quomodo fulgida stella, obscura stella, ambae tamen in coelo." Augustine of Hippo, *Sermo* 354.9, *PL* 39:1568, trans. Hill, 3.10:162. See the same idea in *Sermones* 87.5 and 132.3. See also Leyser, *Authority and Asceticism*, 13. In fact, Pelagius was also not adverse to such a view of differentiated rewards in heaven—see, for example, *Epistula ad Demetriadem* 17.2.

71. Bonner, "Augustine and Modern Research," 14; Brown, "Pelagius and his Supporters," 103.

72. Brown, "Pelagius and his Supporters," 112; Markus, *End of Ancient Christianity*, 45–62; Demacopoulos, *Five Models*, 91.

73. Demacopoulos, *Five Models*, 85–105.

74. "uenire quidem ad eremum summa perfectio est, non perfecte in eremo uiuere summa damnatio est." *Eusebius Gallicanus* 44.1, ed. Glorie, 522. See also *Eusebius Gallicanus* 39.3: "Venire quidem ad eremum summa perfectio est, sed non perfecte in eremo uiuere summa damnatio est." Ed. Glorie, 458. See also 39.2, 40.2–3, 42.8 and 42.10, and the same idea in Cassian, *Institutiones* 4.33–38.

75. "Certum est, carissimi: nisi hic nostras quotidie resecemus et circumcidamus passiones, deteriores multo nos effici quam fuimus dum in saeculo uiueremus." *Eusebius Gallicanus* 42.6, ed. Glorie, 500. See also 40.5, 42.7.

76. "Nec hoc nobis sufficere putemus ad plenam salutem: quod inter seruos dei uel habitatione censemur uel nomine computamur; quod in insula uiuere atque inter monachos psallere uidemur." *Eusebius Gallicanus* 40.3, ed. Glorie, 476.

77. *Eusebius Gallicanus* 40.3.

78. "Aliquanti sufficere nobis putamus, quod secretum istud conscendimus, quod locum habitumque mutauimus, quod hic aliquantum temporis duximus, spem omnem in annorum numerum collocantes . . . Sed non ita est." *Eusebius Gallicanus* 40.2, ed. Glorie, 472.

79. *Eusebius Gallicanus* 39.3.

80. "Nescio de quibus delictis debeant esse securi: etiam de peccatis ignorantiae iudicandi ac *rationem de otiosis sermonibus* ac de cogitationibus *reddituri*. Nescio quae debeant delicta neglegere: de quibus et ipse dominus cum quadam definitione declarat: *Amen dico uobis: si quis dixerit fratri suo: Fatue, reus erit gehennae ignis*." *Eusebius Gallicanus* 42.8, ed. Glorie, 503. Hebrews 13.17, Matthew 5.22.

81. *Eusebius Gallicanus* 42.10.

82. "Quapropter non nobis sufficere credamus quod nos in hanc scholam cernimus congregatos, nisi quod uehementius in nobis neglegentias nostras professa perfectio quam nec assumpta condemnat." *Eusebius Gallicanus* 39.2, ed. Glorie, 456–57.

83. *Eusebius Gallicanus* 39.2. Cf. Luke 12.48.

84. "Inde ergo euenit, dilectissimi, sicut dixi: quod nos interdum deteriores esse sentimus quam in saeculo fuimus: quia hosti, quem ipsa conuersione prouocauimus, in medio certamine manus damus; nec in feruore, quo

coepimus, perseueramus, sed debellante tepore succumbimus." *Eusebius Gallicanus* 42.7, ed. Glorie, 502.

85. "At uero nunc, postquam uoluntatibus illius renuntiauimus . . . *Dirigit contra eos* uitiorum *acies, exhibens secum septem spiritus nequiores se:* si forte *domum nostram* spiritalibus bonis *inueniat uacuam* ac *uacantem,* et cum turbis suis eam ualeat occupare, ac sibi in ea, praemissis uitiis quasi quibusdam metatoribus, praeparet mansionem." *Eusebius Gallicanus* 42.6, ed. Glorie, 501. Genesis 14.8, Matthew 12.44–45.

86. *Eusebius Gallicanus* 40.5. See also 41.1. Compare Cassian, *Conlationes* 2.7–8.

87. "Certum est, carissimi: nisi hic nostras quotidie resecemus et circumcidamus passiones, deteriores multo nos effici quam fuimus dum in saeculo uiueremus." *Eusebius Gallicanus* 42.6, ed. Glorie, 500.

88. "Hic sumus, et tuti non sumus." *Eusebius Gallicanus* 40.6, ed. Glorie, 480. The preacher repeats the point again in 40.7. This is in contrast to other Lérinian writers, who describe the monastery as a place of peace and respite. Caesarius of Arles, for example, repeatedly refers to the monastery as a "haven" and a "safe port." *Sermones* 233.1, 234.1, 235.1–2, 236.2, 237.4. See discussion of this point in Markus, *End of Ancient Christianity*, 162.

89. "Sapiens ergo semper in compunctione et semper in metu est." *Eusebius Gallicanus* 40.2, ed. Glorie, 471.

90. "Non leui agendum est contritione ut debita illa redimantur quibus mors aeterna debetur, nec transitoria opus est satisfactione pro malis illis propter quae paratus est ignis aeternus." *Eusebius Gallicanus* 40.2, ed. Glorie, 473.

91. *Eusebius Gallicanus* 40.3.

92. "si me, de uigiliis reuertentem, inoboedientiae passio, si spiritus inuidiae, si consuetudo obtrectationis excipiat, si ad transgressionem regulae praesumptio furtiua sollicitet: et *zizania tritico miscui,* quod uidebar congregasse dispersi, spem messis auibus ferisque donaui; ac sic uno momento laborem totius noctis effudi." *Eusebius Gallicanus* 43.4, ed. Glorie, 514.

93. See, for example, *Eusebius Gallicanus* 8.3, 36.2–6, 39.5, 43.5, 44.8.

94. See, for example, *Eusebius Gallicanus* 36.7, 39.5, 43.5.

95. Compare *Eusebius Gallicanus* 40.3 with *Eusebius Gallicanus* 4.5.

96. Pricoco identifies this optimism as a defining feature of Lérinian thought. *Isola dei santi*, 182–83.

97. Weaver, *Divine Grace*, 69.

98. "Et ubi uiderit deus deuotionem animi ardentiorem, insinuabit affectum; et quanto nos addiderimus ad studium, tanto ille apponet ad adiutorium; quanto nos apposuerimus ad diligentiam, tanto ille addet ad gloriam: Qui habet dabitur ei, et abundabit." *Eusebius Gallicanus* 38.7, ed. Glorie, 448. Matthew 13.12.

99. "Gratia ergo de gratia nascitur, et profectus profectibus seruiunt. Lucra lucris, et merita meritis locum faciunt: ut, quanto quis plus acquirere coeperit, tanto plus conetur et delectetur inquirere." *Eusebius Gallicanus* 38.7, ed. Glorie, 448.

100. "*Petite*, inquit, *et accipietis, quaerite et inuenietis, pulsate et aperietur uobis*; id est: ut *petamus* orando; *quaeramus* laborando; *pulsemus* desiderando, *pulsemus* proficiendo, *pulsemus* perseuerando; et in spem caelestium promissorum tanto incitemur studio, tantoque inardescamus affectu: ut cum praemiorum dignitate, desideriorum magnitudo concordet." *Eusebius Gallicanus* 38.1, ed. Glorie, 435. Matthew 7.7, Luke 11.9. See the parallel passage in a sermon to the laity, *Eusebius Gallicanus* 64.1.

101. "lentum enim et parum gratum quaerere gratiam diuini muneris, maxima est iniuria remuneratoris." *Eusebius Gallicanus* 38.1, ed. Glorie, 435.

102. "Ergo totis licet et animae et corporis laboribus desudemus, totis licet oboedientiae uiribus exerceamur, nihil tamen condignum merito pro caelestibus bonis compensare et offerre ualebimus. Non ualent uitae praesentis obsequia, aeternae uitae gaudia; lassescant licet membra uigiliis, pallescant licet ora ieiuniis, *non erunt* tamen *condignae passiones huius temporis ad futuram gloriam quae reuelabitur in nobis*." *Eusebius Gallicanus* 38.1, ed. Glorie, 436. Romans 8.18.

103. *Eusebius Gallicanus* 38.1.

104. "Vrgeamus itaque, carissimi, cursum nostrum, ut crescat in nouissimo uita nostra; quaeramus usque in finem, unde sine fine gaudere mereamur." *Eusebius Gallicanus* 38.8, ed. Glorie, 448.

105. See for example *Eusebius Gallicanus* 8.2, 37.2, 39.3, 40.2–4.

106. On Cassian's conception of "purity of heart" see Stewart, *Cassian the Monk*, 41–44.

107. On the role of fasting, prayers and vigils see *Eusebius Gallicanus* 8.2, 37.2, 38.5.

108. "Quid prodest, quod nos pretiosis uigiliis laboribusque conficimus, et ea quae maxime deus noster in nobis desiderat non habemus— hoc est: *cor mundum* . . . ?" *Eusebius Gallicanus* 41.1, ed. Glorie, 487. Psalm

50.12. A rewritten version of this passage appears in Defensor, *Liber scintil-larum* 1.49, where it is attributed to Caesarius.

109. "non nobis sufficere putemus terram corporis nostri uigiliarum exercitiis edomare uel ieiuniorum labore conficere, sed imprimis mentem exstirpatione uitiorum mundare conemur." *Eusebius Gallicanus* 43.1, ed. Glorie, 511–12. See the parallel passage in the *Instructiones* now attributed to Columbanus, 2.2. The motif also found favour with Caesarius. See, for example, *Sermo* 6.4–7.

110. "Quid prodest quod affligis corpus tuum, quando nihil proficit cor tuum?" *Eusebius Gallicanus* 39.4, ed. Glorie, 461.

111. See for example *Eusebius Gallicanus* 43.4: "Quod si solum laboret corpus, et spiritus non repugnet: quid prodest passiones impugnari a fam-ula, quae pacem inueniuntur habere cum domina?" Ed. Glorie, 513. See parallel passage in Columbanus, *Instructiones* 2.2. Another example can be found in *Eusebius Gallicanus* 39.4: "Noueritis itaque, fratres, nihil prodesse si carnem nostram ieiuniis ac uigiliis affligamus, et mentem nostram non emendemus aut quae interiora sunt non curemus . . . Ieiunare, uigilare, et mores non corrigere, sic est: quomodo si aliquis extra uineam aut circa uin-eam exstirpet aut colat, et uineam ipsam desertam atque incultam dimittat, ut *spinas ac tribulos germinet,* quae insistente cultore iucundissimos ex se fructus proferre potuisset. Agnoscite itaque, carissimi, quod, ad salutem perpetuam conquirendam, abstinentia corporalis sola non sufficit nisi et animae quoque ieiunium per abstinentiam uitiorum fuerit sociatum . . . Et idcirco, dilectissimi, ita corpus exerceamus ieiuniis: ut mentem purgemus a uitiis." Ed. Glorie, 459–62. Genesis 3.18. See parallel passages in Defensor, *Liber scintillarum* 10.58, 10.61; Columbanus, *Instructiones* 2.2.

112. *Eusebius Gallicanus* 43.4.

113. "Quod si concupiscentia peccati arcem mentis obtineat: quid mihi prodest, si nondum maculatus uideatur exterior homo, meliore sui parte uitiata? Si enim interior uictus est, iam uterque captiuus est. Quid prodest, si extra ciuitatem geramus bellum, et intus patiamur excidium?" *Eusebius Gallicanus* 43.4, ed. Glorie, 514. See parallel passage in Colum-banus, *Instructiones* 2.2.

114. "Quid prodest, si locus quietus tantum corporaliter teneatur, et inquietudo in corde uersetur; si in habitatione silentium sit, et in habitatori-bus uitiorum sit tumultus et colluctatio passionum; si exteriora nostra se-renitas teneat, et interiora tempestas?" *Eusebius Gallicanus* 44.1, ed. Glorie, 522. See also 39.3: "Quid, inquam, prodest, si in habitatione silentium sit, et in habitatoribus uitiorum tumultus sit et colluctatio passionum; si ex-

teriora nostra serenitas teneat, et interiora tempestas?" Ed. Glorie, 458. These passages appear, excerpted and rewritten, in Defensor, *Liber scintillarum* 16.47.

115. *Eusebius Gallicanus* 39.4.

116. "Studeamus ergo ut cum obsequiis labiorum uita concordet et consonet . . . quando enim praeualent in nobis terrenae superfluae cupiditates, quando tyrannico dominatu malitia in nobis regnat, quando ira superequitat: nos, illi laudabiles eremitae qui extra mundum nos credimus, mundum intra nos inclusum tenemus." *Eusebius Gallicanus* 44.1A, ed. Glorie, 521.

117. Nürnberg, *Askese als sozialer Impuls*, 230. I find Nürnberg's characterisation of the Lérinian social impulse very persuasive, but her work should be used with caution. Not only does she assume that the Eusebian sermons are entirely the work of Faustus of Riez (an issue which is unsettled at best), she also treats the sermons edited by Engelbrecht as Faustus' work, despite the fact that Faustus' authorship of them has been persuasively disproved. See Morin, "Critique des sermons," 49–61; Bergmann, *Studien zu einer kritischen Sichtung*, 3–8; Leroy, "Oeuvre oratoire," 1:4–5.

118. The passage as a whole reads: "uidemus aliquotiens etiam illas animas paenitentiam petere quae ab ineunte adolescentia consecratae pretiosum deo thesaurum deuouerunt, inspirare hoc deum pro ecclesiae nostrae profectibus nouerimus: ut medicinam quam inuadunt sani, discant quaerere uulnerati; ut bonis etiam parua deflentibus, ingentia ipsi mala lugere consuescant. Ac sic, quando iam illa persona, quae forte minus indiget paenitentia, aliquid fide dignum atque compunctum sub oculis ecclesiae gerit, fructum suum etiam de aliena aedificatione multiplicat et meritum suum de lucro proficientis accumulat, ut, dum perfectione illius emendatur alterius uita, spiritali fenore ad ipsum boni operis recurrat usura." *Eusebius Gallicanus* 8.5, ed. Glorie, 87.

119. "Felix per quem etiam in aliena salute exundant merita propria! felix in cuius mentem redundat salus aliena!" *Eusebius Gallicanus* 8.5, ed. Glorie, 87.

120. "crescit deuotio meritorum turba mirantium." *Eusebius Gallicanus* 8.5, ed. Glorie, 88.

121. "Vir ille praecipuus illic doctus, ut hic doceret; illic ditatus, ut hic feneraret; illic illuminatus, ut hic refulgeret; illic purificatus, ut hic sanctificaret; et, ut hic exercere posset confectionem curationum, illuc quaesiuit aromata et pigmenta uirtutum." *Eusebius Gallicanus* 35.5, ed. Glorie, 404. 1 Corinthians 12.9–10.

122. On the prevalence of this theme in Lérinian hagiography in particular, see Markus, *End of Ancient Christianity*, 194.

123. See for example Rousseau, "Cassian: Monastery and World," 68–89; Markus, *End of Ancient Christianity*, 199–213; Weigel, *Faustus of Riez*, 101.

124. This point is emphasised by Casiday, *Tradition and Theology*, 54–56.

125. Leyser, *Authority and Asceticism*, 65–83; Christophe, *Cassien et Césaire*, 74–77.

126. On the prominence of these themes in Augustine's writings, see Leyser, *Authority and Asceticism*, 11–13; Markus, *End of Ancient Christianity*, 77–78, 158. On the extensive direct borrowings from Augustine in the Eusebian sermons, see Glorie, *Eusebius "Gallicanus,"* 1048–52.

127. Rousseau, *Ascetics, Authority and the Church*, 188; Demacopoulos, *Five Models*, 107–26. This conception of community was inherently conservative and the Lérinian monks saw it as their guarantor of orthodoxy. The *Commonitoria* of Vincent of Lérins is a prime example of this way of thinking, in which orthodoxy is defined primarily in terms of which traditions have been handed down by his predecessors. See in particular *Commonitoria* 1–2. On the conservatism of Lérins see also Kasper, *Theologie und Askese*, 18, 66, 266.

128. For each sin that Cassian focused on, he brought out the ways in which it threatened community. Thus his account of gluttony highlighted the dangers of ostentatious virtue and of judging the fasts of fellow monks. Avarice created inequality among those who were supposed to be brothers in Christ, anger brought discord, sadness made monks give up contact with their brethren, and acedia produced disdain for companions and the desire to run away (*Institutiones*, 5.23.2–3, 5.30, 7.7–16, 8.14, 9.7, 10.2.1–2). Pride was the worst shortcoming because it made monks disobedient and harsh, no longer content to bear the yoke of the monastery or to be instructed by their elders. It made them long to leave the discipline of the coenobium in order to live as a solitary or to gather their own disciples and start a new monastery. It destroyed the humility and equality upon which asceticism should be based (*Institutiones*, 12.25–30). Community was also the solution to sin, however. Monks could only conquer avarice by residing in a monastery and being content with the food and clothing provided there (*Institutiones*, 7.29). They should not flee into the desert to avoid anger with others, since no one could claim to be truly virtuous if he had never been tested by company (*Institutiones*, 8.18–19). Pride could be destroyed only

through true humility and complete submission of the will under the yoke of obedience, "such that there is no desire alive in us whatsoever apart from the abba's command." *Institutiones*, 9.13 and 10.25.

129. On the role of the ascetic expert in Cassian's writings, see Leyser, *Authority and Asceticism*, 55.

130. On the influence of Augustine and Cassian on Caesarius' pastoral work, see Leyser, *Authority and Asceticism*, 82–100.

131. See, for example, Caesarius of Arles, *Sermones* 6, 196.

132. Markus, *End of Ancient Christianity*, 205; Klingshirn, *Caesarius of Arles*, 182; Diem, *Keusch und rein,* 171.

133. Caesarius of Arles, *Sermones* 53.2. For an example of how to reprimand your "brother or neighbour," see 42.2. For expansion of some of the ideas here, see Bailey, "Monks and Lay Communities."

134. See discussion of this in chapter 3.

135. *Vita Caesarii* 1.6.

136. For Cassian's imprecations against vainglorious ascetic acts, see *Institutiones* 1.2.4, 3.9–10, 4.3–4, 5.9, 5.23, 6.23, 11.4, and *Conlationes* 2.16–22.

137. *Vita Caesarii* 1.7. Leyser describes Caesarius' time at Lérins as "a relentless show of moral superiority." *Authority and Asceticism*, 86. Klingshirn notes that the *Vita* "casts doubt on [Caesarius'] suitability for the common life." *Caesarius of Arles*, 29.

138. Caesarius of Arles, *Sermones* 233.2–7, 234.2, 235.5, 236.3, 237.4, 238.5.

139. Caesarius of Arles, *Sermones* 233.6.

140. Caesarius of Arles, *Sermones* 233.3, 235.3.

141. "Et quia pro sancta oboedientia et inmaculata opera vestra universus mundus vos et admiratur et diligit . . . oportet, ut honorem et amorem, quem ab omnibus excipitis, assiduis orationibus et inmaculatis actibus repensetis." Caesarius of Arles, *Sermones* 236.3, ed. Morin, 942, trans. Mueller, 66:212.

142. Caesarius of Arles, *Sermones* 234.1. For other examples of this idea, see *Sermones* 233.7, 235.6, 236.5, 237.5.

143. In a sermon directed to the monks of Lérins, Caesarius sought to dissuade them from following the clerical path which he had himself taken. True humility, he insisted, would mean turning down the opportunity of office. Caesarius of Arles, *Sermones* 236.4.

144. Markus, *End of Ancient Christianity*, 199.

145. Markus, *End of Ancient Christianity*, 199, 214.

146. Markus, *End of Ancient Christianity*, 200.

147. Markus also uses the term "ascetic take-over," 17.

148. Markus, *End of Ancient Christianity*, 203–5.

149. Markus, *End of Ancient Christianity*, 206–8. Note this argument also in Christophe, *Cassien et Césaire*, 59, 66.

150. Markus, *End of Ancient Christianity*, 202.

151. See chapter 3.

152. See chapter 3.

153. See chapters 4 and 5.

154. Markus himself notes that "specifically monastic and ascetic virtues are less easy to detect in pastoral work and preaching," an admission which rather undercuts the force of his argument. *End of Ancient Christianity*, 202. For scepticism as to the extent and impact of the ascetic invasion, see Jussen, "Über 'Bischofsherrschaften,'" 682–84; Rousseau, review of Markus, *End of Ancient Christianity*, in *Prudentia* 23.2 (1991): 62–66.

155. For the evidence of opposition to Caesarius, see chapter 3.

156. This complexity and variety has been explored by several other authors, though different patterns of division emerge from their work. See in particular Courtois, "Évolution du monachisme," 42–3; Leyser, "This Sainted Isle," 192; Pricoco, *Isola dei santi*, 14; Dunn, *Emergence of Monasticism*, 83–84; Prinz, *Frühes Mönchtum*, 19–117.

Conclusion

1. McKitterick, *Frankish Church*, esp. 81–112; Amos, "Origin and Nature"; Klingshirn, *Caesarius of Arles*, 273–86.

Epilogue

1. There are extensive excerpts from the Eusebius Gallicanus sermons in the seventh-century *florilegia* the *Liber scintillarum*, and sermons from the collection appear in the homiliaries of Paul the Deacon and Alain of Farfa. The Eucharistic theology of Eusebian sermon 17 and the rite of confirmation in sermon 29 were very influential. On these last two, see Carle, "Homélie de pâques" and "Sermon de s. Fauste de Riez"; Buchem,

Homélie pseudo-Eusébienne. See also the summary of excerpts in Glorie, *Eusebius "Gallicanus,"* 192–23, 334–36. On the liturgical contributions of the Eusebius Gallicanus, see Leroy, "Oeuvre oratoire," 1:484–87.

2. See, in particular, Leroy, "Oeuvre oratoire," 1:57–191, and Glorie, *Eusebius "Gallicanus,"* xxvi–xxxvii, 903–50.

3. Cerquiglini, *In Praise of the Variant,* 27. Taylor, *Textual Situations,* 11, and Nichols, "Introduction," 8–9, both also point to the "multiplicity" of medieval texts in manuscript form. Note, however, that this concept of multiplicity has been extended to printed books as well, especially in the early modern era. See Johns, *Nature of the Book;* McKitterick, *Print, Manuscript.* I owe these references to Meridee Bailey.

4. Cerquiglini, *In Praise of the Variant,* 35.

5. Cerquiglini, *In Praise of the Variant,* 34.

6. There are interesting parallels to the situation which Rio describes in relation to early medieval *formulae.* "Charters, Law Codes and Formulae."

7. Taylor, *Textual Situations,* 10. See also Rasmussen, "Célébration épiscopale," 586; Hen, *Royal Patronage,* 13–15; Cross, "Early Western Liturgical Manuscripts," 64.

8. For example, K^0 is 430 × 297mm; Be is 309 × 310mm and P^0 is 320 × 230mm. The manuscript *sigla* used are those in Glorie's edition. See the appendix for their full titles.

9. Q^0. See Yitzhak Hen on similar portable handbooks from the Carolingian period. "Knowledge of Canon Law," 125–28.

10. Sermon 12 and its variation 12A occur a combined total of ninety-one times in the manuscripts. Sermons 13 and 17 occur sixty-nine and eighty-four times respectively. All the other sermons in this series, including sermon 24, which is often found with it, occur at least thirty times. These figures are dwarfed, however, by the popularity of the *ad monachos* series. Sermons 39, 40, 41 and 44 (which are frequently found together in manuscripts) each occur between 164 and 178 times. Sermon 38 was also very popular, appearing a total of 114 times. The others in the series all occur at least forty-seven times. Leroy, "Oeuvre oratoire," 1:57–58, and Buchem, *Homélie pseudo-Eusébienne,* 47–48, have useful analyses of sermon groupings in the manuscripts.

11. Sermon 51 appears forty-two times, 47 appears forty-nine times, 28 appears twenty-seven times, 49 appears twenty times.

12. Sermon 1 appears fifteen times, 9 and 10 appear twenty-one and nineteen times respectively, 27 appears thirteen times, 34 appears seventeen times, and 61 appears twenty-one times.

13. For a description of the elaborate frontispiece to this work, see *Livre illustre en Occident,* 6–7.

14. For the contents of this manuscript, see Van Den Gheyn, *Catalogue des manuscrits de la Bibliothèque royale de Belgique,* 2:224–6.

15. Hen, "Merovingian Commentary."

16. Hen, "Merovingian Commentary."

17. For a full list of the contents of this very interesting manuscript see Denis, *Codices Manuscripti Theologici,* 2:628–47. On the lower layers of the palimpsest see Bick, "Wiener Palimpseste," 1–109.

18. For descriptions of this manuscript, see Scherer, *Verzeichnis der Handschriften,* 81–82; Lowe, *Codices Latini Antiquiores,* 7:929.

19. The sermons of Caesarius in SΣ[1] are numbers 4, 233–36, and 155–56 in Morin's *CCSL* edition. On the other works, see Hofman, "Regula magistri," 145–46; Bruckner, *Scriptoria Medii Aevi Helvetica,* 2:69.

20. Chavasse, "Composition et date," 82–86.

21. For the contents of this manuscript, see Lauer, *Bibliothèque Nationale: Catalogue général des manuscrits latins,* 2:166–67; Verbraken, "Manuscrit latin 1771," 67–81, and "Pièces inédites du manuscrit latin 1771," 51–63.

22. Verbraken, "Manuscrit latin 1771," 70.

23. For a full list of contents, see Löw, "Stadrömisches Lektionar," 20–37. The homiliary was originally three volumes, but the first of these is now lost.

24. Bouhot, "Homéliaire des *sancti catholici Patres,*" 132–34; Chavasse, "Sermonnaire d'Agimond," 801.

25. Gamber, *Codices Liturgici Latini Antiquiores,* 2:597–98.

26. See the prologue to the collection, edited by Rose, *Verzeichnis der lateinischen Handschriften,* 1:81–82.

27. Rose, *Verzeichnis der lateinischen Handschriften,* 1:82–83.

28. On the very complicated relationships between the surviving homiliaries from this period, see Bouhot, "Homéliaire de Saint-Pierre," 87–115.

29. See Grégoire, "Homéliaires mérovingiens," 901–17, and *Homéliaires liturgiques médiévaux.*

30. See discussion of this issue in Gatch, *Preaching and Theology,* 25–30; d'Avray, *Preaching of the Friars,* 18–20, 62; McKitterick, *Frankish Church,* 92–97; Amos, "Preaching and the Sermon," 45–49.

31. McKitterick, *Frankish Church,* 6–7, 122–23, 160–1; Amos, "Origin and Nature," 1–3.

32. d'Avray, *Preaching of the Friars,* 123–6. See also Amos, "Early Medieval Sermons," 231.

33. d'Avray, *Preaching of the Friars,* 123.

34. d'Avray, *Preaching of the Friars,* 126.

35. Amos, "Origin and Nature," 14–15, 143, 164. McKitterick notes that the Carolingians turned in particular to the fifth and sixth centuries. *Frankish Church,* 64, 88–90.

36. Leroy, "Oeuvre oratoire," 1:70–77. The beginning and end of the manuscript are missing, which is why the collection does not appear in full.

37. Cunningham, "Contents of the Newberry Library Homiliarium," 267–301.

38. Cunningham, "Contents of the Newberry Library Homiliarium," 270–71.

39. Holder, *Handschriften der Grossherzoglich-Badischen Hof- und Landesbibliothek zu Karlsruhe,* 1:33–45.

40. These include thirty homilies or prefaces attributed to Gregory the Great, twenty-eight attributed to Bede, eighteen to Maximus, sixteen to John Chrysostom, fourteen to Augustine, thirteen to Leo, seven to Jerome, two to Ambrose, and one each to Isidore, Fulgentius, Faustinus, and Eusebius the bishop. The last two are sermons 13 and 12 from the Eusebius Gallicanus. Thirty sermons are either anonymous, or the attribution is illegible. There is some debate over the dating of this manuscript. See the different views in Leroy, "Oeuvre oratoire," 1:107; Libri, "Notice des manuscrits," 484.

41. For a discussion of biblical readings during this period, see Willis, *St. Augustine's Lectionary,* 1–3, 80–84.

42. Grégoire, *Homéliaires du Moyen Âge,* 142–60.

43. Wilmart, *Bibliothecae Apostolicae Vaticanae—Codices Reginenses Latini,* 1:337–42.

44. For a full account of the contents, see Wilmart, "Developpement patristique," 276–78.

45. Prete, "Note di agiographia ascolana," 59.

46. This is the conclusion of Étaix, "Lectionnaire d l'office à Cluny," 155–56.

47. Delisle, *Inventaire des manuscrits de la Bibliothèque Nationale, Fonds de Cluny,* 31–43.

48. For example P^3, P^5, P^8, and P^9.

49. It is difficult to know, however, whether this is a fair representation of the original manuscript, since it was clearly longer before it was rebound in the sixteenth century. Leroy, "Oeuvre oratoire," 1:66–67; Engelbrecht, *Studien über die Schriften,* 49–53.

50. Particularly connected, of course, to the Cistercian order. See Wenzel, *Latin Sermon Collections,* 278–83; Kienzle, "Twelfth-Century Monastic Sermon," in Kienzle, ed., *Sermon,* 310.

51. Bériou, "Sermons latins après 1200," in Kienzle, ed. *Sermon,* 363–67; d'Avray, *Preaching of the Friars,* 20–22; Longère, *Prédication médiévale,* 78–93.

52. d'Avray, *Preaching of the Friars,* 61.

53. d'Avray, *Preaching of the Friars,* 13, 57.

54. d'Avray emphasises the novelties of the thirteenth century, *Preaching of the Friars,* 20–22.

55. *Catalogue général des manuscrits des Bibliothèques publiques des Départements,* 3:317.

56. Van Den Gheyn, *Catalogue des manuscrits de la Bibliothèque royale de Belgique,* 5:135–41.

BIBLIOGRAPHY

Primary Works

Ambrose of Milan. *De Nabuthe,* edited by Karl Schenkl. *CSEL* 32:2, *Sancti Ambrosii opera.* Prague: Tempsky, 1897.

———. *Sermones. PL* 17, *Sancti Ambrosii Mediolanensis episcopi opera omnia.* Paris: Garnier, 1845.

Audoenus of Rouen. *Vita Eligii,* edited by Bruno Krusch. *MGH SRM* 4, *Passiones vitaeque sanctorum aevi Merovingici et antiquiorum aliquot.* Hanover: Hahn, 1902.

Augustine of Hippo. *Confessiones,* edited by James J. O'Donnell. *Confessions.* Oxford: Clarendon Press, 1992.

———. *De civitate dei,* edited by Bernhard Dombart and Alfons Kalb. *CCSL* 47 and 48, *Sancti Aurelii Augustini de civitate dei.* Turnhout: Brepols, 1955.

———. *De doctrina christiana,* edited by Joseph Martin. *CCSL* 32, *Sancti Aurelii Augustini de doctrina christiana, de uera religione.* Turnhout: Brepols, 1962.

———. *Enarrationes in Psalmos,* edited by Eligius Dekkers and J. Fraipont. *CCSL* 38, 39, and 40. *Sancti Aurelii Augustini enarrationes in Psalmos.* Turnhout: Brepols, 1954.

215

————. *Sermones* Dolbeau, edited by François Dolbeau. *Vingt-six sermons au peuple d'Afrique.* Paris: Institut d'Études Augustiniennes, 1996.

————. *Sermones. MA* 1, *Sancti Augustini sermones post Maurinos reperti.* Rome: Tipografia Polioglotta Vaticana, 1930.

————. *Sermones. PL* 38 and 39. *Sancti Aurelii Augustini Hipponensis episcopi opera omnia.* Turnhout: Brepols, 1845–86. Translated by Edmund Hill. *The Works of Saint Augustine: A Translation for the Twenty-first Century,* 11 vols. Hyde Park: New City Press, 1990–.

[Where reference is made to Augustinian sermons published elsewhere, the edition is noted in the endnote.]

Avitus of Vienne. *Epistulae,* edited by Rudolf Peiper. *MGH AA* 6:2, *Alcimi Ecdicii Aviti Viennensis episcopi opera quae supersunt.* Berlin: Weidmannos, 1883.

————. *Sermones,* edited by Ulysse Chevalier. *Oeuvres complètes de Saint Avit, évêque de Vienne.* Lyon: Emmanuel Vitte, 1890.

Caesarius of Arles. *Sermones,* edited by Germain Morin. *CCSL* 103 and 104, *Sancti Caesarii Arelatensis sermones.* Turnhout: Brepols, 1953. Translated by Mary Magdeleine Mueller. *FC* 31, 47 and 66, *Saint Caesarius of Arles: Sermons.* Washington, D.C.: Catholic University of America Press, 1956–73.

Celestine I. *Epistulae. PL* 50, *S. Coelestinus I: Epistola et decreta.* Turnhout: Brepols, 1975.

Columbanus. *Instructiones,* edited and translated by G. S. M. Walker. *Scriptores latini Hiberniae* 2: *Sancti Columbani opera.* Dublin: Dublin Institute for Advanced Studies, 1970.

Concilia Galliae a. 314–a. 506, edited by Charles Munier. *CCSL* 148. Turnhout: Brepols, 1963.

Concilia Galliae a. 511–695, edited by Charles de Clercq. *CCSL* 148A. Turnhout: Brepols, 1963.

Constantius of Lyon. *Vita Germani,* edited by René Borius. *SC* 112, *Constance de Lyon: Vie de saint Germain d'Auxerre.* Paris: Éditions du Cerf, 1965.

Defensor. *Liber scintillarum,* edited by Henri M. Rochais. *CCSL* 117, *Defensoris Locogiacensis monachi liber scintillarum.* Turnhout: Brepols, 1957.

Eucherius of Lyon. *Passio Agaunensium martyrum,* edited by Karl Wotke. *CSEL* 31, *Sancti Eucherii Lugdunensis formulae spiritalis intelligentiae.* Vienna: Tempsky, 1894.

Eusebius Gallicanus, edited by Fr. Glorie. *CCSL* 101, 101A, and 101B, *Eusebius "Gallicanus": Collectio homiliarum.* Turnhout: Brepols, 1970.

Faustus of Riez. *Epistulae et sermones,* edited by Augustus Engelbrecht. *CSEL* 21, *Fausti Reiensis praeter sermones pseudoeusebianoa opera.* Prague: Tempsky, 1891.

Gennadius of Marseille. *Liber de viris illustribus. PL* 58, *Gennadius Massiliensis liber de scriptoribus ecclesiasticis.* Turnhout: Brepols, n.d.

Gregory of Tours. *GC, GM, VJ, VM, VP,* edited by Bruno Krusch. *MGH SRM* 1:2, *Gregorii episcopi Turonensis miracula et opera minora.* Hanover: Hahn, 1969.

———. *LH,* edited by Bruno Krusch and Wilhelm Levison. *MGH SRM* 1:1, *Gregorii episcopi Turonensis libri historiarum X.* Hanover: Hahn, 1951. Translated by Lewis Thorpe. *The History of the Franks.* Harmondsworth, UK: Penguin Books, 1974.

Gregory the Great. *Regula pastoralis,* edited by Floribert Rommel. *SC* 381 and 382, *Règle pastorale.* Paris: Éditions du Cerf, 1992.

Hilary of Arles. *Sermo sancti Honorati,* edited by Marie-Denise Valentin. *SC* 46, *Sermo sancti Hilarii de vita sancti Honorati.* Paris: Éditions du Cerf, 1977.

John Cassian. *Conlationes,* edited by Michael Petschenig. *CSEL* 13, *Iohannis Cassiani conlationes XXIII.* Vienna: Apud C. Geroldi filium, 1886.

———. *Institutiones,* edited by Michael Petschenig. *CSEL* 17, *Iohannis Cassiani de institutis coenobiorum.* Vienna: Tempsky, 1888. Translated by Boniface Ramsey. *John Cassian: The Institutes.* New York: The Newman Press, 2000.

John Chrysostom. *Homilies.* Translated by Gus G. Christo. *St. John Chrysostom on Repentance and Almsgiving.* Washington, D.C.: Catholic University of America Press, 1988.

Martin of Braga. *De correctione rusticorum,* edited by Claude W. Barlow. *Martini episcopi Bracarensis opera omnia.* New Haven: Yale University Press, 1950.

Maximus of Turin. *Sermones,* edited by Almut Mutzenbecher. *CCSL* 23, *Maximi episcopi Taurenensis sermones.* Turnhout: Brepols, 1962.

Paulinus the Deacon. *Vita Ambrosii,* edited by Mary S. Kaniecka. *Vita sancti Ambrosii Mediolanensis episcopi: A Paulino eius notario ad beatum Augustinum conscripta.* Washington, D.C.: Catholic University of America Press, 1928.

Pelagius. *Epistula ad Demetriadem.* Translated by Bryn R. Rees, *The Letters of Pelagius and his Followers.* Woodbridge, UK: Boydell Press, 1991.

Peter Chrysologus. *Sermones. PL* 52, *Sancti Petri Chrysologi archiepiscopi Ravennatis opera omnia.* Turnhout: Brepols, 1973. Translated by George E. Ganss. *FC* 17, *Saint Peter Chrysologus: Selected Sermons and Saint Valerian: Homilies.* Washington, D.C.: Catholic University of America Press, 1965. Translated by William B. Palardy. *FC* 109 and 110, *St. Peter Chrysologus: Selected Sermons.* Washington, D.C.: Catholic University of America Press, 2004–5.

Prudentius. *Liber peristephanon,* edited by Maurice Cunningham. *CCSL* 126, *Aurelii Prudentii Clementis carmina.* Turnhout: Brepols, 1966.

Regulae Patrum, edited by Adalbert De Vogüé. *SC* 297 and 298, *Les Règles des Saints Pères: Tome I: Trois règles de Lérins au Ve siècle.* Paris: Éditions du Cerf, 1982.

Rufinus of Aquileia. *Expositio symboli,* edited by Manlio Simonetti. *CCSL* 20, *Tyrannii Rufuni opera.* Turnhout: Brepols, 1961.

Sidonius Apollinaris. *Epistulae,* edited and translated by William B. Anderson. *Sidonius: Poems and Letters,* 2 vols. Cambridge: Harvard University Press, 1936 and 1965.

Sulpicius Severus. *Vita Martini,* edited by Jacques Fontaine. *SC* 133, 134, and 135, *Vie de saint Martin.* Paris: Éditions du Cerf, 1967–69.

Valerian of Cimiez. *Homiliae. PL* 52, *S. Valerianus Cemeliensis episcopus.* Translated by George E. Ganss. *FC* 17, *Saint Peter Chrysologus: Selected Sermons and Saint Valerian: Homilies.* Washington, D.C.: Catholic University of America Press, 1965.

Victricius of Rouen. *De laude sanctorum,* edited and translated by René Herval. *Origines chrétiennes de la IIe Lyonnaise gallo-romaine à la Normandie ducale (IVe–XIe siècles): Avec le texte complet et la traduction intégrale du de laude sanctorum de saint Victrice (396).* Paris: A. et J. Picard, 1966.

Vincent of Lérins. *Commonitoria,* edited by Reginald S. Moxon. *The Commonitorium of Vincentius of Lerins.* Cambridge: Cambridge University Press, 1915.

Vita Caesarii, edited by Bruno Krusch. *MGH SRM* 3, *Passiones vitaeque sanctorum aevi Merovingici et antiquiorum aliquot.* Hanover: Hahn, 1977.

Vita Eugendii, edited by François Martine. *SC* 142, *Vie des pères du Jura.* Paris: Éditions du Cerf, 1968.

Vita Hilarii. PL 50, *S. Hilarii Arelatensis vita.* Turnhout: Brepols, 1975.

Secondary Works

Allen, Pauline. "The Homilist and the Congregation: A Case-Study of Chrysostom's Homilies on Hebrews." *Augustinianum* 36 (1996): 397–421. .

———. "John Chrysostom's Homilies on I and II Thessalonians: The Preacher and his Audience." *Studia Patristica* 31 (1997): 3–21.

———. "The Identity of Sixth-Century Preachers and Audiences in Byzantium." *Mediterranean Archaeology* 11 (1998): 245–53.

Allen, Pauline, and Wendy Mayer. "Through a Bishop's Eyes: Towards a Definition of Pastoral Care in Late Antiquity." *Augustinianum* 40 (2000): 345–97.

Amore, Agostino. "Epipodio e Alessandro." In *Bibliotheca sanctorum,* 4:1274–45. Rome: Istituto Giovanni XXIII nella Pontificia Università Lateranense, 1964.

Amos, Thomas. "The Origin and Nature of the Carolingian Sermon." Ph.D. dissertation, Michigan State University, 1983.

———. "Monks and Pastoral Care in the Early Middle Ages." In *Religion, Culture and Society in the Early Middle Ages: Studies in Honor of Richard E. Sullivan,* edited by Thomas X. Noble and John J. Contreni, 165–80. Kalamazoo, Mich.: Medieval Institute Publications, 1987.

———. "Preaching and the Sermon in the Carolingian World." In *De Ore Domini: Preacher and Word in the Middle Ages,* edited by Thomas L. Amos, Eugene A. Green, and Beverly Mayne Kienzle, 41–60. Kalamazoo, Mich.: Medieval Institute Publications, 1989.

———. "Early Medieval Sermons and their Audiences." In *De l'homélie au sermon: histoire de la prédication médiévale,* edited by Jacqueline Hamesse and Xavier Hermand, 1–14. Louvain-la-Neuve: Publications de l'Institute d'Études Médiévales, 1993.

Antier, Jean-Jacques. *Lérins: L'île sainte de la Côte d'Azur.* Paris: Éditions S.O.S., 1973.

Arnold, Carl F. *Caesarius von Arelate und die gallische Kirche seiner Zeit.* Leipzig: J. C. Hinrichs, 1894.

Astell, Ann W. "Introduction." In *Lay Sanctity: A Search for Models,* edited by Ann W. Astell, 1–26. Notre Dame, Ind.: University of Notre Dame Press, 2000.

Atwood, Margaret. *Alias Grace.* New York: Doubleday, 1996.

Aubrun, Michel. "Le clergé rural dans le royaume franc du VIe au XIIe siècle." In *Le clergé rural dans l'Europe médiévale et moderne,* edited by Pierre Bonnassie, 15–27. Toulouse: Presses Universitaires du Mirail, 1995.

Auerbach, Erich. *Literary Language and its Public in Late Latin Antiquity and in the Middle Ages.* Translated by Ralph Manheim. London: Routledge and Kegan Paul, 1965.

Bailey, Lisa. "Building Urban Christian Communities: Sermons on Local Saints in the Eusebius Gallicanus Collection." *Early Medieval Europe* 12 (2003): 1–24.

———. "Monks and Lay Communities in Late Antique Gaul: The Evidence of the Eusebius Gallicanus Sermons." *Journal of Medieval History* 32 (2006): 315–32.

———. "'These Are Not Men': Sex and Drink in the Sermons of Caesarius of Arles." *Journal of Early Christian Studies* 15 (2007): 23–43.

———. "'No Use Crying over Spilt Milk': The Challenge of Preaching God's Justice in Fifth- and Sixth-Century Gaul." *Journal of the Australian Early Medieval Association* 4 (2008): 19–31.

———. "'Our Own Most Severe Judges': The Power of Penance in the Eusebius Gallicanus Sermons." In *The Power of Religion in Late Antiquity,* edited by Andrew Cain and Noel Lenski, 201–11. Burlington, Vt.: Ashgate, 2009.

Baldovin, John. *The Urban Character of Christian Worship: The Origins, Development and Meaning of Stational Liturgy.* Rome: Pont. Institutum Studiorum Orientalium, 1987.

Banniard, Michel. "Latin et communication orale en Gaule franque: Le témoignage de la 'Vita Eligii.'" In *The Seventh Century: Change and Continuity,* edited by Jacques Fontaine and J. N. Hillgarth, 57–86. London: Warburg Institute, 1992.

———. *Viva Voce: Communication écrite et communication orale du IVe au IXe siècle en Occident latin.* Paris: Institut d'Études Augustiennes, 1992.

———. "Variations langagières et communication dans la prédication d'Augustin." In *Augustin Prédicateur (395–411),* edited by Goulven Madec, 73–93. Paris: Institut d'Études Augustiniennes, 1998.

Barbero, Alessandro. *Un santo in famiglia: Vocazione religiosa e resistenze sociali nell'agiografia latina medievale.* Turin: Rosenberg & Sellier, 1991.

Barcellona, Rossana. "Fausto di Riez, *defensor ciuitatis et defensor orthodoxiae:* Sul ruolo del vescovo in Gallia nel V secolo." In *Vescovi e pastori in epoca*

Teodosiana: In occasione del XVI centenario della consacrazione episcopale de s. Agostino, 396–1996, 2:777–802. Rome: Institutum Patristicum Augustinianum, 1997.

———. "Norme conciliari e società cristiana nella Gallia tardoantica: La penitenza." In *I Concili della cristianità occidentale secoli III–V [XXX Incontro di studiosi dell'antichità cristiana, Roma, 3–5 maggio 2001],* 345–61. Rome: Institutum patristicum Augustinia, 2002.

Bardy, Gustave. "Le répercussions des controverses théologiques des Ve et VIe siècles dans les églises de Gaule." *Revue d'histoire de l'église de France* 24 (1938): 23–46.

———. "La prédication de saint Césaire d'Arles." *Revue d'histoire de l'église de France* 29 (1943): 201–36.

———. "L'église et l'enseignement en Occident au Ve siècle." In *Mélanges offerts au R. P. Ferdinand Cavallera,* 191–214. Toulouse: Bibliothèque de l'Institut Catholique, 1948.

Barré, Henri. *Les homéliaires Carolingiens de l'école d'Auxerre: Authenticité, inventaire, tableaux comparatifs.* Vatican City: Biblioteca Apostolica Vaticana, 1962.

Beaujard, Brigitte. "Dons et piété à l'égard des saints dans la Gaule de Ve et VIe siècles." In *Haut Moyen Âge: Culture, éducation et société: Études offertes à Pierre Riché,* edited by Claude Lepelley et al., 59–67. Nanterre: Editions Publidix, 1990.

———. "Cités, évêques et martyrs en Gaule à la fin de l'époque romaine." In *Les fonctions des Saints dans le monde occidental (IIIe–XIIIe siècle),* 175–91. Rome: École Française de Rome, 1991.

———. "L'évêque dans la cité en Gaule aux Ve et VIe siècles." In *La fin de la cité antique et le début de la cité médiévale de la fin du IIIe siècle à l'avènement de Charlemagne,* edited by Claude Lepelley, 127–45. Bari: Edipuglia, 1996.

———. "Les pèlerinages vus par Grégoire de Tours." In *Grégoire de Tours et l'espace gaulois: Actes du Congès International Tours, 3–5 Novembre 1994,* edited by Nancy Gauthier and Henri Galinié, 263–70. Tours: Revue archéologique du Centre de la France, 1997.

———. *Le culte des saints en Gaule: Les premiers temps, d'Hilaire de Poitiers à la fin du VIe siècle.* Paris: Les Éditions du Cerf, 2000.

Beck, Henry G. J. "A Note on the Frequency of Mass in Sixth-Century France." *American Ecclesiastical Review* 120 (1949): 480–85.

———. *The Pastoral Care of Souls in South-East France during the Sixth Century.* Rome: Apud Aedes Universitatis Gregorianae, 1950.

Bell, Catherine. *Ritual Theory, Ritual Practice*. Oxford: Oxford University Press, 1992.

Benoît, François. "Arles." In *Villes épiscopales de Provence: Aix, Arles, Fréjus, Marseille et Riez de l'époque gallo-romaine au Moyen Âge*, edited by François Benoît, Paul-Albert Février, Jules Formigé, and Henri Rolland, 15–21. Paris: Librairie C. Klincksieck, 1954.

Bergmann Wilhelm. *Studien zu einer kritischen Sichtung der südgallischen Predigtliteratur des fünften und sechsten Jahrhunderts*. Leipzig: Dieterich, 1898.

Bériou, Nicole. "Les sermons latins après 1200." In *The Sermon*, edited by Beverly Mayne Kienzle, 363–447. Turnhout: Brepols, 2000.

Bertelli, Carlo. "The Production and Distribution of Books in Late Antiquity." In *The Sixth Century: Production, Distribution, and Demand*, edited by Richard Hodges and William Bowden, 41–60. Leiden: Brill, 1998.

Biarne, Jacques. "La vie quotidienne des moines en Occident du IVe au VIe siècle." *Collectanea Cisterciensia* 49 (1987): 3–19.

Bick, Josef. "Wiener Palimpseste." In *Sitzungsberichte der philosophisch-historischen Klasse der kaiserlichen Akademie der Wissenschaft*, 1–109. Vienna: K.K. Hof- und Staatsdruckerei, 1908.

Bieler, Ludwig. "The Irish Penitentials: Their Religious and Social Background." *Studia Patristica* 8, *Texte und Untersuchungen* 93 (1966): 329–39.

Biller, P., and A. J. Minnis, eds. *Handling Sin: Confession in the Middle Ages*. Rochester, UK: York Medieval Press, 1998.

Bitton-Ashkelony, Brouria. "Penitence in Late Antique Monastic Literature." In *Transformations of the Inner Self in Ancient Religions*, edited by Jan Assmann and Guy G. Strousma, 179–94. Leiden: Brill, 1999.

Bloch, Maurice. "Symbols, Song, Dance, and Features of Articulation: Is Religion an Extreme Form of Traditional Authority?" *Archives européennes de sociologie* 15 (1974): 55–81.

Bonner, Gerald. "Augustine and Modern Research on Pelagianism." In *God's Decree and Man's Destiny: Studies on the Thought of Augustine of Hippo*. London: Variorum, 1987.

Bosl, Karl. "Cultura cittadina e cultura rurale tra mondo antico e medioevo a confronto nella Cristianizzazione delle campagne." In *Cristianizzazione ed organizzazione ecclesiastica delle campagne nell'alto medioevo: Espansione e resistenze*, 17–50. Spoleto: Presso la Sede del Centro, 1982.

Bouhot, Jean-Paul. "L'homéliaire des *sancti catholici Patres:* Sources et composition." *Revue des études augustiniennes* 24 (1978): 131–37.

———. "L'homéliaire de Saint-Pierre du Vatican au milieu du VIIe siècle et sa postérité." *Recherches augustiniennes* 20 (1985): 87–115.

Bowes, Kimberly D. "Possessing the Holy: Private Churches and Private Piety in Late Antiquity." Ph.D. dissertation, Princeton University, 2002.

———. "'Christianization' and the Rural Home." *Journal of Early Christian Studies* 15.2 (2007): 143–70.

Bradshaw, Paul F. *Daily Prayer in the Early Church: A Study of the Origin and Early Development of the Divine Office.* London: S.P.C.K., 1981.

———. "The Use of the Bible in Liturgy: Some Historical Perspectives." *Studia Liturgica* 22 (1992): 35–52.

Braun, Willi. *Rhetoric and Reality in Early Christianities.* Waterloo, Ont.: Wilfrid Laurier University Press, 2005.

Brown, Peter. *Augustine of Hippo: A Biography.* London: Faber and Faber, 1967.

———. "The Rise and Function of the Holy Man in Late Antiquity." *The Journal of Roman Studies* 61 (1971): 80–101.

———. "Pelagius and His Supporters: Aims and Environment." In *Religion and Society in the Age of Saint Augustine,* 93–114. London: Faber and Faber, 1972.

———. *The Cult of the Saints: Its Rise and Function in Latin Christianity.* Chicago: University of Chicago Press, 1981.

———. *Power and Persuasion in Late Antiquity: Towards a Christian Empire.* Madison: University of Wisconsin Press, 1992.

———. "Vers la naissance du purgatoire: Amnistie et pénitence dans le christianisme occidental de l'Antiquité tardive au Haut Moyen Age." *Annales HSS* 52 (1997): 1247–61.

———. "The Decline of the Empire of God: From Amnesty to Purgatory." In *The Tanner Lectures on Human Values* 20, 51–85. Salt Lake City: University of Utah Press, 1999.

———. "Enjoying the Saints in Late Antiquity." *Early Medieval Europe* 9 (2000): 1–24.

———. "Gregory of Tours: Introduction." In *The World of Gregory of Tours,* edited by Kathleen Mitchell and Ian Wood, 1–28. Leiden: Brill, 2002.

———. *The Rise of Western Christendom: Triumph and Diversity, A.D. 200–1000.* Malden, Mass.: Blackwell Publishers, 2003.

Bruckner, A. *Scriptoria Medii Aevi Helvetica II. Schreibschulen der Diözesa Konstanz.* Genf: Druck und Verlag Roto-Sadag A.G., 1936.

Bruzzone, Antonella. "Similitudine, metafore e contesto sociale nella lingua degli evangelizzatori (saggio di ricerca su Eusebio 'Gallicano')." In *Evangelizzazione dell'Occidente dal terzo all'ottavo secolo: Lingua e linguaggi; dibattitio teologio,* edited by Innocenzo Mazzini and Lucia Bacci, 125–36. Rome: Herder Editrice e Liberia, 2001.

Buc, Philippe. *The Dangers of Ritual: Between Early Medieval Texts and Social Scientific Theory.* Princeton, N.J.: Princeton University Press, 2001.

Buchem, L.A., van. *L'homélie pseudo-Eusébienne de Pentecôte: L'origine de la* confirmatio *en Gaule Méridionale et l'interpretations de ce rite par Fauste de Riez.* Nimwegen: Drukkerij Gebr. Janssen, 1967.

Burke, Trevor J. "Paul's Role as 'Father' to His Corinthian 'Children' in Socio-historical Context (1 Corinthians 4:14–21)." In *Paul and the Corinthians: Studies on a Community in Conflict. Essays in Honour of Margaret Thrall,* edited by Trevor J. Burke and J. Keith Elliott, 95–113. Leiden: Brill, 2003.

Buytaert, Éloi M. *L'héritage littéraire d'Eusèbe d'Émèse: Étude critique et historique textes.* Louvain: Bureaux de Muséon, 1949.

———. *Eusèbe d'Émèse: Discours conservé en latin, textes en partie inédits.* Louvain: Spicilegium Sacrum Lovaniense, 1953–57.

Cabié, Robert. "Les lettres attribuées à saint Germain de Paris et les origines de la liturgie gallicane." *Bulletin de littérature ecclésiastique* 73 (1972): 13–57.

Cabrol, Fernand. "Le 'liber testimoniorum' de St. Augustin et deux traités de Fauste de Riez." *Revue des questions historiques* 47 (1890): 232–43.

Cameron, Alan. *Claudian: Poetry and Propaganda at the Court of Honorius.* Oxford: Clarendon Press, 1970.

Cameron, Averil. *Christianity and the Rhetoric of Empire: The Development of Christian Discourse.* Berkeley: University of California Press, 1991.

———. "The Cult of the Virgin in Late Antiquity: Religious Development and Myth-Making." In *The Church and Mary: Papers Read at the 2001 Summer Meeting and the 2002 Winter Meeting of the Ecclesiastical History Society,* edited by R. N. Swanson, 1–21. Woodbridge, UK: Boydell Press, 2004.

Carle, Paul-Laurent. "L'homélie de pâques 'magnitudo' de saint Fauste de Riez (ou de Lérins) (fin du Ve siècle)." *Divinitas* 27 (1983): 123–54 and 28 (1984): 3–42 and 203–41.

———. "Sermon de s. Fauste de Riez (ou de Lérins) pour la fête de pentecôte sur la confirmation." *Nova et Vetera* 61 (1986): 90–104.

Carrias, Michel. "Vie monastique et règle à Lérins au temps d'Honorat." *Revue d'histoire de l'église de France* 74 (1988): 191–211.

Casiday, A. M. C. *Tradition and Theology in St John Cassian.* Oxford: Oxford University Press, 2006.

Caspari, Carl P. *Kirchenhistorische Anecdota,* vol. 1, *Lateinische Schriften: Die Texte und Anmerkungen.* Christiana: Mallingsche Buchdr., 1883.

Caspers, Charles and Marc Schneiders, eds. *Omnes Circumstantes: Contributions towards a History of the Role of the People in the Liturgy.* Kampen: Uitgeversmaatschapiij J. H. Kok, 1990.

Catalogue général des manuscrits des Bibliothèques publiques des Départements, vol. 3, Paris, 1886.

Cavalieri, Franchi de'. "S. Genesio di Arelate, s. Ferreolo di Vienna, s. Giuliano di Brivas." In *Note agiografiche, studi e testi* 65, 203–29. Vatican City: Biblioteca Apostolica Vaticana, 1935.

Cavallin, Samuel. "Saint Genès le notaire." *Eranos* 43 (1945): 150–75.

Cerquiglini, Bernard. *In Praise of the Variant: A Critical History of Philology.* Translated by Betsy Wing. Baltimore: Johns Hopkins University Press, 1999.

Chadwick, Owen. *John Cassian.* Cambridge: At the University Press, 1968.

Chaffin, Christopher. "Civic Values in Maximus of Turin and his Contemporaries." In *Forma futuri: Studi in onore di M. Pellegrino,* 1041–53. Turin: Bottega d'Erasmo, 1975.

Chavasse, Antoine. "Composition et date des recueils anciens passés dans la seconde partie du «Parisinus» lat. 1771." *Revue bénédictine* 78 (1968): 82–6.

———. "Le sermonnaire d'Agimond: Ses sources immédiates." *Kyriakon: Festschrift Johannes Quasten,* 2:800–10. Münster: Verlag Aschendorff, 1970.

———. "Un utilisation inattendu du recueil dit 'Léonien.'" *Archiv für Liturgie-wissenschaft* 26 (1984): 18–37.

Chelini, Jean. "La pratique dominicale des laics dans l'église franque sous le regne de Pépin." *Revue d'histoire de l'église de France* 42 (1956): 161–74.

Chéné, J. "Les origines de la controverse semi-pélagienne." *L'année théologique augustinienne* 14 (1953): 53–109.

———. "Le semi-pélagianisme du Midi de la Gaule." *Recherches de science religieuse* 43 (1955): 322–41.

Christophe, Paul. *Cassien et Césaire: Prédicateurs de la morale monastique.* Paris: P. Lethielleux, 1969.

Chryssavgis, John. *In the Heart of the Desert: The Spirituality of the Desert Fathers and Mothers.* Bloomington, Ind.: World Wisdom, 2003.

Clark, Elizabeth A. *The Origenist Controversy: The Cultural Construction of an Early Christian Debate.* Princeton, N.J.: Princeton University Press, 1992.

Clark, Gillian. "Victricius of Rouen: *Praising the Saints.*" *Journal of Early Christian Studies* 7 (1999): 365–99.

———. "Pastoral Care: Town and Country in Late Antique Preaching." In *Urban Centers and Rural Contexts in Late Antiquity,* edited by Thomas S. Burns and John W. Eadie, 265–84. East Lansing: Michigan State University Press, 2001.

Clerici, Ergisto. "Il sermo humilis di Cesario d'Arles." *Rendiconti: Classe di letter, scienze morali e storiche* 105 (1971): 339–64.

Colish, Marcia L. *The Stoic Tradition from Antiquity to the Early Middle Ages.* Leiden: Brill, 1985.

Congar, Yves. *Lay People in the Church: A Study for a Theology of Laity,* translated by Donald Attwater. London: Bloomsbury Publishing Co., 1957.

Conroy, Marietta Cashen. *Imagery in the "Sermones" of Maximus, Bishop of Turin.* Washington, D.C.: Catholic University of America Press, 1965.

Constable, Giles. "Monasteries, Rural Churches and the *cura animarum* in the Early Middle Ages." In *Cristianizzazione ed organizzazione ecclesiastica delle campagne nell'alto medioevo: Espansione e resistenze,* 349–89. Spoleto: Presso la Sede del Centro, 1982.

———. "The Language of Preaching in the Twelfth Century." In *Culture and Spirituality in Medieval Europe,* 131–52. Aldershot, UK: Variorum, 1996.

Cooper-Marsdin, Arthur C. *The History of the Islands of the Lerins: The Monastery, Saints and Theologians of S. Honorat.* Cambridge: At the University Press, 1913.

Countryman, Louis W. *The Rich Christian in the Church of the Early Empire.* New York: Edwin Mellen Press, 1980.

Courcelle, Pierre. "Nouveaux aspects de la culture lérinienne." *Revue des études latines* 46 (1968): 379–409.

Courtois, Christian. "L'évolution du monachisme en Gaule de St Martin à St Columban." In *Il monachesimo nell'alto medioevo e la formazione della civiltà occidentale,* 47–72. Spoleto: Centro italiano di studi sull'alto Medioevo, 1957.

Coville, Alfred, *Recherches sur l'histoire de Lyon du Vme siècle au IXme siècle (450–800)*. Paris: Éditions Auguste Picard, 1928.

Cramer, Peter. *Baptism and Change in the Early Middle Ages, c. 200–c. 1150*. Cambridge: Cambridge University Press, 1993.

Cross, Frank. "Early Western Liturgical Manuscripts." *Journal of Theological Studies* n.s. 16 (1965): 61–67.

Cunningham, Mary B. "Preaching and the Community." In *Church and People in Byzantium,* edited by Rosemary Smith, 29–47. Birmingham, UK: Centre for Byzantine, Ottoman and Modern Greek Studies, 1990.

———. "Andreas of Crete's Homilies on Lazarus and Palm Sunday: The Preacher and his Audience." *Studia Patristica* 31 (1995): 22–41.

Cunningham, Mary B., and Pauline Allen, eds. *Preacher and Audience: Studies in Early Christian and Byzantine Homiletics*. Leiden: Brill, 1998.

Cunningham, Maurice. "Contents of the Newberry Library Homiliarium." *Sacris Erudiri* 7 (1995): 267–301.

Daly, William M. "Caesarius of Arles: A Precursor of Medieval Christendom." *Traditio* 26 (1970): 1–28.

Dargan, Edwin Charles. *A History of Preaching*. Grand Rapids: Baker Book House, 1954.

d'Avray, D. L. *The Preaching of the Friars: Sermons Diffused from Paris before 1300*. Oxford: Clarendon Press, 1985.

De Bruyn, Theodore S. "Ambivalence within a 'Totalizing Discourse': Augustine's Sermons on the Sack of Rome." *Journal of Early Christian Studies* 1 (1993): 405–21.

De Clerck, Paul. "Pénitence seconde et conversion quotidienne aux IIIème et IVème siècles." *Studia Patristica* 20 (1989): 352–74.

De Filippis Cappai, Chiara. *Massimo: Vescovo di Torino e il suo tempo*. Turin: Società Editrice Internazionale, 1995.

De Gaiffier, Baudouin. "La lecture des actes des martyrs dans la prière liturgique en Occident." *Analecta Bollandiana* 72 (1954): 134–66.

De Jong, Mayke. "What Was Public about Public Penance? *Paenitentia publica* and Justice in the Carolingian World." In *La giustizia nell'alto medioevo,* vol. 2, *Secoli IX–XI,* 863–902. Spoleto: Presso la Sede del Centro, 1997.

———. "Transformations of Penance." In *Rituals of Power from Late Antiquity to the Early Middle Ages,* edited by Frans Theuws and Janet L. Nelson, 185–224. Leiden: Brill, 2000.

Dekkers, Eligius. "Des prix et du commerce des livres à l'époque patristique." *Sacris Erudiri* 31 (1989–1990): 99–115.

DeLeeuw, Patricia A. "Gregory the Great's 'Homilies on the Gospels' in the Early Middle Ages." *Studi Medievali,* 3rd ser. 26 (1985): 859–65.

Delisle, Leopold. *Inventaire des manuscrits de la Bibliothèque Nationale, Fonds de Cluny.* Paris: H. Champion, 1884.

Demacopoulos, George. *Five Models of Spiritual Direction in the Early Church.* Notre Dame, Ind.: University of Notre Dame Press, 2007.

De Margerie, Bertrand. "L'exégèse de Saint Pierre Chrysologue: Théologien biblique." In *Introduction à l'histoire de l'exégèse: IV. L'Occident latin de Léon le Grand à Bernard de Clairvaux,* 75–108. Paris: Cerf, 1990.

Denis, Michael. *Codices manuscripti theologici bibliothecae palatinae Vindobonensis latini aliarumque Occidentis linguarum.* Vienna: Typis et sumpt. Joan. Thomae Nob. de Trattnern, 1793–1802.

Descombes, François. "La topographie chrétienne de Vienne des origines à la fin du VIIe siècle." In *Les Martyrs de Lyon (177),* 267–77. Paris: Centre National de la Recherche Scientifique, 1978.

———. "Hagiographie et topographie religieuse: L'exemple de Vienne en Dauphiné." In *Hagiographie, cultures et sociétés: IVe–XIIe siècles,* 361–79. Paris: Études Augustiniennes, 1981.

Devailly, Guy. "La pastorale en Gaule au IXe siècle." *Revue d'histoire de l'église en France* 59 (1973): 23–54.

De Vogüé, Adalbert. "Sur une série des emprunts de saint Colomban à Fauste de Riez." *Studia Monastica* 10 (1968): 119–23.

———. "Understanding Cassian: A Survey of the Conferences." *Cistercian Studies Quarterly* 19 (1984): 101–21.

———. "Aux origines de Lérins: La règle de s. Basile?" *Studia Monastica* 31 (1989): 259–66.

———. "Les débuts de la vie monastique à Lérins: Remarques sur un ouvrage récent." *Revue d'histoire ecclésiastique* 58 (1993): 5–53.

———. *Histoire littéraire du mouvement monastique dans l'antiquité.* Paris: Éditions du Cerf, 1997.

Devoti, Domenico. "Massimo di Torino e il suo pubblico." *Augustinianum* 21 (1981): 153–67.

Dictionnaire de spiritualité. Paris: Beauchesne, 1937–67.

Diem, Albrecht. *Keusch und rein: Eine Untersuchung zu den Ursprüngen des frühmittelalterlichen Klosterwesens und seinen Quellen.* Utrecht: Universiteit Utrecht, 2000.

Dix, Gregory. *The Shape of the Liturgy.* Westminster, UK: Dacre Press, 1954.

Dodaro, Robert. "Christus Iustus and Fear of Death in Augustine's Dispute with Pelagius." In *Signum pietatis: Festgabe für Cornelius Petrus Mayer O.S.A. zum 60. Geburtstag,* 341–61. Würzburg: Augustinus-Verlag, 1989.

Dodaro, Robert, and George Lawless, eds. *Augustine and His Critics: Essays in Honour of Gerald Bonner.* London: Routledge, 2000.

Dolbeau, François. "'Serminator uerborum': Réflexions d'un editeur de sermons d'Augustin." In *Augustin et la prédication en Afrique: Recherches sur les divers sermons authentique, apocryches ou anonymes,* 71–86. Paris: Institut d'Études Augustiennes, 2005.

Driscoll, Michael S. "Penance in Transition: Popular Piety and Practice." In *Medieval Liturgy: A Book of Essays,* edited by Lizette Larson-Miller, 121–63. New York: Garland Publishing, 1997.

Duchesne, Louis. "Sur l'origine de la liturgie gallicane." *Revue d'histoire et de littérature religieuse* 5 (1900): 31–47.

———. *Christian Worship: Its Origin and Evolution. A Study of the Latin Liturgy up to the Time of Charlemagne.* Translated by M. L. McClure. London: S.P.C.K., 1912.

Dunn, Marilyn. *The Emergence of Monasticism: From the Desert Fathers to the Early Middle Ages.* Oxford: Blackwell Publishers, 2000.

Durliat, Jean. "*Episcopus, civis* et *populus* dans les *historiarum libri* de Grégoire." In *Grégoire de Tours et l'espace gaulois: Actes du Congès International Tours, 3–5 Novembre 1994,* edited by Nancy Gauthier and Henri Galinié, 185–93. Tours: Revue archéologique du Centre de la France, 1997.

Effros, Bonnie. "Appearance and Ideology: Creating Distinctions between Clerics and Lay Persons in Early Medieval Gaul." In *Encountering Medieval Textiles and Dress: Objects, Texts, Images,* edited by Désirée G. Koslin and Janet E. Synder, 7–24. New York: Palgrave MacMillan, 2002.

Engelbrecht, August G. *Studien über die Schriften des Bischofes von Reii, Faustus: Ein Beitrag zur spätlateinischen Literaturgeschichte.* Vienna: Verlag der Theresianischen Akademie, 1889.

Étaix, Raymond. "Un homéliaire ancien dans le manuscrit LII de la Bibliothèque capitulaire de Vérone." *Revue bénédictine* 73 (1963): 289–306.

———. "Le lectionnaire d l'office à Cluny." *Recherches augustiniennes* 11 (1976): 91–159.

————. "Le sermonnaire carolingien de Beaune." *Revue des études augustiniennes* 25 (1979): 106–49.

————. *Homéliaires patristiques latins: Recueil d'études de manuscrits médiévaux.* Paris: Institut d'Études Augustiniennes, 1994.

Evans, Robert F. *Four Letters of Pelagius.* London: Seabury Press, 1968.

Faivre, Alexandre. "Clerc/ Laïc: Histoire d'une frontière." *Revue des sciences religieuses* 57 (1983): 195–220.

Fanning, Steven. "Emperors and Empires in Fifth-Century Gaul." In *Fifth-Century Gaul: A Crisis of Identity?* edited by John Drinkwater and Hugh Elton, 288–97. Cambridge: Cambridge University Press, 1992.

————. "Clovis Augustus and Merovingian *Imitatio Imperii.*" In *The World of Gregory of Tours,* edited by Kathleen Mitchell and Ian Wood, 321–35. Leiden: Brill, 2002.

Ferguson, John. *Pelagius: A Historical and Theological Study.* Cambridge: W. Heffer, 1956.

Ferreiro, Alberto. "The Missionary Labours of St. Martin of Braga in Sixth-Century Galicia." *Studia Monastica* 23 (1981): 11–26.

————. "Job in the Sermons of Caesarius of Arles." *Recherches de théologie ancienne et médiévale* 54 (1987): 13–25.

————. "Early Medieval Missionary Tactics: The Example of Martin and Caesarius." *Studia Historica–Historia Antiqua* 6 (1988): 225–38.

————. "'Frequenter legere': The Propagation of Literacy, Education and Divine Wisdom in Caesarius of Arles." *Journal of Ecclesiastical History* 43 (1992): 5–15.

————. "Modèles laïcs de sainteté dans les sermons de Césaire d'Arles." In *Clovis histoire et mémoire: Clovis et son temps l'événement,* 97–114. Paris: Presses de l'Université de Paris-Sorbonne, 1997.

Février, Paul-Albert. "Riez." In *Villes épiscopales de Provence: Aix, Arles, Fréjus, Marseille et Riez de l'époque gallo-romaine au Moyen Âge,* edited by François Benoît, Paul-Albert Février, Jules Formigé, and Henri Rolland, 39–43. Paris: Librairie C. Klincksieck, 1954.

————. *Le développement urbain en Provence de l'époque romaine à la fin du XIVe siècle.* Paris: De Boccard, 1964.

————. "Arles aux IVe et Ve siècles: Ville impériale et capitale régionale." In *Corso di cultura sull'arte ravennate e bizantina* 15, 127–58. Ravenna: Edizioni del Girasole, 1978.

Février, Paul-Albert, Michel Bats, Gabriel Camps, Michel Fixot, Jean Guyon, and Jean Riser. *La Provence des origines à l'an mil: Histoire et archéologie.* Rennes: Editions Ouest-France, 1989.

Finn, Thomas. "Quodvultdeus: Preacher and Audience, the Homilies on the Creed." *Studia Patristica* 31 (1995): 42–58.

Fitzgerald, Allan. "The Relationship of Maximus of Turin to Rome and Milan: A Study of Penance and Pardon at the Turn of the Fifth Century." *Augustinianum* 27 (1987): 465–86.

———. *Conversion through Penance in the Italian Church of the IVth and Vth Centuries: New Approaches to the Experience of Conversion from Sin.* Lewiston, N.Y.: E. Mellen Press, 1988.

———. "Maximus of Turin: How He Spoke of Sin to His People." *Studia Patristica* 23 (1989): 127–32.

Fitzgerald, Allan, ed. *Augustine through the Ages: An Encyclopedia.* Grand Rapids: William B. Eerdmans, 1999.

Flint, Valerie I. J. *The Rise of Magic in Early Medieval Europe.* Princeton: Princeton University Press, 1991.

Fouracre, Paul. "The Work of Audoenus of Rouen and Eligius of Noyon in Extending Episcopal Influence from the Town to the Country in Seventh-Century Neustria." In *The Church in Town and Countryside,* edited by Derek Baker, 77–91. Oxford: Blackwell, 1979.

Fournier, Pierre-François. "Clermont Ferrand au VIe siècle." *Bibliothèque de l'école des Chartes* 128 (1970): 273–344.

Frahier, Louis Jean. "L'interprétation du récit du jugement dernier (Mt 25, 31–46) dans l'oeuvre d'Augustin." *Revue des études augustiniennes* 33 (1987): 70–84.

Gaddis, Michael. *There Is No Crime for Those Who Have Christ: Religious Violence in the Christian Roman Empire.* Berkeley: University of California Press, 2005.

Gadille, Jacques, ed. *Le diocèse de Lyon.* Histoire des diocèses de France 16. Paris: Beauchesne, 1983.

Galinié, Henri. "Reflections on Early Medieval Tours." In *The Rebirth of Towns in the West: A.D. 700–1050,* edited by Richard Hodges and Brian Hobley, 57–62. London: Council for British Archaeology, 1988.

Gamber, Klaus. *Codices liturgici latini antiquiores.* 2d ed. Freiburg: Universitätsverlag, 1968.

Gamble, Harry Y. *Books and Readers in the Early Church: A History of Early Christian Texts.* New Haven: Yale University Press, 1995.

Ganz, David. "The Merovingian Library of Corbie." In *Columbanus and Merovingian Monasticism,* edited by Howard B. Clarke and Mary Brennan, 153–72. Oxford: B.A.R., 1981.

Garrigues, M.-O. "Massimo di Riez." In *Bibliotheca sanctorum* 9.64. Rome: Istituto Giovanni XXIII nella Pontificia Università Lateranense, 1961–70.

Gatch, Milton McC. *Preaching and Theology in Anglo-Saxon England: Aelfric and Wulstan.* Toronto: University of Toronto Press, 1977.

Gaudemet, Jean. "Unanimité et majorité (observations sur quelques études récentes)." In *La société ecclésiastique dans l'Occident médiéval.* London: Variorum, 1980.

Gauthier, Nancy. "Le paysage urbain en Gaule au VIe siècle." In *Grégoire de Tours et l'espace gaulois: Actes du Congès International Tours, 3–5 Novembre 1994,* edited by Nancy Gauthier and Henri Galinié, 49–63. Tours: Revue archéologique du Centre de la France, 1997.

———. "La topographie chrétienne entre idéologie et pragmatisme." In *The Idea and Ideal of the Town between Late Antiquity and the Early Middle Ages,* edited by Gian P. Brogiolo and Bryan Ward-Perkins, 195–209. Leiden: Brill, 1999.

———. "From the Ancient City to the Medieval Town: Continuity and Change in the Early Middle Ages." In *The World of Gregory of Tours,* edited by Kathleen Mitchell and Ian Wood, 47–66. Leiden: Brill, 2002.

Gennaro, Salvatore. *Dinamii vita sancti Maximi episcopi Reiensis: Fausti Reiensis sermo de sancto Maximo episcopo et abbate.* Catania: Università di Catania, 1966.

Gillett, Andrew. "Rome, Ravenna and the Last Western Emperors." *Papers of the British School at Rome* 69 (2001): 131–67.

Glorie, Fr. "La culture lérinienne (Notes de lecture)." *Sacris Erudiri* 19 (1969): 71–76.

Godden, Malcolm R. "The Development of Aelfric's Second Series of Catholic Homilies." *English Studies* 54 (1973): 209–16.

Godding, Robert. *Prêtres en Gaule mérovingienne.* Bruxelles: Société des Bollandistes, 2001.

Graumann, Thomas. "St. Ambrose on the Art of Preaching." *Vescovi e pastori in epoca Teodosiana: In occasione del XVI centenario della consacrazione episcopale de s. Agostino, 396–1996,* 2:587–600. Rome: Institutum Patristicum Augustinianum, 1997.

Greer, Rowan A. "Pastoral care and discipline." In *The Cambridge History of Christianity,* vol. 2, *Constantine to c. 600,* edited by Augustine Cassidy and Frederick W. Norris, 567–84. Cambridge: Cambridge University Press, 2007.

Grégoire, Réginald. *Les homéliaires du Moyen Âge: Inventaire et analyse des manuscrits.* Rome: Herder, 1966.

———. "L'homéliaire romain d'Agimond." *Ephemerides Liturgicae* 82 (1968): 257–305.

———. "Les homéliaires mérovingiens du VIIe–VIIIe siècle." *Studi Medievali* 3rd series, 13 (1972): 901–17.

———. "L'homéliaire de St.-Pierre au Vatican." *Studi Medievali* 3rd series, 13 (1972): 233–55.

———. "La collection homilétique du ms. Wolfenbüttel 4096." *Studi Medievali* 3rd series, 14 (1973): 259–86.

———. *Homéliaires liturgiques médiévaux: Analyse des manuscrits.* Spoleto: Centro Italiano di Studi sull'alto Medioevo, 1980.

———. "Homily" and "Homiliary." In *Encyclopedia of the Early Church,* 1:393–94. New York: Oxford University Press, 1992.

Griffe, Élie. "Aux origines de la liturgie gallicane." *Bulletin de littérature ecclésiastique* 52 (1951): 17–43.

———. "Les sermons de Fauste de Riez: La «collectio gallicana» du pseudo-Eusèbe." *Bulletin de littérature ecclésiastique* 61 (1960): 27–38.

———. "La pratique réligieuse en Gaule au Ve siècle: *Saeculares et sancti.*" *Bulletin de littérature ecclésiastique* 63 (1962): 241–67.

———. *La Gaule chrétienne a l'époque romaine,* vol. 3, *La cité chrétienne.* Paris: Letouzey et Ané, 1965.

———. "Nouveau plaidoyer pour Fauste de Riez." *Bulletin de littérature ecclésiastique* 74 (1973): 187–92.

Guevin, Benedict M. "The Beginning and End of Purity of Heart: From Cassian to the Master and Benedict." In *Purity of Heart in Early Ascetic and Monastic Literature: Essays in Honor of Juana Raasch, O.S.B.,* edited by Harriet Luckman and Linda Kulzer, 197–214. Collegeville, Minn.: Liturgical Press, 1999.

Gurevich, Aron. *Medieval Popular Culture: Problems of Belief and Perception.* Cambridge: Cambridge University Press, 1988.

Habinek, Thomas. *Ancient Rhetoric and Oratory.* Oxford: Blackwell Publishing, 2005.

Hall, Thomas N. "The Early Medieval Sermon." In *The Sermon,* edited by Beverly Mayne Kienzle, 203–69. Turnhout: Brepols, 2000.

Halsall, Guy. "Towns, Societies and Ideas: The Not-So-Strange Case of Late Roman and Merovingian Metz." In *Towns in Transition: Urban Evolution in Late Antiquity and the Early Middle Ages,* edited by Neil Christie and Simon T. Loseby, 235–61. Aldershot, UK: Scolar Press, 1996.

Hamilton, Sarah. *The Practice of Penance: 900–1050.* Woodbridge, UK: Boydell Press, 2001.

Hamman, Adalbert. G. "La transmission des sermons de saint Augustin: Les authentiques et les apocryphes." *Augustinianum* 25 (1985): 311–27.

Hannig, Jürgen. *Consensus fidelium: Frühfeudale Interpretationen des Verhältnisses von Königtum und Adel am Beispiel des Frankenreiches.* Stuttgart: Anton Hiersemann, 1982.

Harmening, Dieter. *Superstitio: Überlieferungs- und theoriegeschichtliche Untersuchungen zur kirchlich-theologischen Aberglaubensliteratur des Mittelalters.* Berlin: E. Schmidt, 1979.

Harmless, William. *Augustine and the Catechumenate.* Collegeville, Minn.: The Liturgical Press, 1995.

Harries, Jill. "Christianity and the City in Late Roman Gaul." In *The City in Late Antiquity,* edited by John Rich, 77–98. London: Routledge, 1992.

———. "Sidonius Apollinaris, Rome and the Barbarians: A Climate of Treason?" In *Fifth-Century Gaul: A Crisis of Identity?* edited by John Drinkwater and Hugh Elton, 298–308. Cambridge: Cambridge University Press, 1992.

———. *Sidonius Apollinaris and the Fall of Rome, A.D. 407–485.* Oxford: Oxford University Press, 1994.

———. *Law and Empire in Late Antiquity.* Cambridge: Cambridge University Press, 1999.

Harvey, Susan Ashbrook. "The Stylite's Liturgy: Ritual and Religious Identity in Late Antiquity." *Journal of Early Christian Studies* 6 (1998): 523–39.

Hausherr, Irénée. "Spiritualité monacale et unité chrétienne," and "Vocation chrétienne et vocation monastique selon le pères." In *Études de spiritualité orientale,* 315–32, 405–85. Rome: Pontificium Institutum Studiorum Orientalium, 1969.

Heather, Peter, "The Emergence of the Visigothic Kingdom." In *Fifth-Century Gaul: A Crisis of Identity?* edited by John Drinkwater and Hugh Elton, 84–94. Cambridge: Cambridge University Press, 1992.

Heene, Katrien. "*Audire, legere, vulgo:* An Attempt to Define Public Use and Comprehensibility of Carolingian Hagiography." In *Latin and the Romance Languages in the Early Middle Ages,* edited by Roger Wright, 146–63. London: Routledge, 1991.

Heffernan, Thomas J. *Sacred Biography: Saints and Their Biographers in the Middle Ages.* New York: Oxford University Press, 1988.

Heinzelmann, Martin. *Bischofsherrschaft in Gallien: Zur Kontinuität römischer Führungsschichten vom 4. bis 7. Jahrhundert. Soziale, prosopographische und bildungsgeschischtliche Aspekte.* Munich: Artemis Verlag, 1976.

————. "Pater populi: Langage familial et détention de pouvoir public (antiquité tardive et très haut Moyen Âge)." In *Aux sources de la puissance: Sociabilité et parenté,* edited by Françoise Thélamon, 47–56. Rouen: Publications de l'Université de Rouen, 1989.

————. "Studia sanctorum: Éducation, milieux d'instruction et valeurs éducatives dans l'hagiographie en Gaule jusqu'à la fin de l'époque mérovingienne." In *Haut Moyen Âge: Culture, éducation et société. Études offertes à Pierre Riché,* 105–38. Nanterre: Éditions Publidix, 1990.

————. "The 'Affair' of Hilary of Arles (445) and Gallo-Roman Identity in the Fifth Century." In *Fifth-Century Gaul: A Crisis of Identity?* edited by John Drinkwater and Hugh Elton, 239–51. Cambridge: Cambridge University Press, 1992.

Hellerman, Joseph H. *The Ancient Church as Family.* Minneapolis: Fortress Press, 2001.

Hen, Yitzhak. *Culture and Religion in Merovingian Gaul, A.D. 481–751.* Leiden: E. J. Brill, 1995.

————. "Unity in Diversity: The Liturgy of Frankish Gaul before the Carolingians." In *Unity and Diversity in the Church,* edited by Robert N. Swanson, 19–30. Oxford: Blackwell Publishers, 1996.

————. "Knowledge of Canon Law among Rural Priests: The Evidence of Two Carolingian Manuscripts from around 800." *Journal of Theological Studies,* n.s. 50 (1999): 117–34.

————. "Martin of Braga's *de correctione rusticorum* and Its Uses in Frankish Gaul." In *Medieval Transformations: Texts, Power and Gifts in Context,* edited by Esther Cohen and Mayke de Jong, 35–49. Leiden: Brill, 2001.

————. *The Royal Patronage of Liturgy in Frankish Gaul to the Death of Charles the Bald (877).* Woodbridge, UK: Boydell and Brewer, 2001.

————. "A Merovingian Commentary on the Four Gospels (CPL 1001)." *Revue des études augustiniennes* 49 (2003): 167–87.

Henriet, Patrick. "*Verbum Dei disseminando:* La parole des ermites prédicateurs d'après les sources hagiographiques (XIe–XIIe siècles)." In *La parole du prédicateur: Ve–XVe siècle,* 153–85. Nice: Centre d'Études Médiévales, 1997.

Herman, József. "Spoken and Written Latin in the Last Centuries of the Roman Empire: A Contribution to the Linguistic History of the Western Provinces." In *Latin and the Romance Languages in the Early Middle Ages,* edited by Roger Wright, 29–43. London: Routledge, 1991.

Hill, Joyce. "Reform and Resistance: Preaching Styles in Late Anglo-Saxon England." In *De l'homélie au sermon: Histoire de la prédication médiévale,* edited by Jacqueline Hamesse and Xavier Hermand, 15–46. Louvain-la-Neuve: Publications de l'Institute d'Études Médiévales, 1993.

———. "The Preservation and Transmission of Aelfric's Saints' Lives: Reader-Reception and Reader-Response in the Early Middle Ages." In *The Preservation and Transmission of Anglo-Saxon Culture,* edited by Joel T. Rosenthal and Paul E. Szarmach, 405–30. Kalamazoo, Mich.: Medieval Institute Publications, 1997.

Histoire littéraire de la France ou l'on traite de l'origine et du progrès de la décadence. Paris: Libraire de Victor Palmé, 1865.

Hofman, Josef. "Regula magistri xlvii und xlviii in St. Galler und Würzburger Caesarius-Handschriften." *Revue bénédictine* 61 (1951): 141–66.

Holder, Alfred. *Die Handschriften der Grossherzoglich-Badischen Hof- und Landesbibliothek zu Karlsruhe.* Karlsruhe: C.T. Groos, 1891–1926.

Hopkins, Keith. "Christian Number and Its Implications." *Journal of Early Christian Studies* 6.2 (1998): 185–226.

Hosp, E. "Il sermonario di Alano di Farfa." *Ephemerides Liturgicae* 50 (1936): 375–83 and 51 (1937): 210–41.

Howard-Synder, Daniel, ed. *The Evidential Argument from Evil.* Bloomington: Indiana University Press, 1996.

Hubert, Jean. "La topographie religieuse d'Arles au VIe siècle." *Cahiers archéologiques* 2 (1947): 17–27.

Hunt, E. D. "Gaul and the Holy Land in the Early Fifth Century." In *Fifth-Century Gaul: A Crisis of Identity?* edited by John Drinkwater and Hugh Elton, 264–74. Cambridge: Cambridge University Press, 1992.

Hunter, David G. "Resistance to the Virginal Ideal in Late Fourth-Century Rome: The Case of Jovinian." *Theological Studies* n.s. 48 (1987): 45–64.

———. "Vigilantius of Calagurris and Victricius of Rouen: Ascetics, Relics and Clerics in Late Roman Gaul." *Journal of Early Christian Studies* 7 (1999): 401–30.

———. "Rereading the Jovinianist Controversy: Asceticism and Clerical Authority in Late Ancient Christianity." *Journal of Medieval and Early Modern Studies* 33 (2003): 454–70.

Johns, Adrian. *The Nature of the Book: Print and Knowledge in the Making.* Chicago: University of Chicago Press, 1988.

Jones, A. H. M. *The Later Roman Empire, 284–602: A Social, Economic and Administrative Survey.* Baltimore: Johns Hopkins University Press, 1986.

Jouassard, Georges. "Saint Césaire d'Arles et Sedatus de Nîmes." *Recherches de science religieuse* 31 (1943): 211–15.

Judic, Bruno. "Grégoire le Grand, un maître de la parole." In *La parole du prédicateur: Ve–XVe siècle,* 49–107. Nice: Centre d'Études Médiévales, 1997.

Jussen, Bernhard. "Über 'Bischofsherrschaften' und die Prozeduren politisch-sozialer Umordnung in Gallien zwischen 'Antike' und 'Mittelalter.'" *Historische Zeitschrift* 260 (1995): 673–718.

———."Liturgy and Legitimation, or How the Gallo-Romans Ended the Roman Empire." In *Ordering Medieval Society,* edited by Bernhard Jussen, 147–99. Philadelphia: University of Philadelphia Press, 2000.

Kantorowicz, Ernst H. *The King's Two Bodies: A Study in Medieval Political Theology.* Princeton: Princeton University Press, 1957.

Kasper, Clemens M. *Theologie und Askese: Die Spiritualität des Inselmönchtums von Lérins im 5. Jahrhundert.* Münster: Aschendorff, 1991.

Kaster, Robert A. *Guardians of Language: The Grammarian and Society in Late Antiquity.* Berkeley: University of California Press, 1988.

Kelly, John N. D. *Early Christian Creeds.* London: Longmans, 1950.

———. *Early Christian Doctrines.* New York: Harper and Brothers Publishers, 1958.

Kennedy, George. *The Art of Rhetoric in the Roman World, 300 B.C.–A.D. 300.* Princeton: Princeton University Press, 1972.

Kienzle, Beverly Mayne. "The Typology of the Medieval Sermon and Its Development in the Middle Ages: Report on Work in Progress." In *De l'homélie au sermon: Histoire de la prédication médiévale,* edited by Jacqueline Hamesse and Xavier Hermand, 83–101. Louvain-la-Neuve: Publications de l'Institute d'Études Médiévales, 1993.

———. "Preaching as a Touchstone of Orthodoxy and Dissidence in the Middle Ages." *Medieval Sermon Studies* 43 (1999): 19–54.

———. "Medieval Sermons and their Performance: Theory and Record." In *Preacher, Sermon and Audience in the Middle Ages,* edited by Carolyn Muessig, 89–124. Leiden: Brill, 2002.

Kienzle, Beverly Mayne, ed. *The Sermon.* Turnhout: Brepols, 2000.

Kierkegaard, Søren. *Concluding Unscientific Postscript.* Translated by David F. Swenson and Walter Lowrie. Princeton: Princeton University Press, 1968.

Kleinberg, Aviad M. "*De agone christiano:* The Preacher and his Audience." *Journal of Theological Studies* n.s. 38 (1987): 16–33.

Klingshirn, William. "Caesarius' Monastery for Women in Arles and the Composition and Function of the 'Vita Caesarii.'" *Revue bénédictine* 100 (1992): 441–81.

———. "Church Politics and Chronology: Dating the Episcopacy of Caesarius of Arles." *Revue des études augustiniennes* 38 (1992): 80–88.

———. *Caesarius of Arles: The Making of a Christian Community in Late Antique Gaul.* Cambridge: Cambridge University Press, 1994.

Koziol, G. *Begging Pardon and Favor: Ritual and Political Order in Early Medieval France.* Ithaca, N.Y.: Cornell University Press, 1992.

Kremer, Elmar J. and Michael J. Latzer, eds. *The Problem of Evil in Early Modern Philosophy.* Toronto: University of Toronto Press, 2001.

Labrousse, Mireille. *Saint Honorat, fondateur de Lérins et évêque d'Arles: Étude et traduction de textes d'Hilaire d'Arles, Fauste de Riez et Césaire d'Arles.* Maine and Loire: Abbaye de Bellefontaine, 1995.

LaCapra, Dominick. "*The Cheese and the Worms:* The Cosmos of a Twentieth-Century Historian." In *History and Criticism,* 45–69. Ithaca: Cornell University Press, 1985.

Laistner, Max L. W. *Thought and Letters in Western Europe A.D. 500 to 900.* Ithaca, N.Y.: Cornell University Press, 1957.

Lakeland, Paul. *The Liberation of the Laity: In Search of an Accountable Church.* New York and London: Continuum, 2003.

Lara, María Pía, ed. *Rethinking Evil: Contemporary Perspectives.* Berkeley: University of California Press, 2001.

Latouche, Robert. "Nice et Cimiez (Ve–Xe siècle)." In *Mélanges d'histoire du Moyen Âge offerts à M. Ferdinand Lot,* 331–58. Paris: Librairie ancienne Édouard Champion, 1925.

Lauer, Philippe. *Bibliothèque Nationale: Catalogue général des manuscrits latins.* Paris: Bibliothèque Nationale, 1939–.

Leeming, Bernard. "The False Decretals, Faustus of Riez and the Pseudo-Eusebius." *Studia Patristica* 2 (1957): 122–40.

Lejay, Paul. "Le rôle théologique de Césaire d'Arles." *Revue d'histoire et de littérature religieuses* 10 (1905): 135–82.

Le livre illustre en Occident du haut moyen-âge à nos jours. Brussels: Bibliotheque Royale Albert, 1977.

Lemarié, Joseph. "La liturge de Ravenne au temps de Pierre Chrysologue et l'ancienne liturgie d'Aquilée." In *Antichitá Altoadriatiche XIII: Aquileia e Ravenna,* 355–73. Udine: Arti Grafiche Friulane, 1978.

Leroy, Jean. "L'oeuvre oratoire de s. Fauste de Riez: La collection gallicane dite d'Eusèbe d'Émèse." Ph.D. dissertation, University of Strasbourg, 1954.

Leroy, Jean, and Fr. Glorie. "«Eusèbe d'Alexandrie» source d'«Eusèbe de Gaule»," *Sacris Erudiri: Jaarboek voor Godsdientwetenschappen* 19 (1969–70): 33–70.

Lewis, C. S. "On Obstinacy in Belief." In *They Asked for a Paper,* 183–96. London: Geoffrey Bles Ltd., 1962.

Leyser, Conrad. "'This Sainted Isle': Panegyric, Nostalgia and the Invention of a 'Lerinian Monasticism.'" In *The Limits of Ancient Christianity: Essays on Late Antique Thought and Culture in Honor of R. A. Markus,* edited by William Klingshirn and Mark Vessey, 188–206. Ann Arbor: University of Michigan Press, 1999.

———. "Semi-Pelagianism." In *Augustine through the Ages: An Encyclopedia,* edited by Allan Fitzgerald, 761–66. Grand Rapids: William B. Eerdmans, 1999.

———. *Authority and Asceticism from Augustine to Gregory the Great.* Oxford: Oxford University Press, 2000.

Libri, G. "Notice des manuscrits de quelques bibliothèques des départements." *Journal des Savants* (1841): 477–86.

Liebescheutz, Wolfgang "The End of the Ancient City." In *The City in Late Antiquity,* edited by John Rich, 1–49. Routledge: London, 1992.

Lim, Richard. "Christian Triumph and Controversy." In *Late Antiquity: A Guide to the Postclassical World,* edited by G. W. Bowersock, Peter Brown, and Oleg Grabar, 196–218. Cambridge: Belknap Press, 1999.

Lizzi, Rita. *Vescovi e strutture ecclesiastiche nelle città tardoantica: L'Italia Annonaria nel IV–V secolo d.C.* Como: Edizoni New Press, 1989.

Lloyd, Paul M. "On the Names of Languages (and Other Things)." In *Latin and the Romance Languages in the Early Middle Ages,* edited by Roger Wright, 9–18. London: Routledge, 1991.

Lodi, E. "La preghiera in S. Pietro Crisologo." In *La preghiera nel tardo antico: Dalle origini ad Agostino: XXVII Incontro di studiosi dell'antichità cristiana,* 389–417. Rome: Institutum Patristicum Augustinianum, 1999.

Longère, Jean. *La prédication médiévale.* Paris: Études Augustiniennes, 1983.

Loseby, Simon T. "Bishops and Cathedrals: Order and Diversity in the Fifth-Century Urban Landscape of Southern Gaul." In *Fifth-Century*

Gaul: A Crisis of Identity? edited by John Drinkwater and Hugh Elton, 144–55. Cambridge: Cambridge University Press, 1992.

———. "Marseilles: A Late Antique Success Story?" *Journal of Roman Studies* 82 (1992): 165–85.

———. "Arles in Late Antiquity: Gallula Roma Arelas and urbs Genesii." In *Towns in Transition: Urban Evolution in Late Antiquity and the Early Middle Ages,* edited by Neil Christie and Simon T. Loseby, 45–70. Brookfield, Vt.: Scolar Press, 1996.

———. "Gregory's Cities: Urban Functions in Sixth-Century Gaul." In *Franks and Alamanni in the Merovingian Period: An Ethnographic Perspective,* edited by Ian Wood, 239–70. Woodbridge, UK: Boydell Press, 1998.

Löw, P. Josef. "Ein stadrömisches Lektionar des VIII. Jahrhunderts (Cod. Vatic. No. 3835 und 3836)." *Römische Quartalschrift für christliche Altertumskunde und für Kirchengeschichte* 37 (1929): 20–37.

Lowe, Elias A. *Codices Latini Antiquiores.* Oxford: The Clarendon Press, 1934–66.

Maas, Michael. "Ethnicity, Orthodoxy and Community in Salvian of Marseilles." In *Fifth-Century Gaul: A Crisis of Identity?* edited by John Drinkwater and Hugh Elton, 275–84. Cambridge: Cambridge University Press, 1992.

MacCoull, Leslie S. B. "Who Was Eusebius of Alexandria?" *Byzantinoslavica* 60 (1999): 9–18.

MacMullen, Ramsey. "A Note on *sermo humilis.*" *Journal of Theological Studies* n.s. 16 (1966): 108–12.

———. "The Preacher's Audience (A.D. 350–400)." *Journal of Theological Studies* n.s. 40 (1989): 503–11.

Manselli, Raoul. *La religion populaire au Moyen Âge: Problèmes de méthode et d'histoire.* Montréal: Institut d'Études Médiévales Albert-le-Grand, 1975.

———. "Resistenze dei culti antichi nella practica religiosa dei laici nelle campagne." In *Cristianizzazione ed organizzazione ecclesiastica delle campagne nell'alto Medioevo: Espansione e resistenze,* 57–108. Spoleto: Presso la Sede del Centro, 1982.

Mara, Maria Grazia. "Mass." In *Encyclopedia of the Early Church,* 2:541. New York: Oxford University Press, 1992.

Markus, Robert. "The Roman Empire in Early Christian Historiography." *The Downside Review* 81 (1963): 343–44.

———. *"Alienatio:* Philosophy and Eschatology in the Development of an Augustinian Idea." *Studia Patristica* 9, *Texte und Untersuchungen* 94 (1966): 431–50.

———. *Saeculum: History and Society in the Theology of St. Augustine.* Cambridge: Cambridge University Press, 1970.

———. "St. Augustine on Signs." In *Augustine: A Collection of Critical Essays,* edited by Robert Markus, 61–91. Garden City, N.Y.: Anchor Books, 1972.

———. "The Legacy of Pelagius: Orthodoxy, Heresy and Conciliation." In *The Making of Orthodoxy: Essays in Honour of Henry Chadwick,* edited by Rowan Williams, 214–34. Cambridge: Cambridge University Press, 1989.

———. *The End of Ancient Christianity.* Cambridge: Cambridge University Press, 1990.

———. *"De ciuitate dei:* Pride and the Common Good." In *Sacred and Secular: Studies on Augustine and Latin Christianity.* Aldershot, UK: Variorum, 1994.

———. "From Caesarius to Boniface: Christianity and Paganism in Gaul." In *Sacred and Secular: Studies on Augustine and Latin Christianity.* Aldershot, UK: Variorum, 1994.

———. *Signs and Meanings: World and Text in Ancient Christianity.* Liverpool: Liverpool University Press, 1996.

———. *Gregory the Great and His World.* Cambridge: Cambridge University Press, 1997.

Marrou, Henri-Irénée. *Histoire de l'éducation dans l'antiquité,* 2d ed. Paris: Éditions du Seuil, 1950.

Mathisen, Ralph W. "Epistolography, Literary Circles and Family Ties in Late Roman Gaul." *Transactions of the American Philological Association* 111 (1981): 95–109.

———. *Ecclesiastical Factionalism and Religious Controversy in Fifth-Century Gaul.* Washington, D.C.: Catholic University of America Press, 1989.

———. "Fifth-Century Visitors to Italy: Business or Pleasure?" In *Fifth-Century Gaul: A Crisis of Identity?* edited by John Drinkwater and Hugh Elton, 228–38. Cambridge: Cambridge University Press, 1992.

———. "For Specialists Only: The Reception of Augustine and his Teachings in Fifth-Century Gaul." In *Augustine: Presbyter factus sum,* edited by Joseph T. Lienhard, Earl C. Muller, and Roland J. Teske, 29–41. New York: Peter Lang, 1993.

————. "The 'Second Council of Arles' and the Spirit of Compilation and Codification in Late Roman Gaul." *Journal of Early Christian Studies* 5 (1997): 511–54.

————. "The *Codex sangallensis* 190 and the Transmission of the Classical Tradition during Late Antiquity and the Early Middle Ages." *International Journal of the Classical Tradition* 5 (1998): 163–94.

————. "A New Fragment of Augustine's *De nuptiis et concupiscentia* from the *Codex sangallensis* 190." *Zeitschrift für Antikes Christentum* 3 (1999): 165–83.

————. "The Letters of Ruricius of Limoges and the Passage from Roman to Frankish Gaul." In *Society and Culture in Late Antique Gaul: Revisiting the Sources,* edited by Ralph W. Mathisen and Danuta Shanzer, 101–15. Aldershot U.K.: Ashgate, 2001.

Maxwell, Jaclyn L. *Christianization and Communication in Late Antiquity.* Cambridge: Cambridge University Press, 2006.

Mayeski, Marie Anne. "Reading the Word in a Eucharistic Context: The Shape and Methods of Early Medieval Exegesis." In *Medieval Liturgy: A Book of Essays,* edited by Lizette Larson-Miller, 61–84. New York: Garland Publishing, 1997.

McDermott, William C. "Felix of Nantes: A Merovingian Bishop." *Traditio* 31 (1975): 1–24.

McGoldrick, Patrick. "Liturgy: The Context of Patristic Exegesis." In *Scriptural Interpretation in the Fathers: Letter and Spirit,* edited by Thomas Finan and Vincent Twomey, 27–37. Dublin: Four Courts Press, 1995.

McKitterick, David. *Print, Manuscript, and the Search for Order, 1450–1830.* New York: Cambridge University Press, 2003.

McKitterick, Rosamond. *The Frankish Church and the Carolingian Reforms, 789–895.* London: Royal Historical Society, 1977.

————. "Town and Monastery in the Carolingian Period." In *The Church in Town and Countryside,* edited by Derek Baker, 93–102. Oxford: Blackwell, 1979.

————. *The Carolingians and the Written Word.* Cambridge: Cambridge University Press, 1989.

————. "Nuns' Scriptoria in England and France in the Eighth Century." *Francia* 19 (1989): 1–35.

————. "Latin and Romance: An Historian's Perspective." In *Latin and the Romance Languages in the Early Middle Ages,* edited by Roger Wright, 130–45. London: Routledge, 1991.

———. "Some Carolingian Law-Books and their Function." In *Books, Scribes and Learning in the Frankish Kingdoms, 6th–9th Centuries,* 13–27. Aldershot, UK: Variorum, 1994.

McKitterick, Rosamond, ed. *The Uses of Literacy in Early Mediaeval Europe.* Cambridge: Cambridge University Press, 1990.

McLaughlin, R. Emmet. "The Word Eclipsed? Preaching in the Early Middle Ages." *Traditio* 46 (1991): 77–122.

Meens, Rob. "Pollution in the Early Middle Ages: The Case of Food Regulations in Penitentials." *Early Medieval Europe* 4 (1995): 3–19.

———. "The Frequency and Nature of Early Medieval Penance." In *Handling Sin: Confession in the Middle Ages,* edited by Peter Biller and A. J. Minnis, 35–61. Woodbridge, UK: York Medieval Press, 1998.

Mensbrugghe, Alexis van der. "Pseudo-Germanus Reconsidered." *Studia Patristica* 5 (1962): 172–84.

Merkt, Andreas. *Maximus I. von Turin: Die Verkündigung eines Bischofs der frühen Reichskirche im zeitgeschichtlichen, gesellschaftlichen und liturgischen Kontext.* Leiden: Brill, 1997.

Milleman, Honoratus. "Caesarius von Arles und die frühmittelälterliche Missionspredigt." *Zeitschrift für Missionswissenschaft und Religionswissenschaft* 23 (1933): 12–27.

Mitchell, Kathleen. "Marking the Bounds: The Distant Past in Gregory's History." In *The World of Gregory of Tours,* edited by Kathleen Mitchell and Ian Wood, 295–306. Leiden: Brill, 2002.

Mitchell, Margaret M. *Paul and the Rhetoric of Reconciliation: An Exegetical Investigation of the Language and Composition of 1 Corinthians.* Tübingen: J. C. B. Mohr, 1991.

Mohrmann, Christine. "*Praedicare–tractare–sermo:* Essai sur la terminologie de la prédication paleochrétienne." *La Maison-Dieu* 39 (1954): 97–107.

Morin, Germain. "Hiérarchie et liturgie dans l'église gallicane au Ve siècle d'après un écrit restitué à Fauste de Riez." *Revue bénédictine* 8 (1891): 97–104.

———. "Critique des sermons attribués à Fauste de Riez dans la récente édition de l'Académie de Vienne." *Revue bénédictine* 9 (1892): 49–61.

———. "L'homéliaire de Burchard de Würzburg: Contribution à la critique des sermons de saint Césaire d'Arles." *Revue bénédictine* 13 (1896): 97–111.

———. "Notes sur un manuscrit des homélies du Pseudo-Fulgence." *Revue bénédictine* 26 (1909): 223–28.

———. "Le plus ancien *comes* ou lectionnaire de l'église romaine." *Revue bénédictine* 27 (1910): 47–74.

———. "Liturgie et basiliques de Rome au milieu du VIIe siècle." *Revue bénédictine* 28 (1911): 296–330.

———. "Les éditions des sermons de s. Césaire d'Arles du XVIe siècle jusqu'à nos jours." *Revue bénédictine* 43 (1931): 23–37.

———. "Le symbole de saint Césaire d'Arles." *Revue bénédictine* 46 (1934): 178–89.

———. "La collection gallicane dite d'Eusèbe d'Émèse et les problèmes qui s'y rattachant." *Zeitschrift für Neutestamentliche Wissenschaft* 34 (1935): 92–115.

———. "Le «breviarium fidei» contre les ariens: Produit de l'atelier de Césaire d'Arles?" *Revue d'histoire ecclésiastique* 35 (1939): 35–53.

———. "The Homilies of St. Caesarius of Arles: Their Influence on the Christian Civilisation of Europe." *Orate Fratres* 14 (1940): 481–86.

Moris, Henri. *L'abbaye de Lérins: Histoire et monuments*. Paris: Plon-Nourrit, 1909.

Morstein-Marx, Robert. *Mass Oratory and Political Power in the Late Roman Republic*. Cambridge: Cambridge University Press, 2004.

Muessig, Carolyn. "Preacher, Sermon, and Audience in the Middle Ages: An Introduction." In *Preacher, Sermon, and Audience in the Middle Ages*, edited by Carolyn Muessig, 3–9. Leiden: Brill, 2002.

———. "Sermon, Preacher, and Society in the Middle Ages." *Journal of Medieval History* 28 (2002): 73–91.

Muessig, Carolyn, ed. *Medieval Monastic Preaching*. Leiden: Brill, 1998.

Munz, Peter. "John Cassian." *Journal of Ecclesiastical History* 2 (1960): 1–22.

Muschiol, Gisela. *Famula Dei: Zur Liturgie in merowingischen Frauernklöstern*. Münster: Aschendorff, 1994.

Nathan, Geoffrey. "The Rogation Ceremonies of Late Antique Gaul: Creation, Transmission and the Role of the Bishop." *Classica et Mediaevalia* 49 (1998): 275–303.

Neill, Stephen Charles, "Introduction." In *The Layman in Christian History*, edited by Stephen Charles Neill and Hans-Ruedi Weber, 15–27. London: SCM Press, 1963.

Nelson, Janet L. "Ritual and Reality in the Early Medieval *Ordines*." In *The Materials, Sources, and Methods of Ecclesiastical History*, edited by Derek Baker, 41–51. New York: Barnes and Noble Books, 1975.

———. "The Merovingian Church in Carolingian Perspective." In *The World of Gregory of Tours,* edited by Kathleen Mitchell and Ian Wood, 241–59. Leiden: Brill, 2002.

Nichols, Stephen G. "Introduction: Philology in a Manuscript Culture." *Speculum* 65 (1990): 1–10.

Noble, Thomas F. X. "Gregory of Tours and the Roman Church." In *The World of Gregory of Tours,* edited by Kathleen Mitchell and Ian Wood, 145–61. Leiden: Brill, 2002.

Nodes, Daniel J. "Avitus of Vienne's Spiritual History and the Semi-Pelagian Controversy: The Doctrinal Implications of Books I–III." *Vigiliae Christianae* 38 (1984): 184–95.

———. "*De subitanea paenitentia* in the Letters of Faustus of Riez and Avitus of Vienne." *Recherches de théologie ancienne et médiévale* 55 (1988): 30–40.

Nouailhat, René. *Saints et patrons: Les premiers moines de Lérins.* Paris: Les Belles Lettres, 1988.

Nürnberg, Rosemarie. *Askese als sozialer Impuls: Monastisch-asketische Spiritualität als Wurzel und Triebfeder sozialer Ideen und Aktivitäten der Kirche in Südgallien im 5. Jahrhundert.* Bonn: Borengässer, 1988.

Oberhelman, Steven M. *Rhetoric and Homiletics in Fourth-Century Christian Literature: Prose Rhythm, Oratorical Style and Preaching in the Works of Ambrose, Jerome and Augustine.* Atlanta: Scholars Press, 1991.

O'Donnell, James J. "The Authority of Augustine." *Augustinian Studies* 22 (1991): 7–35.

Oehler, Klaus. "Der Consensus omnium als Kriterium der Wahrheit in der antiken Philosophie und der Patristik: Eine Studie zur Geschichte des Begriffs der Allgemeinen Meinung." *Antike und Abendland* 10 (1961): 103–29.

Old, Hughes Oliphant. *The Reading and Preaching of the Scriptures in the Worship of the Christian Church.* Grand Rapids: Eerdmans, 1998.

Orselli, Alba Maria. *L'idea e il culto del santo patrono cittadino nella letteratura latina cristiana.* Bologna: Zanichelli, 1965.

———. "L'idée chrétienne de la ville: Quelques suggestions pour l'antiquité tardive et le haut Moyen Âge." In *The Idea and Ideal of the Town between Late Antiquity and the Early Middle Ages,* edited by Gian P. Brogiolo and Bryan Ward-Perkins, 181–93. Leiden: Brill, 1999.

Padovese, Luigi. *L'originalita cristiana: Il pensiero etico-sociale di alcuni vescovi norditaliani del IV secolo.* Rome: Laurentianum, 1983.

Penn, Michael Philip. *Kissing Christians: Ritual and Community in the Late Ancient Church*. Philadephia: University of Pennsylvania Press, 2005.

Perrin, Michel-Yves. "Grégoire de Tours et l'espace extra-gaulois: La gallo-centrisme grégorien revisité." In *Grégoire de Tours et l'espace gaulois: Actes du Congès International Tours, 3–5 Novembre 1994*, edited by Nancy Gauthier and Henri Galinié, 35–45. Tours: Revue archéologique du Centre de la France, 1997.

———. "À propos de la participation des fidèles aux controverses doctrinales dans l'antiquité tardive: Considérations introductives." *Antiquité Tardive* 9 (2001): 179–99.

Pfaff, Richard W. *Medieval Latin Liturgy: A Select Bibliography*. Toronto: University of Toronto Press, 1982.

Pierce, Joanne M. "The Evolution of the *Ordo missae* in the Early Middle Ages." In *Medieval Liturgy: A Book of Essays,* edited by Lizette Larson-Miller, 3–24. New York: Garland Publishing, 1997.

Pietri, Luce. "Culte des saints et religiosité politique dans la Gaule du Ve et du VIe siècle." In *Les fonctions des saints dans le monde occidental (IIIe–XIIIe siècle),* 353–69. Rome: École Française de Rome, 1991.

Pirenne, Henri. "De l'état de l'instruction des laïques à l'époque mérovingienne." *Revue bénédictine* 46 (1934): 165–77.

Pontal, Odette. *Histoire des conciles mérovingiens*. Paris: Éditions du Cerf, 1989.

Porter, William S. *The Gallican Rite*. London: Mowbray, 1958.

Poschmann, Bernhard. *Penance and the Anointing of the Sick*. Translated by Francis Courtney. New York: Herder and Herder, 1964.

Prete, Serafino. "Genesio di Arles." In *Bibliotheca sanctorum* 6:115–17. Rome: Istituto Giovanni XXIII nella Pontificia Università Lateranense, 1961–70.

———. "Note di agiographia ascolana." *Studia picena* 40 (1973): 58–66.

Pricoco, Salvatore. *L'isola dei Santi: Il cenobio de Lerino e le origini del monachesimo gallico*. Rome: Edizioni dell'Ateneo & Bizarri, 1978.

Price, Richard M. "Marian Piety and the Nestorian Controversy." In *The Church and Mary: Papers Read at the 2001 Summer Meeting and the 2002 Winter Meeting of the Ecclesiastical History Society,* edited by R. N. Swanson, 31–38. Woodbridge, UK: Boydell Press, 2004.

Prince, Georgia M. "A Mood of Self-Reliance: A Study of Pelagianism in Fifth-Century Gaul." M.A. thesis, University of Auckland, 1977.

Prinz, Friedrich. *Frühes Mönchtum im Frankenreich: Kultur und Gesellschaft in Gallien, den Rheinlanden und Bayern am Beispiel der monastischen Entwicklung (4. bis 8. Jahrhundert)*. Munich: Oldenbourg Verlag, 1965.

Ramsey, Boniface. "Almsgiving in the Latin Church: The Late Fourth and Early Fifth Centuries." *Theological Studies* n.s. 43 (1982): 226–59.

Rapisarda, Carmelo A. "Lo stile umile nei sermoni di Cesario d'Arles." *Orpheus* 17 (1970): 115–59.

Rapp, Claudia. *Holy Bishops in Late Antiquity: The Nature of Christian Leadership in an Age of Transition*. Berkeley: University of California Press, 2005.

Rasmussen, Niels. "Célébration épiscopale et célébration presbytérale: Un essai de typologie." In *Segni et riti nella chiesa altomedievale occidentale*, 581–603. Spoleto: Presso la Sede del Centro, 1987.

Rebillard, Éric. *In hora mortis: Évolution de la pastorale chrétienne de la mort aux IVe et Ve siècles dans l'Occident latin*. Rome: École Française de Rome, 1994.

———. "*Quasi funambuli:* Cassien et la controverse pélagienne sur la perfection." *Revue des études augustinienne* 40 (1994): 197–210.

———. "Interaction between the Preacher and the Audience: The Case-Study of Augustine's Preaching on Death." *Studia Patristica* 31 (1997): 86–96.

Rebillard, Éric and Claire Sotinel, eds. *L'évêque dans la cité du VIe et Ve siècle: Image et authorité*. Rome: École Française de Rome, 1998.

Rees, Bryn R. *Pelagius: A Reluctant Heretic*. Woodbridge, UK: Boydell Press, 1988.

Rees, Roger. *Layers of Loyalty in Latin Panegyric, A.D. 289–307*. Oxford: Oxford University Press, 2002.

Reydams-Schils, Gretchen. *The Roman Stoics: Self, Responsibility, and Affection*. Chicago: University of Chicago Press, 2005.

Reynaud, Jean-François. "Les premiers édifices de culte à Lyon, IVe–VIIe siècle." In *Les martyrs de Lyon (177)*, 279–87. Paris: Éditions du C.N.R.S, 1978.

Reynolds, Roger E. *Clerics in the Early Middle Ages: Hierarchy and Image*. Aldershot, UK: Variorum, 1999.

Riché, Pierre. *Education and Culture in the Barbarian West, 6th to 8th Centuries*. Translated by John J. Contreni. Columbia: University of South Carolina Press, 1976.

———. "La pastorale populaire en Occident, VIe–XIe siècles." In *Histoire vécue au peuple chretien,* edited by Jean Delumeau, 195–219. Toulouse: Privat, 1979.

———. "Columbanus, His Followers and the Merovingian Church." In *Columbanus and Merovingian Monasticism,* edited by Howard B. Clarke and Mary Brennan, 59–72. Oxford: B.A.R., 1981.

Richter, Michael. "A quelle époque a-t-on cessé de parler Latin en Gaule? A propos d'une question mal posée." *Annales* 38 (1983): 439–48.

Rio, Alice. "Charters, Law Codes and Formulae: The Franks between Theory and Practice." In *Frankland: The Franks and the World of the Early Middle Ages,* edited by Paul Fouracre and David Ganz, 7–27. Manchester: Manchester University Press, 2008.

Rivet, *Histoire litteraire de la France.* Paris, De Boccard, 1733–.

Rivière, Jean. "Rédemption chez saint Césaire d'Arles." *Bulletin de littérature ecclésiastique* 44 (1943): 3–20.

Roberts, Phyllis. "Sermon Studies Scholarship: The Last Thirty-Five Years." *Medieval Sermon Studies* 43 (1999): 9–18.

———. "The *Ars praedicandi* and the Medieval Sermon." In *Preacher, Sermon, and Audience in the Middle Ages,* edited by Carolyn Muessig, 41–62. Leiden: Brill, 2002.

Rochais, Henri M. "Le manuscrits du *Liber scintillarum.*" *Scriptorium* 4 (1950): 294–309.

———. "Contribution à l'histoire des florilèges ascétiques." *Revue bénédictine* 63 (1953): 246–91.

Rose, Valentin. *Verzeichnis der lateinischen Handschriften.* Berlin: A. Asher & Co., 1893–1914.

Rouse, Mary A., and Richard H. Rouse. *Preachers, Florilegia and Sermons: Studies on the "Manipulus florum" of Thomas of Ireland.* Toronto: Pontifical Institute of Mediaeval Studies, 1979.

———. *Authentic Witnesses: Approaches to Medieval Texts and Manuscripts.* Notre Dame, Ind.: University of Notre Dame Press, 1991.

———. "*Ordinatio* and *compilatio* Revisted." In *Ad litteram: Authoritative Texts and their Medieval Readers,* edited by Mark D. Jordan and Kent Emery, Jr., 113–34. Notre Dame, Ind.: University of Notre Dame Press, 1992.

Rousseau, Philip. "The Spiritual Authority of the 'Monk-Bishop': Eastern Elements in Some Western Hagiography of the Fourth and Fifth Centuries." *Journal of Theological Studies,* n.s. 22 (1971): 380–419.

———. "Cassian, Contemplation and the Coenobitic Life." *Journal of Ecclesiastical History* 26 (1975): 113–26.

———. *Ascetics, Authority and the Church in the Age of Jerome and Cassian.* Oxford: Oxford University Press, 1978.

———. *Basil of Caesarea.* Berkeley: University of California Press, 1994.

———. "Cassian: Monastery and World." In *The Certainty of Doubt: Tributes to Peter Munz,* edited by Miles Fairburn and W. H. Oliver, 68–89. Wellington, NZ: Victoria University Press, 1997.

———. *The Early Christian Centuries.* London: Longman, 2002.

Russell, Frederick H. "Persuading the Donatists: Augustine's Coercion by Words." In *The Limits of Ancient Christianity: Essays on Late Antique Thought and Culture in Honor of R. A. Markus,* edited by William E. Klingshirn and Mark Vessey, 115–30. Ann Arbor: University of Michigan Press, 1999.

Salvatore, A. "Uso delle similitudini e pedagogia pastorale nei *Sermones* di Cesario di Arles." *Rivista di cultura classica e medioevale* 9 (1967): 177–225.

Salzman, Michele R. *The Making of a Christian Aristocracy: Religious and Social Change in the Western Roman Empire.* Cambridge, Mass.: Harvard University Press, 2001.

Scherer, Gustav. *Verzeichnis der Handschriften der Stiftsbibliothek von Sankt-Gallen.* Halle: G. Olms, 1875.

Schmitt, Jean-Claude. "Du bon usage du «credo»." In *Faire croire: Modalités de la diffusion et de la réception des messages religieux du XIIe au XVe siècle,* 337–61. Rome: École Française de Rome, 1981.

Schneyer, Johann Baptist. *Geschichte der katholischen Predigt.* Freiburg: Seelsorge Verlag, 1969.

Schofield, Malcolm. *The Stoic Idea of the City.* Chicago: The University of Chicago Press, 1999.

Simonetti, Manlio. *Biblical Interpretation in the Early Church: An Historical Introduction to Patristic Exegesis.* Translated by John A. Hughes. Edinburgh: T & T Clark, 1994.

———. "Eusebius Gallicanus," in *Encyclopedia of the Early Church,* 1:298. New York: Oxford University Press, 1992.

Smetana, Cyril L. "Aelfric and the Early Medieval Homiliary." *Traditio* 15 (1959): 163–204.

———. "Paul the Deacon's Patristic Anthology." In *The Old English Homily and Its Backgrounds,* edited by Paul E. Szarmach and Bernard F. Huppé, 75–97. Albany: State University of New York Press, 1978.

Smith, Jonathan Z. *To Take Place: Toward Theory in Ritual.* Chicago: University of Chicago Press, 1987.

Smith, Julia M. H. "Gender and Ideology in the Early Middle Ages." In *Gender and Christian Religion,* edited by Robert N. Swanson, 51–73. Woodbridge, UK: Boydell Press, 1998.

———. "Old Saints, New Cults: Roman Relics in Carolingian Francia." In *Early Medieval Rome and the Christian West: Essays in Honour of Donald A. Bullough,* edited by Julia Smith, 317–39. Leiden: Brill, 2000.

———. *Europe after Rome: A New Cultural History, 500–1000.* Oxford: Oxford University Press, 2005.

Smith, Thomas A. *De gratia: Faustus of Riez's Treatise on Grace and its Place in the History of Theology.* Notre Dame, Ind.: University of Notre Dame Press, 1990.

Sotinel, Claire. *Rhétorique de la faute et pastorale de la reconciliation dans la "lettre apologétique contre Jean de Ravenne": Un texte unédit de la fin du VIe siècle.* Rome: École Française de Rome, 1994.

Souter, Alexander. "Observations on the Pseudo-Eusebian Collection of Gallican Sermons." *Journal of Theological Studies* 41 (1940): 47–57.

Stalley, Roger. *Early Medieval Architecture.* Oxford: Oxford University Press, 1999.

Stancliffe, Clare. "From Town to Country: The Christianization of the Touraine, 370–600." In *The Church in Town and Countryside,* edited by Derek Baker, 43–59. Oxford: Blackwell, 1979.

———. "The Thirteen Sermons Attributed to Columbanus and the Question of Their Authorship." In *Columbanus: Studies on the Latin Writings,* edited by Michael Lapidge, 93–202. Woodbridge, UK: Boydell Press, 1997.

Stansbury, Mark. "Early Medieval Biblical Commentaries, Their Writers and Readers." *Frühmittelalterliche Studien* 33 (1999): 49–82.

Stark, Rodney. *The Rise of Christianity: A Sociologist Reconsiders History.* Princeton: Princeton University Press, 1996.

Sterk, Andreas. *Renouncing the World Yet Leading the Church: The Monk-Bishop in Late Antiquity.* Cambridge: Harvard University Press, 2004.

Stevenson, Thomas R. "The Ideal Benefactor and the Father Analogy in Greek and Roman Thought." *Classical Quarterly* 42 (1992): 421–36.

Stewart, Columba. *Cassian the Monk.* New York: Oxford University Press, 1998.

Stocking, Rachel L. *Bishops, Councils and Consensus in the Visigothic Kingdom, 589–633.* Ann Arbor: University of Michigan Press, 2000.

Straw, Carole. "Augustine as Pastoral Theologian: The Exegesis of the Parables of the Field and Threshing Floor." *Augustinian Studies* 14 (1983): 129–51.

Stroumsa, G. G. "From Repentance to Penance in Early Christianity: Tertullian's *De paenitentia* in Context." In *Transformations of the Inner Self in Ancient Religions,* edited by J. Assmann and G. G. Stroumsa, 167–78. Leiden: Brill, 1999.

Swanson, Robert N. *Religion and Devotion in Europe, c. 1215–c. 1515.* Cambridge: Cambridge University Press, 1995.

Taylor, Andrew. *Textual Situations: Three Medieval Manuscripts and Their Readers.* Philadephia: University of Pennsylvania Press, 2002.

Teitler Hans C. "Un-Roman Activities in Late Antique Gaul: The Cases of Arvandus and Seronatus." In *Fifth-Century Gaul: A Crisis of Identity?* edited by John Drinkwater and Hugh Elton, 309–17. Cambridge: Cambridge University Press, 1992.

Thibaut, Jean-Baptiste. *L'ancienne liturgie gallicane: Son origine et sa formation en Provence aux Ve et VIe siècles sous l'influence de Cassien et de Saint Césaire d'Arles.* Paris: Maison de la Bonne Presse, 1929.

Thompson, Augustine. "From Texts to Preaching: Retrieving the Medieval Sermon as an Event." In *Preacher, Sermon and Audience in the Middle Ages,* edited by Carolyn Muessig, 13–37. Leiden: Brill, 2002.

Tibiletti, Carlo. "La salvezza umana in Fausto di Riez." *Orpheus* 1 (1980): 371–90.

———. "Rassegna di studi e testi sui «semipelagiani»." *Augustinianum* 25 (1985): 507–22.

———. "La teologia della grazia in Giuliano Pomerio: Alle origini dell'agostinismo provenzale." *Augustinianum* 25 (1985): 489–506.

Topographie chrétienne des cités de la Gaule des origines au milieu du VIIIe siècle, edited by Nancy Gauthier and Jean-Charles Picard. Paris: De Boccard, 1986–98.

Triacca, Achille M. "«Cultus» in Eusebio «Gallicano»." *Ephemerides Liturgicae* 100 (1986): 96–110.

———. "La maternità feconda di Maria Vergine e della chiesa: Ana riconferma dalle omelie di Eusebio «Gallicano» (contributo alla teologia liturgica)." In *Virgo fidelis: Miscellanea in onore di Don Domenico Bertetto S.D.B.,* edited by Ferdinando Bergamelli and Mario Cimosa, 341–93. Rome: C. L.V.–Edizioni liturgiche, 1986.

Uhalde, Kevin. *Expectations of Justice in the Age of Augustine.* Philadelphia: University of Pennsylvania Press, 2007.

Van Dam, Raymond. *Leadership and Community in Late Antique Gaul.* Berkeley: University of California Press, 1985.

———. "The Pirenne Thesis and Fifth-Century Gaul." In *Fifth-Century Gaul: A Crisis of Identity?* edited by John Drinkwater and Hugh Elton, 321–33. Cambridge: Cambridge University Press, 1992.

———. *Saints and Their Miracles in Late Antique Gaul.* Princeton: Princeton University Press, 1993.

———. *Becoming Christian: The Conversion of Roman Cappadocia.* Philadelphia: University of Pennsylvania Press, 2003.

Van Den Gheyn, Joseph. *Catalogue des manuscrits de la Bibliothèque royale de Belgique.* Brussels: H. Lamertin and Des Presses de J. Leherte Courtin, 1901–32.

Van Uytfanghe, Marc. "The Consciousness of a Linguistic Dichotomy (Latin-Romance) in Carolingian Gaul: The Contradictions of the Sources and of their Interpretation." In *Latin and the Romance Languages in the Early Middle Ages,* edited by Roger Wright, 114–29. London: Routledge, 1991.

———. "La Bible et l'instruction des laïcs en Gaule mérovingienne: Des témoignages textuels à une approche langagière de la question." *Sacris Eruditi* 34 (1994): 67–123.

Vasey, Vincent R. *The Social Ideas in the Works of St. Ambrose: A Study on de Nabuthe.* Rome: Institutum Patristicum «Augustinianum», 1982.

Verbraken, Pierre-Patrick. "Le manuscrit latin 1771 de la Bibliothèque Nationale de Paris et ses sermons augustiniennes." *Revue bénédictine* 78 (1968): 67–81.

———. "Les pièces inédites du manuscrit latin 1771 de la Bibliothèque Nationale de Paris." *Revue bénédictine* 80 (1970): 51–63.

Vessey, Mark. "The Origins of the *Collectio Sirmondiana:* A New Look at the Evidence." In *The Theodosian Code: Studies in the Imperial Law of Late Antiquity,* edited by Jill Harries and Ian Wood, 178–99. London: Duckworth, 1993.

———. "The *Epistula Rusticii ad Eucherium:* From the Library of Imperial Classics to the Library of the Fathers." In *Society and Culture in Late Antique Gaul: Revisiting the Sources,* edited by Ralph W. Mathisen and Danuta Shanzer, 278–97. Aldershot, UK: Ashgate, 2001.

Viard, Paul. "Fauste de Riez." In *Dictionnaire de spiritualité,* 5:113. Paris, Beauchesne, 1937–67.

Vogel, Cyrille. *La discipline pénitentielle en Gaule des origines a la fin du VIIe siècle.* Paris: Letouzey et Ané, 1952.

———. "La discipline pénitentielle en Gaule des origines au IXe siècle: Le dossier hagiographique." *Revue des sciences religieuses* 30 (1956): 1–26.

———. "Une mutation cultuelle inexpliquée: Le passage de l'eucharistie communautaire à la messe privée." *Revue de sciences religieuses* 54 (1980): 231–50.

Ward-Perkins, Bryan. "Urban Continuity?" In *Towns in Transition: Urban Evolution in Late Antiquity and the Early Middle Ages,* edited by Neil Christie and Simon T. Loseby, 4–17. Aldershot, UK: Scolar Press, 1996.

Weaver, Rebecca Harden. *Divine Grace and Human Agency: A Study of the Semi-Pelagian Controversy.* Macon: Mercer University Press, 1996.

Weigel, Gustave. *Faustus of Riez: An Historical Introduction.* Philadephia: The Dolphin Press, 1938.

Weisberger, Andrea M. "The Argument from Evil." In *The Cambridge Companion to Atheism,* edited by Michael Martin, 166–81. Cambridge: Cambridge University Press, 2007.

Weiss, Jean-Pierre. "Valerien de Cimiez et Valère de Nice." *Sacris Erudiri* 21 (1972–73): 109–46.

———. "La fondation de la communauté des moines de Lérins." In *Bulletin de l'Association Guillaume Budé,* 338–51. Paris: The Association, 1988.

———. "Valerien de Cimiez et la société de son temps." In *Melanges Paul Gonnet,* 281–89. Nice: Laboratoire d'analyse spatiale Raoul Blanchard, 1989.

———. "Le statut du prédicateur et les instruments de la prédication dans la Provence du Ve siècle." In *La parole du prédicateur: Ve–Xe siècle,* edited by Rosa Maria Dessì and Michel Lauwers, 23–47. Nice: Centre d'Études Médiévales, 1997.

Wenzel, Siegfried. *Latin Sermon Collections from Later Medieval England: Orthodox Preaching in the Age of Wyclif.* Cambridge: Cambridge University Press, 2005.

Willis, Geoffrey Grimshaw. *St. Augustine's Lectionary.* London: S.P.C.K., 1962.

Wilmart, Andreas. "Un developpement patristique sur l'Eucharistie dans la lettre de Pascase Radbert a Fredigard." *Studi e Testi* 59 (1933): 267–78.

———. *Bibliothecae Apostolicae Vaticanae–Codices Reginenses latini,* t. 1, codices 1–250, In Bibliotheca Vaticana, 1937.

Wood, Ian. "Early Merovingian Devotion in Town and Country." In *The Church in Town and Countryside,* edited by Derek Baker, 61–76. Oxford: Blackwell, 1979.

———. "A Prelude to Columbanus: The Monastic Achievement in the Burgundian Territories." In *Columbanus and Merovingian Monasticism,* edited by Howard B. Clarke and Mary Brennan, 3–32. Oxford: B.A.R., 1981.

———. "The Missionary Life." In *The Cult of Saints in Late Antiquity and the Middle Ages: Essays on the Contribution of Peter Brown,* edited by James Howard-Johnson and Paul Antony Hayward, 167–83. Oxford: Oxford University Press, 1999.

———. *The Missionary Life: Saints and the Evangelisation of Europe, 400–1050.* Harlow: Longman, 2001.

———. "Topographies of Holy Power in Sixth-Century Gaul." In *Topographies of Power in the Early Middle Ages,* edited by Mayke de Jong and Francis Theuws with Carine van Rhijn, 137–54. Leiden: Brill, 2001.

Wright, Roger. *Late Latin and Early Romance in Spain and Carolingian France.* Liverpool: Francis Cairns, 1982.

Young, Bailey K. "Que restait-il de l'ancien paysage religieux à l'époque de Grégoire de Tours?" In *Grégoire de Tours et l'espace gaulois: Actes du Congès International Tours, 3–5 Novembre 1994,* edited by Nancy Gauthier and Henri Galinié, 241–50. Tours: Revue archéologique du Centre de la France, 1997.

———. "Autun and the Civitas Aeduorum: Maintaining and Transforming a Regional Identity in Late Antiquity." In *Urban Centers and Rural Contexts in Late Antiquity,* edited by Thomas S. Burns and John W. Eadie, 25–46. East Lansing: Michigan State University Press, 2001.

Young, Frances M. "The Rhetorical Schools and their Influence on Patristic Exegesis." In *The Making of Orthodoxy: Essays in Honour of Henry Chadwick,* edited by Rowan Williams, 182–99. Cambridge: Cambridge University Press, 1989.

———. *Biblical Exegesis and the Formation of Christian Culture.* Cambridge: Cambridge University Press, 1997.

LISA KAAREN BAILEY

is a senior lecturer in the Departments of Classics

and Ancient History and of History at the University of Auckland.